Manchester Medieval Sources Series

series advisers Rosemary Horrox and Janet L. Nelson

This series aims to meet a growing need among students and teachers of medieval history for translations of key sources that are directly usable in students' own work. It provides texts central to medieval studies courses and focuses upon the diverse cultural and social as well as political conditions that affected the functioning of all levels of medieval society. The basic premise of the series is that translations must be accompanied by sufficient introductory and explanatory material, and each volume, therefore, includes a comprehensive guide to the sources' interpretation, including discussion of critical linguistic problems and an assessment of the most recent research on the topics being covered.

also available in the series

SAINTS AND CITIES IN MEDIEVAL ITALY

D1738291

WITHDRAWN
UTSA LIBRARIES

MANCHESTER
1824

Manchester University Press

MedievalSources*online*

Complementing the printed editions of the Medieval Sources series, Manchester University Press has developed a web-based learning resource which is now available on a yearly subscription basis.

Medieval Sources*online* brings quality history source material to the desktops of students and teachers and allows them open and unrestricted access throughout the entire college or university campus. Designed to be fully integrated with academic courses, this is a one-stop answer for many medieval history students, academics and researchers keeping thousands of pages of source material 'in print' over the Internet for research and teaching.

titles available now at Medieval Sources*online include*

Trevor Dean *The towns of Italy in the later Middle Ages*

John Edwards *The Jews in Western Europe, 1400–1600*

Paul Fouracre and Richard A. Gerberding *Late Merovingian France: History and hagiography 640–720*

Chris Given-Wilson *Chronicles of the Revolution 1397–1400: The reign of Richard II*

P. J. P. Goldberg *Women in England, c. 1275–1525*

Janet Hamilton and Bernard Hamilton *Christian dualist heresies in the Byzantine world c. 650–c. 1450*

Rosemary Horrox *The Black Death*

Graham A. Loud and Thomas Wiedemann *The history of the tyrants of Sicily by 'Hugo Falcandus', 1153–69*

Janet L. Nelson *The Annals of St-Bertin: Ninth-century histories, volume I*

Timothy Reuter *The Annals of Fulda: Ninth-century histories, volume II*

R. N. Swanson *Catholic England: Faith, religion and observance before the Reformation*

Elisabeth van Houts *The Normans in Europe*

Jennifer Ward *Women of the English nobility and gentry, 1066–1500*

Visit the site at *www.medievalsources.co.uk* for further information and subscription prices.

SAINTS AND CITIES
IN MEDIEVAL ITALY

selected sources translated and annotated with an introduction

by Diana Webb

Manchester University Press
Manchester and New York

distributed exclusively in the USA by Palgrave

Published by Manchester University Press
Oxford Road, Manchester M13 9NR, UK
and Room 400, 175 Fifth Avenue, New York, NY 10010, USA
www.manchesteruniversitypress.co.uk

Distributed exclusively in the USA by
Palgrave, 175 Fifth Avenue, New York, NY 10010, USA

Distributed exclusively in Canada by
UBC Press, University of British Columbia, 2029 West Mall,
Vancouver, BC, Canada V6T 1Z2

British Library Cataloguing-in-Publication Data
A catalogue record for this book is available from the British Library

Library of Congress Cataloging-in-Publication Data applied for

ISBN   0 7190 7292 1 *hardback*
EAN   978 0 7190 7292 5

ISBN   0 7190 7293 X *paperback*
EAN   978 0 7190 7293 2

First published 2007

15 14 13 12 11 10 09 08 07   10 9 8 7 6 5 4 3 2 1

Typeset in Monotype Bell
by Koinonia Ltd, Manchester
Printed in Great Britain
by Bell & Bain Ltd, Glasgow

For Tony again

CONTENTS

ACKNOWLEDGEMENTS

This book was first drafted during a period of sabbatical leave in 1997–8 and completed in another such period in 2004–5. I owe one debt of gratitude to King's College for granting me this leave and another to my friend and colleague in the History Department, Jinty Nelson, who has been consistently enthusiastic and encouraging about the project. She, Rosemary Horrox and Peter Biller have read and very helpfully commented on two versions of the text; grateful thanks to them. I must also offer very special thanks to Don Daniele Piazzi of Cremona, who most generously sent me copies of both his invaluable work on Homobonus (which I had been told was no longer obtainable) and André Vauchez's *Omobono di Cremona*; the usefulness of this entirely unexpected gift can scarcely be overstated. My life has as ever been made easier and pleasanter, whether working in London or at home in Kent, by the existence of the London Library; the Institute of Historical Research has also been indispensable. My thanks go to everyone at Manchester University Press who has been involved in the production of the book.

My family are best aware of the reasons why 2004–5 has been a difficult year. The dedication rather inadequately acknowledges what I owe to the person who has done most to help me surmount the difficulties.

INTRODUCTION

The saints whose Lives (*vitae*) are translated in this book have in common the fact that they were laypeople (five men and two women) who lived, died and achieved their holy reputations in central or north Italian cities during what may be termed the long thirteenth century. Earliest in date were Homobonus of Cremona and Raimondo Palmario of Piacenza, near-contemporaries and inhabitants of neighbouring cities, who died in 1197 and 1200 respectively; the latest was Enrico ('Rigo') of Bolzano, who died in Treviso in 1315. This was a period of rapid demographic and economic growth in the Italian urban environment; it witnessed much social and political upheaval, accompanied by religious change. It is hoped that the Lives translated here will open a window on to this world by showing how the sanctity of these men and women was perceived and described by observers who were familiar with their social and religious setting, whether as contemporary eyewitnesses or as members of a closely succeeding generation. The chief purpose of this Introduction is to point out some issues which the reader might like to bear in mind while reading the translations. More narrowly focused comments on the Lives are to be found in the short introductions which precede each one.[1]

Five of the Lives translated here were published in *Acta sanctorum* in the course of the seventeenth and eighteenth centuries. *Acta sanctorum* was a product of the seventeenth-century explosion in religious and historical scholarship, a massive and ambitious project intended to produce a comprehensive edition of the lives of the saints based on the best manuscript sources. Specifically it was the brainchild of the Jesuit Heribert

---

1 All the saints and many of the issues raised in this introduction are discussed by André Vauchez in *La sainteté en occident aux derniers siècles du moyen âge* (Rome, 1981). All subsequent references are to the translation by J. Birrell, *Sainthood in the later middle ages* (Cambridge, 1997). There are also articles (in Italian) and further bibliography on all the saints mentioned in this book in the alphabetically organised *Biblioteca sanctorum* (12 vols, Rome, 1960–70). Four Lives of thirteenth-century Italian female saints are translated in E. Petroff, *Consolation of the blessed* (New York, 1979). For women's spirituality, see also A. Benvenuti Papi, *'In castro poenitentiae': santità e società femminile nell' Italia medievale* (Rome, 1990); D. Bornstein and R. Rusconi (eds), *Women and religion in medieval and renaissance Italy* (Chicago, 1996). For the urban religious context in general, see A. Thompson, *Cities of God: the religion of the Italian communes 1125–1325* (University Park, PA, 2005).

Rosweyde (d. 1629) and after him John van Bolland (d. 1665), the first directing editor. Bolland bequeathed his name to a group of Jesuits, the Société des Bollandistes, based in what is now Belgium. Their labours have continued to the present day, interrupted only between 1773, when the order was suppressed in the Belgian Netherlands, and 1837.[2]

Acta sanctorum is arranged in calendar order, so that saints commemorated in January appear in one set of volumes, the saints for February in a succeeding set and so on.[3] The volumes are physically large and in the seventeenth and eighteenth centuries were produced with the full panoply of engraved title-pages and Latin dedications to the great and good of the contemporary Catholic world. Inevitably the project was overtaken by the passage of time and the advances in hagiographical scholarship which the Bollandists themselves helped to bring about. For all the energy and assiduity with which they pursued and collected manuscripts it was not invariably the case that Lives were edited from the best possible sources (that of Zita of Lucca is a conspicuous example), and new material naturally kept coming to light. Some of the earlier volumes were later slightly updated, but only a preliminary volume has yet appeared for the month of December. Since 1882 the annual volumes of *Analecta Bollandiana* have made available a stream of editions of individual Lives in a much more compact format, as well as critical hagiographical studies.

Whatever the shortcomings of *Acta sanctorum*, the student of hagiography would find life a lot harder without it; but it has to be acknowledged that some of the procedures adopted by its early editors would now be regarded as unacceptable or simply unnecessary. They were working in a scholarly environment in which Latin was still an international standard language, which accounts for the dress in which the Life of Raimondo Palmario now appears: an eighteenth-century Latin translation of an early sixteenth-century Italian version of the original Latin life, now lost. It was also their common practice to ignore the original chapters or rubrics of medieval Lives and to divide the text into much longer chapters according to their own discretion. It is often therefore the case that a Life, as it appears in *Acta sanctorum*, has lost some of the features that its first readers would have found in it, even when its language is reasonably trustworthy.

---

2 For a succinct account see M. D. Knowles, *Great historical enterprises* (London, 1963), pp. 3–32.

3 Cited hereafter as *AS*, followed by the month and the volume number within the month.

Miracle collections are another important hagiographical genre; for some saints we have both Life and miracle collection, for others only the one or the other. Limitations of space have forbidden the translation of miracle collections here which are not integral to the Lives. Andrea Gallerani's miracles are so integrated, in an abbreviated form derived from a fuller record now apparently no longer extant. Miracles were often recorded by notaries, sometimes with the intention of providing evidence for a canonisation enquiry; the process was independent of the composition of a Life. Hagiographers often however included one or more post mortem miracles towards the end of a Life, and sometimes, as in the Life of Raimondo Palmario, it is possible to find the source for these stories among the separately surviving notarial records. By contrast, there is no cross-reference between the Lives of Zita of Lucca and Rigo of Bolzano and their extensive miracle collections (which are published in *Acta sanctorum*).[4] The hagiographers of Homobonus of Cremona drew on a record of his miracles which we no longer have. Both the miracles which Umiliana de' Cerchi did in the first three years after her death and her posthumous appearances to her devotees were separately recorded, constituting, together with the Life which is translated here, a hagiographical dossier.[5]

As Innocent III explained when canonising Homobonus, it was official doctrine that miracles post mortem counted for more as evidence of sanctity than miracles performed by the saint *in vita*, which might just be the product of diabolical illusion. The latter nonetheless clearly gratified a profound conviction that if a man or woman was God's chosen the fact would surely be demonstrated during his or her lifetime, and they remained part of the hagiographer's stock in trade. There were several different kinds. Helpful supernatural interventions on behalf of the saint, as when Zita and Rigo remain dry in the rain to the chagrin of mischievous onlookers, shade into the familiar replenishment miracles, for example when the beans that Zita has covertly given to the poor are replaced before her master can find the bin empty or when water is transformed into wine by (or on behalf of) Homobonus, Umiliana, Andrea Gallerani and Zita. Visions and conversations with heavenly visitants are by definition *in vita* experiences. More carefully rationed by hagiographers, at least in this period, are curative miracles carried out by the living saint, but Pier Pettinaio was responsible for several.

---

4 Respectively in *AS*, April, 3, pp. 510–27, and June, 2, pp. 376–91.

5 The apparitions and miracles are in *AS*, May, 4, pp. 401–7. Some of the apparitions were also included in the Life.

Like Rigo of Bolzano on the one occasion when the latter performed such a miracle, he prudently enjoined the beneficiaries and witnesses of his cures to silence until he himself was dead, a traditional demonstration of humility.

Hagiography: some basic characteristics

Hagiography is not biography, but it has sufficient in common with it for confusion between the two to be unsurprising. The most obvious point of resemblance is structural. Both forms normally follow the life-cycle of the human individual from birth to death, but it was not the hagiographer's business to narrate the events of his subject's life for their own sake, nor to place him or her in a social or historical setting (as the modern biographer usually does) unless that served his over-riding purpose, which was to illustrate the saint's possession and exercise of the virtues which justified the claim to sanctity.

This all-important purpose was frequently served by the use of the *topos* or commonplace, which could be anything from a biblical parallel or quotation to a model story derived from an earlier Life and possibly ultimately from a biblical precedent. Miracles furnish particularly obvious examples of this procedure: saints regularly turn water into wine or replenish exhausted stocks of wine or bread or other foodstuffs, as Christ did at the Wedding at Cana and when multiplying the loaves and fishes. The technique could easily spill over into a more thorough-going adaptation of a pre-existing model, which would not be regarded as good practice by modern biographers but was far from unknown in medieval and renaissance biography, where, for example, Suetonius's *Lives of the Caesars* provided helpful hints for describing rulers both good and bad. The notion that the individual saint was, like St Paul, a 'vessel of election' and inevitably resembled other saints could not but promote such borrowings. Originality was no more required of the author who described the saint's life than it was of the saint himself.

Sometimes *topoi* are prominently signposted. An example is the episode in which Zita of Lucca borrows her master's cloak to go to church on a bitterly cold night and gives it to a poor man; back home, her master heaps reproaches upon her until the poor man (either Christ himself or an angel) reappears and restores the cloak. Zita's likeness to St Martin, who divided his cloak with the beggar, is specifically pointed out to us. Saints' Lives vary, however, in the extent and in the style with which

they utilise such devices, and it is important not to approach any particular Life with rigid preconceptions about its individuality or lack of it.
Where alternative versions of a Life exist, the historian may sometimes
need to suppress the impulse to ask which of them gives the most accurate account of the saint's biography. The issue may rather be what
model of sanctity the authors had in mind or for exactly what purpose
or audience they were writing.

The modern reader of medieval hagiography may sometimes be struck
by unconvincing characterisation and muddled chronology. Episodes
and examples are produced in the order which the author judges
appropriate in order to illustrate the saint's virtues, rather than to tell
a connected story or portray a personality 'in the round'. There is an
accompanying tendency to treat virtues sequentially rather than as co-
existing aspects of a rounded personality. The result is often a somewhat
prismatic effect; it is the writer's purpose to depict not a convincing
character but rather a series of facets, virtues which one by one catch
the light. The aim is to show that the saint at all times epitomised the
virtue that is under discussion, whether it be abstinence or humility. If
the subject is prudence, he or she always displays a practical wisdom
perfectly adapted to the best interests of whoever seeks their counsel.
Only rarely does a hagiographer acknowledge that the exercise of one
virtue might cut across another or at least modify it. The need to rebuke
or edify, for example, might require the saint to abandon his or her
normally lowly and submissive demeanour and the silence which is also
taken to be an attribute of perfection. Umiliana's unsurpassed humility
did not stop her using an extremely tart tongue to repress talk of which
she disapproved. Pier Pettinaio could scarcely have achieved the reputation he did as a spiritual counsellor if he had been afraid to speak his
mind when appropriate, but his commitment to silence was regarded
as so characteristic that artists represented him with his finger laid to
his lips. It was, of course, a part of prudence to know when words were
required and when they were idle or superfluous; Pier had particularly
good judgement in this respect. Zita too knew when to abandon her
excessive humility in order to correct members of the household.

A cavalier attitude to chronology is a common characteristic. André
Vauchez observes of the Life of Fazio of Cremona (d. 1272), goldsmith,
frequent pilgrim and charitable activist: 'The text is very badly composed;
events succeed one another without apparent connection and chronological order is not in the least respected.' Vauchez also remarked on the
'imprecision' of the chronology in the Life of Fazio's contemporary Pier

Pettinaio of Siena.[6] As if forestalling such criticism, Pier's Franciscan hagiographer in fact made it plain that he was following not the order of events but what to him was a more important order of inner substance. In expounding the saint's virtues, he drew illustrations from different periods of his life as seemed appropriate, precisely (he said) in order to avert confusion.[7] An event which occurred when the saint had moved to live in the Franciscan convent of Siena may therefore be followed by one which took place while he was still living in his own house in the Ovile district, or while his wife was still alive and they were living near the Dominican church on the other side of town; nor is it made at all clear when he ceased to ply the active trade of making and selling combs. The Dominican syndicate which compiled the life of another Sienese saint, Ambrogio Sansedoni, consisted of four learned men, doctors of theology, but their chronology was little less than chaotic.[8]

It follows from what has been said that the information we might like to glean from hagiography is not necessarily the information its authors were trying or intending to convey. This is not just because their purposes were didactic and edifying. The audience they expected to reach was often already familiar with the saint's life and background as well as with the value-system espoused by the hagiographer. Lives also came in a variety of forms which depended on the purpose to which they were to be put and to some degree on their potential audience. At one extreme there was the full narrative, sometimes intended to accompany and support a campaign for canonisation and therefore including everything about the saint that was deemed necessary or relevant. At the other there was the abbreviated version, arranged in readings (*lectiones*) for liturgical use, which constituted a 'legend' in the literal sense (*legenda*, 'things to be read [aloud])'. Lives also often incorporated material for preaching. The rather short Life of Andrea Gallerani of Siena contains a number of colourful, not to say fanciful, anecdotes which would have served that purpose; a longer version may well once have existed. The Life of Zita of Lucca is much lengthier and includes not only similar improving anecdotal material but a great deal of homiletic content, most of it unacknowledged quotations from Gregory the Great.[9]

6 A. Vauchez, 'Sainteté laïque au XIIIe siècle: la Vie du Bienheureux Facio de Crémone (v. 1196–1272)', *Mélanges de l'Ecole Française de Rome*, 84 (1972), p. 19. His remarks on the Life of Pier Pettinaio are in *Biblioteca sanctorum*, 10, cols 719–22.

7 Below, p. 194.

8 *AS*, March, 3, pp. 180–209.

9 See further below, p. 161.

This Life was probably composed within about a decade of Zita's death. It was written, as the author says in obedience to a time-hallowed convention, to preserve the memory of the saint's great achievements from oblivion. Zita's miracles were recorded by a notary in the immediate aftermath of her death, but there is no evidence of a canonisation campaign on her behalf. The Life of Umiliana de' Cerchi is accompanied by a miracle collection and may have been composed with a view to canonisation, but if so nothing came of it. Sometimes Lives seem to have been intended as commemorative accounts written for the pleasure and improvement of the community which conserved the saint's relics. Rufino's Life of Raimondo Palmario, for example, was explicitly written for the benefit of the brethren of the hospital the saint had founded at Piacenza; there is no suggestion that canonisation was envisaged. The Lives of both Pier Pettinaio of Siena and Rigo of Bolzano were written some time after their deaths, apparently to satisfy local and community *pietas*. Unsuccessful attempts had been made to secure Rigo's canonisation many years before.

Lay sanctity

Homobonus of Cremona, canonised by Innocent III in January 1199, was the first of four very different saints whom this pope canonised early in his pontificate. Of the others, Gilbert of Sempringham, who died in 1189 and was canonised in 1202, was the founder of the only uniquely English monastic order. Of an older vintage were the Empress Cunigunde, who died in 1033, and Wulfstan, bishop of Worcester (d. 1095), who were canonised in 1200 and 1203 respectively.[10] Any expectation that the pope was committed to a rolling programme of canonisation was doomed to disappointment, perhaps because he was overtaken by other preoccupations. In particular, anyone who entertained the belief or the hope that the canonisation of Homobonus portended the admission of more pious layfolk of lesser social rank to the number of the officially canonised would have been mistaken.

If Homobonus did not have successors among canonised saints, it was not because there was no one else like him: the strenuously charitable Raimondo Palmario of Piacenza was his almost exact contemporary.

---

10 For the development of canonisation procedures see E. Kemp, *Canonisation and authority in the western church* (Oxford, 1948) and Vauchez, *Sainthood*, pp. 11–84. Gilbert of Sempringham's canonisation is fully documented in R. Foreville and G. Keir (eds), *The book of St Gilbert* (Oxford, 1987).

Nor was it for want of trying on the part of the rulers and clergy of the Italian cities. Over a century later the bishop and magistrates of Treviso resolved to press for the canonisation of the humble layman Rigo, and there were other candidates both male and female.[11] There were many reasons for their failure. Already in the twelfth century the popes had indicated that canonisation was not going to be devalued by overuse. The complexity, long duration and expense of the procedure, which might be regarded as the necessary corollaries of its solemnity, increasingly made both funds and influential backing indispensable. Political upheaval, long papal vacancies and short pontificates (between 1252 and 1305 the average papal reign lasted little more than three years) all contributed to disrupt enquiries already in hand and to prevent others from ever beginning.

Equally important were the changes in the landscape of sanctity which followed on the appearance of the friars. A high proportion of the few saints to be formally canonised between 1200 and 1500 were members or associates of the mendicant orders, such as Francis, Dominic, Antony of Padua and Peter Martyr in the thirteenth century, Thomas Aquinas in the fourteenth, or Bernardino and Catherine, both of Siena, in the fifteenth. Much more numerous than canonised saints were men and women, laity and clergy, who were commemorated and venerated locally, as saints had been for centuries, by the communities which had nurtured them, achieving no higher official recognition. Homobonus apart, the saints included in this book all fall into that category.

Was there a specifically lay type of sanctity? The development of an authoritative papal canonisation process, even if relatively few candidates were ever subjected to it, reinforced the sense that there was a verifiable core of attributes by which a saint could and must be identified. Sanctity did not and could not suddenly become something different from what it had once been. In *Quia pietas*, the bull of canonisation of Homobonus (translated here), the pope succinctly summarised the basic criteria on which canonisation was based, above all the simultaneous insistence on posthumous miracles and evidence of holy life. These criteria were not Innocent's invention. Gregory the Great six centuries before had stated that the 'proof of sanctity' lay in virtues rather in 'signs' (a statement quoted, without acknowledgement, by Zita's hagiographer).[12]

11 Vauchez, *Sainthood*, pp. 72–3, lists requests to the papacy for canonisations which remained without result between 1198 and 1431 (some of the saints concerned were canonised in more recent times).

12 See below, p. 164.

Quia pietas provides a model statement of one layman's qualifications for sanctity, firmly placed within a general framework. There are (and can be) no special rules for lay saints. The destination which Homobonus had approached by an unusual and obscure path was the same which Wulfstan and Gilbert of Sempringham had reached by treading in the footsteps of previous bishops and monastic patriarchs. While the investigation of a monk's sanctity might in fact be somewhat differently focused (with more emphasis on bodily austerities, perhaps, and less on practical charity), the imitation of devotional practices that were in origin monastic was a common feature of lay sanctity. There was a deeply engrained tendency to believe that the relevant virtues were most likely to be perfected by monks and other religious professionals; from a clerical viewpoint it may have seemed desirable to encourage the laity in this belief.

There were however cogent pastoral reasons for seeking saints over a broader area. Clerical saints had limited value as role models and sources of inspiration for men and women who were inevitably going to remain 'in the world' for all or most of their lives but must nonetheless be encouraged to lead Christian lives. If there were to be 'lay' saints they must exemplify the indispensable virtues in ways that were appropriate to the lay condition. This was not a brand-new perception in the thirteenth century, but the sanctity of the immediately preceding centuries had been predominantly monastic and clerical. The 'Gregorian reformers' of the eleventh century, with their powerful emphasis on the superiority and separateness of the priestly order, were arguably unlikely to look for sanctity among laymen and less still among women.

In the early tenth century, however, Odo, abbot of Cluny, a monk of the highest possible standing who was alive to the realities of the world around him, had held up the nobleman Gerald of Aurillac as a model of what was achievable by the pious layman.[13] Assiduous prayer and the limited imitation of monastic austerities, such as fasting, were to be accompanied by the practice of the virtues which were accessible and appropriate to a person living in the world: benevolence and obedience to the church, justice and mercy towards social inferiors, practical charity to the needy, pilgrimage. Pilgrimage, an arduous physical

13 Text in J. P. Migne (ed.), *Patrologia Latina* [hereafter *PL*], 133, cols 639–703; translation in T. F. X. Noble and T. Head (eds), *Soldiers of Christ: saints and saints' Lives from late antiquity and the early middle ages* (London 1995), pp. 295–362. B. Rosenwein, 'St Odo's St Martin: the uses of a model', *Journal of Medieval History*, 4 (1978), pp. 317–31, suggests that Odo's devotion to St Martin, the converted soldier, helped to shape his treatment of Gerald.

activity, was regarded as a penitential exercise suitable for laymen; Gerald went several times to Rome and also to Tours and Limoges. Frequent pilgrimage, whether over long or short distances, remained characteristic of the lay saints of the thirteenth century. [14]

There was nothing urban about Gerald of Aurillac's social setting, but he was, so to speak, the characteristic lay type of his day, the noble who, if unjust, violent and rapacious, could make life a misery for his neighbours and inferiors, both lay and ecclesiastical. By the later twelfth century, attention was increasingly directed to laymen of quite another stamp: the merchants, craftsmen and urban patricians who might not have the knightly capacity to wreak physical havoc but who exerted varying degrees of influence in local society and also possessed wealth which could be tapped for the benefit of the church and of their fellow men. They also of course had souls which needed saving, and there were a lot more of them than there had been in the tenth century.

Andrea Gallerani of Siena (d. 1251) in some respects recalls the older type. He had military experience: it is said that in 1219 he participated in a Sienese expedition against Orvieto and personally killed the leader of the opposing forces.[15] Exiled for a murder, he returned covertly to Siena and hid himself in one of the fortified towers which characterised the Italian urban landscape (Umiliana lived in a 'tower' belonging to her father). On a later occasion Andrea's enemies set an ambush to kill him but in the event could not bring themselves to do so. It is not clear whether this incident was connected with the homicide he had committed, but after his death his victim's brother, Guelfo, was enraged that he should have been so reverently buried by the Dominicans. Struck by 'divine terror', however, Guelfo repented and went barefoot to the church, processing solemnly from the choir to the saint's tomb, a conspicuous witness to his sanctity. Andrea Gallerani did not retire to the cloister to escape violence and feud as St Romuald and St Giovanni Gualberto had done in the tenth and eleventh centuries, but like his social inferior Raimondo Palmario remade himself according to the contemporary model of the lay charitable activist, which he united with the *personae* of the citizen and the noble with a past history of violence.

One eleventh-century glimpse of lay charitable piety in action in a different setting is instructive by contrast. In 1041, the monk Andreas

14 Vauchez, *Sainthood*, pp. 197–9; also Vauchez, 'Sainteté laïque', pp. 30–1.
15 *AS*, March, 3, p. 50.

began work on his section of the lengthy compilation of the miracles of St Benedict which was produced at the abbey of Fleury (Saint Benoît-sur-Loire). Among other reminiscences of his childhood in a noble family he recalls the charitable endeavours of his father Stephanus during a famine year:

> With great fervour and unremitting effort he began to alleviate poverty, to the extent that every day he gave donations, at his own expense, to 200 or more, visited the sick and, confident of his reward, conscientiously kept several infirmaries, constructed for this good purpose, supplied; with his wife he gave honourable burial to a multitude of dead. While they were engaged in this activity it happened that the store of wheat, which contained about ten measures of grain, and from which a crowd of poor people were supplied at a fixed time, began to run out. He was informed of this by his faithful wife, who wanted to know how their work was to continue … He maintained his accustomed faith in God and said, 'Go, don't hesitate, but trust in the strength of God and his servant Benedict, open the container at first light and assuage the hunger of the poor of Christ with what you find in it.' The wise woman gave a believing ear to his command and, after going to the church of the friend of God [Benedict] before dawn, she hastened to the store of alms, which she was amazed to discover so filled and heaped with celestial abundance that she marvelled at the overflowing heaps of grain; nor did this bounty fail for as long as the aforesaid dearth continued. Thus, through the merits of Benedict, the wonders of Elias return, the pious increase of 200 measures is repeated, through the workings of divine mercy.[16]

With filial pride, Andreas gives us a picture of the pious layman in action around the year 1000; but the miraculous element in the story is attributed to St Benedict, the monk-saint, indeed the patron of monks, to whom that layman and his wife were devoted. Two hundred years later it could be suggested that God would perform similar miracles of replenishment and multiplication in response to the merits of a layman such as Homobonus or Andrea Gallerani, not to mention the laywoman Zita.

Andreas was writing in praise of St Benedict, and his frame of reference was that of a monk since childhood. Holiness, in this world-view, was above all a monastic quality; it was not associated even with secular clerks, who often seemed slightly suspect even when they became monks late in life, and certainly not with laymen, who appear for the most part as violent and greedy nobles or as peasants whose 'simplicity' manifests itself in either devout obedience or wilful obtuseness. This was

---

16 E. de Certain (ed.), *Les miracles de Saint Benoît* (Paris, 1858), 7:10, pp. 266–7.

a conventional monastic attitude, well expressed in a phrase Andreas uses elsewhere to describe one of two brothers from Barcelona who came to Fleury. One had been a monk at Ripoll; the other, brought up from youth as a soldier, was 'obedient to God, so far as is possible for a layman'.[17] Andreas doubtless saw it as to his father's credit that he had offered his son to God and St Benedict as a monk. A shift away from child oblation was among the multiple changes which affected monasticism between 1000 and 1200. Not only the friars but a higher proportion of monks had a lengthier experience of exposure to the world, if only as children, and to that extent they had more in common with their lay contemporaries than many earlier monks had had.

The 'Gregorian reformers' may have been disposed to discern sanctity in the priest or the monk rather than in the layman, but in one light, and especially in its Italian setting, the eleventh-century drive for reform can be seen as an episode in the growth of a more self-conscious urban laity to which the parties in the 'church–state' struggle appealed and from which they recruited. Milan, one of the greatest of the Italian cities, played a central part in the papal–imperial struggle and produced an urban saint for the times, the priest Ariald. Himself the son of minor nobility, Ariald had support among the urban laity, not only among aristocrats who were prepared to take up arms against the other members of their class who dominated the Milanese church, but among lowlier, though affluent, individuals such as the moneyer Nazarius, who offered him hospitality and eloquently denounced clergy who were in no way morally superior to the laymen like himself who sought their blessing. Nazarius himself is represented not as a saint but as a devout witness to the sanctity embodied in the true priest Ariald.[18]

To his biographer, the Vallombrosan monk Andrea of Strumi, it was not so much Ariald's social setting as his modernity that required emphasis. The end of the world was nigh but, as no one knew exactly when it was coming, it remained important to transmit to posterity knowledge of the new saints who equalled the ancients.[19] To Andrea, as to St Augustine, Gregory the Great or Gregory of Tours centuries earlier, sanctity and miracles were vital proofs that God was still at work in the world, and the same sense breathes from the Lives which are the subject of this book. Historic change disposed observers to look for sanctity in

17 Ibid., 4:7, pp. 182–3.
18 Andrea da Strumi, Vita Sancti Arialdi, ed. F. Baethgen, Monumenta Germaniae Historiae: Scriptores [hereafter MGH Scriptores], 30:2, p. 1053.
19 Ibid., p. 1050.

new places and indeed made it highly necessary to do so in order to keep the faith in God's continuing activity and presence alive among the populace. At the same time, as these Lives also demonstrate, there were powerful pressures moulding the representation of lay saints in accordance with established models.

Bishops as urban saints

Characteristic of the Italian cities in the chronological gap between the heroic beginnings of Christianity under the later Roman Empire and the thirteenth century was an ancient category of urban patron saints, the bishops. Among the many reasons why Thomas Becket achieved rapid celebrity in Italy as elsewhere in Europe was the fact that the doughty episcopal champion of ecclesiastical rights against a threatening lay power was a familiar figure in a society which had witnessed not only the incursions of the emperors, down to and particularly including Frederick Barbarossa, but also the rapid growth of a more localised but also sometimes aggressive secular political authority, the commune.

Atto of Pistoia, Ubaldo of Gubbio, Galdino of Milan and Lanfranc of Pavia were only some of the twelfth-century Italian bishops to achieve veneration. Not all of them were 'popular' in the sense of attracting lay as well as clerical enthusiasm, but it was characteristic of bishop-saints (as of holy popes in their special relationship to Rome) that, as well as standing up for the church, they were represented as earning the gratitude of their citizens by a variety of means: obtaining important relics for the city, invoking celestial protection for it against hostile neighbours and vigorously dispensing charity.[20] Bishops were not monks (although monks could become bishops). They lived in the world and served the church in the world. They might be distinguished for humility and other virtues, and of course they had to be punctilious in the performance of their religious duties, but visions, ecstasies and extreme austerity were not such essential features of episcopal sanctity as they tended to be of its monastic counterpart. Their lives in fact help to explain much that might at first sight seem distinctive about

---

20 On bishop-saints in the civic context, see A. Benvenuti Papi, *Pastori di popolo: storie e leggende di vescovi e di città nell' Italia medievale* (Florence, 1988) and the essays by A. Orselli collected in *L'immaginario religioso della città medievale* (Ravenna, 1985). There is also much that is relevant in M. C. Miller, *The bishop's palace: architecture and authority in medieval Italy* (Ithaca, 2000), especially pp. 157–63.

the sanctity of Homobonus or Raimondo Palmario late in the twelfth century.

Galdino, archbishop of Milan from 1166 to 1176, was a member of the minor Milanese nobility, who became archdeacon and chancellor in the cathedral church of the city and went into exile with his archbishop, Oberto, during the papal schism that was brought about by Frederick Barbarossa in 1158. On the death of Oberto, Alexander III consecrated Galdino as his successor, but his exile continued until the creation of the Lombard League and the restoration of Milan, which had been sacked by Barbarossa in 1163. Galdino re-entered the city amid general rejoicing in December 1165. From the viewpoint from which the extant Life was written, it was a signal proof of Galdino's merits that he now busied himself restoring ecclesiastical property and redecorating the episcopal palace with some splendour. He was assiduous in the performance of the liturgy, to the extent of wearing the lesser clergy out; he was ever mindful of death and of the transience of all earthly things. These were all distinctively clerical virtues, but he also presented a positive face to the urban laity:

> He had received such a gift of speech from God that when he spoke to the people about holy religion it seemed that not a man but the spirit of God spoke in him. The care of the poor, above all other mortals, was his concern; and although in other expenditures and everyday charges he was touched by human avarice, to the poor he was as generous as if he thought that he possessed nothing for himself but everything for them, so that he was believed to live not for himself but for the poor of Christ. He was however no less concerned for those who laboured under want and poverty but were ashamed to beg for alms; anticipating the call of the petitioner he was compassionate and generous to all.[21]

The curious reference to 'avarice' is perhaps a gloss on Galdino's zeal for the restoration of his church's income. A eulogy of his humility follows – some even thought him contemptible because of it – but he was also determined to resist the arrogant. He was vigorous in defence of the church and could not be moved by threats or flattery; but he was so marvellously kind to all as to furnish a model of compassion, and within his own household he was the soul of amiability and good fellowship.

It was not by the unaided efforts of the church that Galdino was enabled to return to Milan, but with the assistance of laymen, that is the mili-

---

21 Life in *AS*, April, 2, pp. 594–5; also in Boninus Mombritius, *Sanctuarium seu vitae sanctorum*, edited by two monks of Solesmes (2 vols, Paris, 1910), 1, pp. 561–3.

tias of the Lombard League, whose members were happy to espouse the ecclesiastical cause insofar as it was also the anti-imperial cause of urban autonomy. The subsequent spread of heresy in this environment (particularly when the secular authorities seemed to connive at it) indicated that there was no necessary or guaranteed harmony between the civic and ecclesiastical versions of 'liberty'. No sooner had Galdino consecrated all his suffragans and set the church and the city to rights than Catharism began to spread in Milan, to no small degree as a result of the preceding schism. Heresy indirectly claimed the archbishop's life, for it was after a particularly energetic verbal assault on the Cathars from the pulpit of Santa Tecla that he collapsed and commended his soul to God with such signs to the bystanders as he could manage.

The image of episcopal sanctity given in this Life squares, in all essentials, with the portrayal of Galdino's near-contemporary Lanfranc of Pavia (d. 1194) by Bernardo, his successor in the see.[22] Lanfranc too was a warrior against heresy. He surpassed his predecessors in almsgiving (his highly organised daily benefactions are described in some detail) while also greatly increasing his possessions and rents and taking steps to regain properties that his predecessors had lost. He was briefly sent into exile when he quarrelled with his citizens but was restored when 'a friend of the church and enemy of impiety' became *podestà* of Pavia. As the internal contest for control of urban governments intensified, there was increased scope for the factional alignments which, nominally at least, identified themselves as pro-ecclesiastical or pro-imperial and which in the next century would be labelled 'Guelf' and 'Ghibelline'. It was evidently essential to win the most influential members of these societies over to the cause of the church. The defence of ecclesiastical property and privilege must be accompanied by charitable benevolence.

In the closing decades of the twelfth century Homobonus and Raimondo Palmario based their claims to veneration on activities – charity and peacemaking – which were specifically and urgently relevant to their fellow-citizens. Their attributes thus overlapped to some degree with those of the holy bishops of recent times. Like them they exemplified an activist sanctity in which charity was more prominent than extreme forms of spiritual self-development.[23] However, as laymen they were not personally associated, as Galdino and Lanfranc were, with the

22 *AS*, June, 4, pp. 619–30.

23 One version of Homobonus's Life however emphasises the penitential, ascetic elements of his sanctity; see below, pp. 49–53.

defence of ecclesiastical property or jurisdiction. Preaching, other than by example, was not their business. According to Innocent III, Homobonus sternly condemned heretics but, although there were undoubtedly heretics in Piacenza in Raimondo's time, we are not told what, if anything, he had to do with them. Both in what they did and in what they did not do such men were plausible models for imitation.

What might not have been foreseen when Raimondo died in 1200 was that within a few decades the urban apostolate would be to a large extent appropriated by new orders of regular clergy whose hagiography fused the ideals of the active life (*vita activa*) as it might be lived by bishops or laymen with significant elements of monastic sanctity. Henceforth, the ways in which lay aspirants to holiness experienced their lives and were described (often by mendicant biographers) bore this indelible imprint.

There was a considerable overlap between the clerical ideals exemplified by bishops and friars. They had in common a commitment to charity, preaching and other expressions of pastoral care, but there could be tensions between episcopal ideal and religious profession. Friars, like monks, sometimes became bishops (and popes), although not everyone approved. It was not merely humility that might deter an individual friar from accepting such promotion, but the desire to persist in a chosen way of life and a particular form of apostolate which were perceived not to be easily compatible with the episcopal office. A Galdino of Milan or Lanfranc of Pavia expended much energy in defending ecclesiastical property; for the friars, although they later acquired a reputation with satirists for avarice and hypocrisy, the commitment to poverty was of central importance and played a large part in the reputation they enjoyed with the laity. In the thirteenth century bishop-saints, though not unknown, were less prominent in Italy than they had been or than they remained in some other regions, such as England. It has been remarked that thirteenth-century English saints tended to be bishops, while in Italy 'the bishop and the saint were different things'.[24] The Sienese Dominican Ambrogio Sansedoni twice refused a bishopric, and Pier Pettinaio is said to have advised him to do so.[25]

---

24 R. Brentano, *Two churches: England and Italy in the thirteenth century* (Berkeley, CA, 1988), p. 222 (reprint of original 1968 edition). On episcopal sanctity and its regional and chronological variations, see Vauchez, *Sainthood*, pp. 197–203, 329–58.
25 Below, p. 230.

The urban background

It might well be asked what, if anything, was peculiarly 'urban' (as distinct from 'lay') about the sanctity which is the subject of this book. The demographic, urban and economic changes of the eleventh and twelfth centuries in Italy did not pass unnoticed by contemporaries, and, given that those who recorded their observations were most likely to be clergy, it is not surprising that some note was taken of the moral and spiritual implications. One ' Gregorian' bishop, Rangerio of Lucca (d. 1112), was struck by the destructive effects of social and economic change in the urban environment. Reviewing the recent history of Lucca in his vast verse biography of his predecessor Anselm (d. c.1080), Rangerio saw an increasingly ungovernable community, corrupted by affluence and the aping of foreign (notably French) ways, but also enlarged by immigration, which had its own adverse effects. A 'rude' people, sprung from villages and mountains (*genus incultum villis et rupibus ortum*), had come to town in search of an easier life and, finding things not so easy, became embroiled in clashes with the older nobility.[26]

Rangerio's diagnosis has some striking similarities with the one which after another two hundred years of urban growth and factional strife Dante put into the mouth of his ancestor Cacciaguida in *Paradiso*, 16. Cacciaguida complained that Dante's Florence was five times the size of the early twelfth-century city he had known. This enlargement was in itself an evil – the blind bull takes a heavier fall than the blind lamb – but it was also inextricably bound up with an undesirable social mixture deriving from immigration. Would that many families, who had fomented the divisions that had torn Florence apart (and sent Dante himself into exile), had never come to Florence from their rural places of origin to buy and sell! Included in this lament were the Cerchi, who were not only the leaders of the so-called 'White' Guelfs, Dante's party, at the end of the thirteenth century, but earlier in the century had produced one of the saints included in this book, Umiliana.

By 1200 towns in most of Europe were larger and more numerous than they had been. Many shrank in size, at least temporarily, in the plague-ridden years after 1350, but they had by then acquired a collective significance which they would never lose, as centres not only of commercial activity but of government, justice and administration, education, culture and, not least, religious life. In a still overwhelmingly

26 *Vita metrica*, in *MGH Scriptores*, 30:2, pp. 1152–307. The quotation here is from line 4549.

agrarian landscape, towns of a few thousand souls could and did carry considerable weight in these roles. The appearance of these concentrations of people had already before 1200 imposed considerable strains on a parochial system which had grown piecemeal over centuries of scantier and more dispersed population and was served by a clergy for whom there was no systematic training. When the first orders of friars were establishing their convents shortly after 1200, it was in the towns that they located them. At least initially, they were resolved to live on alms, and they had to go where alms were to be had in sufficient quantity, but their mission was also to the inhabitants, both the destitute who like themselves relied on alms if they could get them and the more prosperous householders who had disposable surpluses.

The towns of Italy have with some justification been taken to be the most precocious, richest and largest in this urbanising Europe. It has to be remembered that a city of more than 50,000 people was quite exceptional, and the proportion of the Italian population that lived in towns, about 30 per cent, was probably little, if any, bigger than it was in Flanders, or, rather later, Holland. In Italy, however, there was a substantial number of cities in the 20,000–50,000 range, which north of the Alps would have looked very large, and a host of others of 6,000 or more.[27] In addition, these cities collectively enjoyed a freedom from dynastic overlordship which few cities elsewhere in Europe came anywhere near emulating, although some of their other features could be paralleled, especially in the Low Countries, the Rhineland and the Hanseatic region. In Italy north of Rome centralised territorial power was to a remarkable degree absent or non-existent, at least until rulers such as the Venetians or the dukes of Milan extended and consolidated their spheres of influence in the fifteenth century.

This liberty was far from making life easy for either the rulers or the ordinary inhabitants of the cities. It committed them to an endless series of power struggles, external and internal, which there was no one to prevent or resolve. The freedom which permitted the more substantial Italian citizen to profit from his business activities and to compete for a share in political power also aggravated the social and economic tensions to which both he and the less affluent and influential were subject. In the later twelfth and earlier thirteenth centuries these conditions helped open up niches here and there in which heresy could flourish. It is hardly surprising that the orders of friars looked

27 M. Ginatempo and L. Sandri, *L'Italia delle città* (Florence, 1990), give population estimates for many cities before and after the Black Death.

especially at home in Italy. Francis himself was a product of the small-town mercantile society of central Italy, and Dominic was buried in the great university city of Bologna, where his order had come in search of promising recruits. To mention Francis is to be reminded, however, that sanctity in this society did not bear a single 'urban' face. The quest for eremitical solitude was an important aspect of Francis's spirituality, and it was in a mountain retreat that he received the Stigmata. Only in the centre of the northern plain are Italian cities any distance from the mountains, and many of the smaller ones perch among the foothills of the major mountain ranges. Eremitical 'solitudes' were to be found close to such centres of population.

The difficulties of establishing criteria by which the 'towns' of this period can be distinguished from lesser centres of population, in Italy or elsewhere, are notorious. Determining a minimum size presents its difficulties, and neither the physical characteristics of the 'town' nor the range of goods and services available in it are decisive. Towns had walls, fairs and markets, shrines, notaries and schoolmasters, but all of these things could be found in settlements which would probably strike us as rural rather than urban. Even towns which were identified as such by common consent were more 'rural' than the enormous agglomerations of the present day can possibly be. The open spaces that survived within their walls were not, as they are now, industrial wasteland or parks or playing fields deliberately set aside for purposes of recreation; if land was not 'built up' or inhabited it was as like as not still serving the economic purpose, as vineyard, orchard or 'market garden', of which the modern allotment furnishes a tenuous reminder. The point is underlined by the presence of large numbers of animals within the urban space, for example the pigs which were often identified as a nuisance. Not only was the countryside not far away, but the urban inhabitants, both great and small, owned land which some at least of the latter might work part-time with their own hands or with hired labour. The Life of Homobonus translated here notes that the saint's parents lived in a quarter of Cremona which had recently grown up around the church of Sant' Egidio, but like other moderately affluent town-dwellers, in addition to practising a trade, they 'obtained the necessaries of life from a sufficient landholding, not far from the walls of the city'. Pier Pettinaio for a long time derived both income and enjoyment from his vineyard, which was evidently outside the walls of Siena.

Settlement by one or more of the mendicant orders, in Italy as elsewhere in Europe, can be regarded as a useful indicator of urban status, or at least of a density of population which on the one hand could support the existence of one or more convents and on the other seemed to require the pastoral intervention of the friars. There were many small-town Italian saints in the thirteenth century, and their biographers were not infrequently mendicants. The Life of Fina of San Gimignano (d. 1253) was written by a fourteenth-century Dominican of the place who describes it as a 'flourishing *castello*' but unfortunately sheds no further light on the social setting. San Gimignano may have attained a population of about 8,500 around the year 1300.[28] Lucchesius of Poggibonsi (d. 1241) was a native of the *villa* of Gaggiani, in the Val d' Elsa in the Florentine *contado*.[29] By the standards of local society, he was of 'honourable birth'. He became involved in a feud and took refuge in Poggibonsi, described as a *castrum*, where he was apparently able to indulge a constitutional weakness for social climbing. When he decided, together with his wife, to follow the Franciscan way of life he retained a 'garden' of four *jugera*[30] for his sustenance. Like his counterparts in larger communities, he marked his change of mind by vigorous involvement in charity, and we are given at least an impression of the landscape in which he operated: he toured the roads, *villae*, *castella* and households round about to seek out the needy and the infirm, whom he carried back either himself or on an ass.

Recent population estimates suggest that even the smallest of the cities featured in this book (probably Treviso) was substantially larger than San Gimignano or Poggibonsi. Florence was by far the largest, although the population of 100,000 which may be ventured for about the year 1300 (the fictional date of Cacciaguida's complaints) would have been smaller half a century earlier in Umiliana's lifetime. Cremona and Piacenza, which are estimated to have had, respectively, over 40,000 and over 20,000 inhabitants around 1300, must also be assumed to have grown in the century that had elapsed since Homobonus and Raimondo Palmario died. Around 1300, Siena may have had 45,000–50,000 people, Lucca 20,000–30,000 and Treviso 20,000.[31]

28 Life in *AS*, March, 2, pp. 236–41. For the population estimate see Ginatempo and Sandri, *L'Italia delle città*, p. 148. The word *castello* (in Latin *castrum* or *castellum*) frequently designated a fortified settlement rather than a 'castle'. *Villa* is hard to translate exactly, but 'village' is sometimes a reasonable equivalent.

29 P. M. Bertagna, *S. Lucchese da Poggibonsi: note storiche e documenti* (Florence, 1969); originally in *Archivum Franciscanum Historicum*, 62 (1969). *Contado* (in Latin, *comitatus*) designates the rural territory immediately dependent on an Italian city.

30 The *jugum* was a land-measure of Roman origin equivalent to 240 × 120 Roman feet or about 2500 square metres.

31 Ginatempo and Sandri, *L'Italia delle città*, pp. 100 (northern Italy), 148 (Tuscany).

How important to the hagiographer was the social setting of his subject and what confidence can be reposed in the picture he gives of it? Both in miracle stories and in the narrative body of Lives there was a certain amount of scope for adaptation to the particular landscape in which the saint lived and worked. Both elements were essential: the obedience to convention which located the saint in the great tradition and the local detail which reinforced the verisimilitude of the narrative and related it to the lives of its audience. It is unlikely that hagiographers, who probably assumed the audience's familiarity with the material background, consciously set out to evoke a distinctive 'urban' setting, but there are at least two ways in which, like other contemporary narrative sources, Lives sometimes do so.

In the first place they may describe, or at least mention, the physical aspects of the urban environment. Places with a certain concentration of population boasted gates, squares, market-places and numerous churches, although we must again remember that even quite small settlements possessed surprising numbers of churches and other architectural features, such as walls, which were common to big cities. The frequency with which small children seem to have fallen from upper windows into the streets of Siena, only to be rescued by one of the numerous local saints, hints at an environment distinguished by tall buildings.[32] Windows have a certain importance in these sketches. The beneficiary of Andrea Gallerani's first posthumous miracle was a knight whose eyes were discharging pus and who was cured when he chanced to see the saint's funeral procession passing by from a window in his palace. Here the window links the domestic interior to the passing life of the street. Those characteristic figures of life in a built-up area, the people across the road, also figure in Andrea's story. On several occasions 'the women who lived opposite the holy man' rose early for matins and saw a great light shining from the place where he prayed. When Raimondo Palmario wanted to goad his fellow-citizens into greater generosity to beggars his shouted exhortations brought people to their windows, 'and some opened their doors and ran into the

32 A depiction of one such Sienese miracle, performed by the Augustinian friar Agostino Novello, was included by Simone Martini in an altarpiece celebrating the saint, now in the Sienese Pinacoteca. See A. Martindale, 'The child in the picture: a medieval perspective', in D. Wood (ed.), *The church and childhood* (Oxford, 1994) (*Studies in Church History*, 31), pp. 197–232, and D. Webb, 'Friends of the family: some miracles for children by Italian friars', *ibid.*, pp. 183–95. Andrea Gallerani performed a similar miracle, and Pier Pettinaio's prayers helped to resuscitate another such child: see below, pp. 152, 156, 218. On miracles for children in general see R. Finucane, *The rescue of the innocents: endangered children in medieval miracles* (London, 1997).

piazza'. The piazza too is a characteristic and important element in this urban theatre. We are given some vivid glimpses of the space before the cathedral of Treviso where Rigo used to stand and venerate an image of the Virgin under the portico and where his body was brought, as word of his death 'resounded around the Piazza del Commune and the main street'.

Some of the most vividly evoked spaces in this literature are interiors. The lay saint was often making a conscious effort to reproduce the conditions of monastic seclusion in the secular domestic setting. He or she in effect sought the privacy in which to pursue not only prayer but monastic austerities such as flagellation. This endeavour was reflected, in Umiliana's Life, by the repeated use of the word 'cell' to describe the room in her father's house in which she conducted her spiritual exercises and which, we are told, she often kept locked precisely in order to avoid interruption. Pietro da Baono not only describes the location of the notary's house in Treviso in which Rigo was given a room, but explains that the room was 'at the far end of the house, beyond a courtyard'. The notary's wife, who 'as is usual with women' spent much of her time in the house, heard him in it conversing with saints and angels.

Hagiography may also convey the social atmosphere, the sorts of human interactions, including war and feud, which were fostered by town life. Cities then as now enhanced visibility, partly because the concentration of population within them also concentrated problems in a quantitative sense. They acted as magnets, sometimes for the saints themselves: Zita found employment in Lucca and Rigo at Treviso. At any one moment, in a city like Piacenza which stood at a junction of major roads and at a major river crossing, there was a bigger population of sometimes penniless transients, pilgrims among them, than there would be in a *castello*, and such people were among Raimondo Palmario's clients. The foundlings whom he so tenderly collected from the streets of Piacenza may not all have been natives. The permanent presence of a substantial number of beggars is virtually taken for granted. Unfortunates of all kinds required both spiritual and charitable provision, but in another sense, emphasised in these Lives, they themselves provided opportunities for the display of charismatic power and heroic charity.

There were more criminals in cities, more prostitutes, more people to engage in factional warfare and bigger gangs of youths to join in the dangerous and violent games which could lead to bloodshed and which Raimondo tried to stop. Zita's tenderness for the victims of execution had more scope in the urban setting; she wept copiously when the bells rang to announce that a condemned man was going to his death. We hear of factional conflict at Florence in the life of Umiliana and of war between Cremona and Piacenza in the life of Raimondo. The Lives of Raimondo and Pier Pettinaio are particularly rich in references to the institutions of urban government and justice, including Raimondo's interventions on behalf of criminals and Pier's determination to pay his taxes. More elusive and rarely explicit is the sense that urban living and social relationships were distinctive in ways which impinged on the spiritual life, on the shaping and expression of religious ideals.

Charity and poverty

A sense of obligation to the poor and the sick was deeply embedded in Christianity; had it not been so, practical charity would not have been a virtue to which a high proportion of saints laid claim at all times. However, the medieval emphasis (not least in hagiography) tended to be on the merit of the voluntary giver rather than on the moral obligation of the affluent to yield up their surplus. Charitable provision could easily be ritualised. A testator, lay or ecclesiastical, might make provision in his (or her) will for the regular feeding of a fixed number of 'poor and pilgrims', and if the ceremony was at all public the effect was as much to demonstrate the benevolence of the provider as to alleviate want, which of course it could not do, even for the selected individuals, beyond the very short term. While this kind of semi-symbolic provision continued, growing population and the appearance after the eleventh century of larger concentrations of people, living in insalubrious conditions, did much to force the 'real' poor on the attention of contemporary observers. Equally important was the growing visibility alongside the poor of the newly rich, men who did not derive their wealth from traditional sources. The wealth of such people was less bound up in land and agricultural surpluses, more in liquid cash and household effects, than that of the 'traditional' nobility, and it could readily be mobilised for charitable purposes.

Raimondo Palmario's conversion from lifelong pilgrimage to charitable activism was effected by a vision of Christ, experienced at St Peter's in Rome. Christ's mission, although he was himself garbed as a pilgrim, as it was commonly imagined he had appeared to the disciples on the road to Emmaus, was to divert Raimondo from his present plans.

> You are not to think that I shall be thinking principally of pilgimage, and works of piety of that kind, when at the time of Judgement I say, 'Come, O

blessed of my Father, take possession of the kingdom of Heaven: for I was hungry and you gave me food; I was thirsty, and you gave me to drink; I was naked and you clothed me; I was sick and you visited me; I was in prison and you ransomed me.'

The reference, or quotation, was unmistakable. In the Gospel of St Matthew (25:31–46) Christ imagines himself dividing the saved from the damned at the Last Judgement. The saved will be told that in performing these acts of charity 'even for the least of my brothers' they have performed them for Christ himself. For some reason, Raimondo's biographer, Master Rufino, omits from the gospel list of beneficiaries the 'stranger' or 'guest' (*hospes*) to whom shelter should be offered, although this was to be one of Raimondo's own specialities.

Matthew's account of Christ's words supplied the basic text for an artistic theme which was popular in the later middle ages, especially in northern Europe: the Corporal Works of Mercy.[33] One of the earliest representations of it was carved by Benedetto Antelami's workshop on the west portal of the baptistery of the cathedral of Parma, some time around 1200. On the tympanum above the door the judging Christ is depicted as he had come to be represented in the French twelfth-century sculpture by which Antelami was profoundly influenced. He raises his hands to display his wounds, while angels around him hold up the Instruments of the Passion and other angels, below, summon the dead to arise to damnation or salvation. The Works of Mercy are shown below, on the left-hand jamb of the door as the spectator looks at it, and are thus visually associated with the theme of Judgement. A solemn male figure, dressed in cap and gown, is shown offering hospitality, bathing an injured limb, providing food and drink to the needy, bearing bread to a prisoner and clothing the naked.[34] It is implicit, rather than visually explicit, that the little human figures which receive these charities express Christ's self-identification with mankind, which finds its ultimate expression in his death on the Cross and to which he draws attention by his gesture on the tympanum. On the opposite jamb, the sculptor represented the parable of the Labourers in the Vineyard (Matthew 20:1–16), which also has to do with the themes of service, judgement and reward.

Too much must not be made of a single work of art, but this sculpture was close not only chronologically but geographically to Raimondo

33 See E. Kirschbaum (ed.), *Lexikon der christlichen Ikonographie*, 1 (Rome, 1968), cols 243–51, s.v. 'Barmherzigkeit, Werke der'.

34 G. H. Crichton, *Romanesque sculpture in Italy* (London, 1954), p. 66.

of Piacenza and Homobonus of Cremona. We may not take literally Rufino's account of how Raimondo was converted from a way of life dedicated simply to the saving of his own soul to one orientated to the needs of others but, whether in the saint's own understanding or in his biographer's, its source and its justification were beyond dispute. Christ's summons to Raimondo is remarkable for the distance it sets between pilgrimage and pious exercises of that kind and the more practically useful good works which he was enjoining. It seems to devalue pilgrimage even for the laity, or at least represents it as something from which Raimondo was now supposed to progress. The same note is not struck, however, in any of the other Lives translated here. Insofar as pilgrimage is mentioned it seems simply to be regarded as a meritorious expression of religious devotion. Artistic representations of the Works of Mercy frequently represented the 'strangers' to whom the charitable ministered in the easily recognisable guise of pilgrims. Raimondo's own charities embraced pilgrims, male and female, for whom he provided accommodation as he did for other sick and poor people and foundlings. It is reported without comment of another 'hospitaller' saint, Gualtiero of Lodi, who received part of his training at Raimondo's hospital shortly after the latter's death, that he was a frequent pilgrim to Rome, Santiago and elsewhere.[35]

Christ instructed Raimondo to relieve the poor, widows, the sick and those afflicted by various calamities; he was to lead the rich to almsgiving, those in conflict to peace, and errant women to a right way of living. The injunctions to charity (and against avarice) to be found in the Bible were not, of course, limited to St Matthew's Gospel. When Raimondo went out alms-gathering he used both stick and carrot, on the one hand quoting the Sermon on the Mount ('Blessed be the merciful, for they shall receive mercy') and on the other threatening woe to the rich and avaricious, 'for sentence will be pronounced upon you' (probably an adaptation of the Epistle of St James, chapter 5). One night when Ambrogio Sansedoni of Siena was playing host to pilgrims in his father's house he received an angelic vision which underlined the point that he had obeyed the counsel of Hebrews 13:2, 'Do not forget hospitality, for thereby some have received angels unawares.'[36] A seventh work of mercy which features in the late medieval iconography

---

35 A. Caretta, 'La Vita di S. Gualtiero di Lodi', *Archivio Storico Lodigiano*, 2nd series 17 (1969), p. 20. On Gualtiero see also G. Albini, *Città e ospedali nella Lombardia medievale* (Bologna, 1993), pp. 54–62.

36 *AS*, March, 3, p. 184. In 789, Charlemagne's *Admonitio generalis* (c. 75) quoted both Matthew and Hebrews in encouragement of hospitality.

was the burial of the dead; Innocent III cited the burial of the pauper dead among the good works of Homobonus. This derived its biblical sanction from the speech of the archangel Raphael in Tobias 12:8–12, a powerful statement of the crucial role of works of mercy in salvation. Raimondo Palmario as a head of household modelled himself on Tobit, the pious married man, and Pier Pettinaio too is likened to him.

The modern reader of these Lives may be struck by the recurrent phrase 'the decent poor' (*pauperes verecundi* or *decentes*). Their equivalents are still with us, especially in the form of older people who have 'always paid their way' and 'have never got into debt and aren't going to start now', and also some of the thousands who do not claim benefits to which they are entitled. In the absence of state welfare provision, they represented a category of the poor which, especially perhaps in the urban setting, was likely to escape notice. Poor people of this kind were sometimes quite sharply distinguished from the all too visible beggars from whose condition and behaviour the respectable, the affluent and the proud shuddered. Writing in 1212, Master Rufino says that when Raimondo Palmario began his charitable work in Piacenza he targeted the *verecundi*, those who were ashamed to beg, as well as those who were too infirm to do so. Umiliana had a special tenderness for female members of this group, who were deemed to be vulnerable to the risk of prostitution.

Begging in itself was not unacceptable to Raimondo; after all, he was doing it himself, albeit on behalf of others. When an army of habitual beggars tried to get a share of his charity, he told them to go and beg, because they were not ashamed to do so. They replied that they did not get anything when they did, which stung him into an effort to persuade the affluent citizenry to take notice of all the poverty in their midst. Even though Raimondo's hagiographer laid forcible stress on the obligation of the well-off to support the less fortunate, it was inevitable, given the scriptural matrix of his thinking, that he should stress the rewards of charity as well as the nemesis of avarice. Raimondo would accept only voluntary gifts, because he wanted the giver to earn merit by his or her giving. A more austere and intellectualised view of the unconditional obligations of the well-off as members of a single Christian community, especially in times of need, is to be found in the Life of Zita, written three-quarters of a century later. This concern may betray mendicant influence, but one of its most trenchant expressions is a direct quotation from the *Regula pastoralis* of Gregory the Great.[37]

37 Below, p. 168.

There can be little doubt that the starving poor to whom these saints ministered, as the father of the monk Andreas of Fleury had done centuries before, were genuinely indigent; but the word *pauper* did not always mean what we automatically take 'the poor' to mean today, a person or people bereft of material resources through no choice of their own. As Giles Constable emphasised long ago in his discussion of the high medieval debate about the allocation of tithe income, the authentic poor could be taken to mean those who had voluntarily embraced a condition of individual propertylessness and by abandoning their own wills to that of a superior had furthermore become 'poor in spirit'.[38] The triumph of the mendicant and especially the Franciscan ideal in the thirteenth century not only lent muscle to the demand that the rich should do their duty but reinforced an old belief in the spiritual value of voluntary poverty. Real want was sad and uncomfortable, like the physical suffering that so often accompanied it, but not in itself meritorious. Zita was wedded to 'voluntary poverty', and so, unsurprisingly, was the Franciscan tertiary Pier Pettinaio. He was bound to believe that poverty was to be embraced as a positive spiritual good, and one day he fell into an ecstasy as he tried to impress this truth on some acquaintances who were lamenting their penury. Generosity to the 'real' poor or sick nonetheless was a great virtue, and the tendency to identify the *pauper* as the image of Christ himself likewise remained strong.

The reader of these translations should also bear in mind that at least since the Carolingian period, the word *pauper* had had the connotation of 'powerless'; the *pauperes* were contrasted with the *potentes*, who were both wealthy and powerful. The monk or holy man who embraced poverty of spirit abjured not only earthly riches but earthly power, while the saint who took upon himself the cause of the poor, like Raimondo in Piacenza, undertook both to relieve their material distress and to defend their interests in the public arena, for example in the law courts, where the 'powerful' had a natural advantage.

Varieties of religious living

One of the most striking features of the thirteenth-century religious landscape was the variety and fluidity of the forms of life that were open

---

38 G. Constable, *Monastic tithes from their origins to the twelfth century* (Cambridge, 1964), pp. 169–70, 173, 185–6, 262–3.

to the spiritual enthusiast.[39] Pious laypeople sometimes went through a series of stages in their lives, moving, as Pier Pettinaio seems to have done, from a period of charitable activity and devout religious observance which was compatible with marriage and the pursuit of a trade to a more advanced stage of quasi-monastic withdrawal from the world under the direction of the friars, which coincided with widowhood. At an earlier date and in a very much shorter life Umiliana de' Cerchi of Florence followed a similar course, with inevitable differences because she was not only a young woman but a person of some wealth and social standing. Of the saints included in this book, we can be certain only of Zita of Lucca that she was never married, while Homobonus (probably), Raimondo, Umiliana and Rigo of Bolzano all had children.

Zita was a servant all her life from the age of twelve, but, like the humble Rigo a little later, she made assiduous use of the religious provision that was available from local clergy. She was a devout attender at the church of San Frediano (a house of regular canons), while Rigo, although we are told that he had much to do with the Augustinian Hermits of Treviso, frequented most of all the cathedral, where he was eventually buried. Umiliana and Pier Pettinaio were associated with the Franciscans, while Homobonus and Raimondo Palmario lived and died before 'the coming of the friars'. Homobonus seems to have been simply a pious layman. After his 'conversion' Raimondo devoted himself to charitable work and established his own hospital under the wing of the canons who served the church of the Twelve Apostles in Piacenza, but it is not clear from his Life that he took formal vows or followed (or created) any kind of 'rule'. When on his deathbed he urged his sole surviving son Gerardo to embrace the religious life, the latter applied for admission to the community of canons of the Twelve Apostles.

The friars undertook the urban apostolate which thoughtful observers around 1200 (such as Innocent III) could not have doubted was necessary. This did not mean that the laity were reduced to inactivity but that their pious observances were increasingly given shape by mendicant direction. The friars, albeit not to the exclusion of other clergy, provided the framework – 'third orders', charitable and flagellant confraternities – within which the layman operated, and to some extent at least they found a place for the laywoman which she might otherwise have found it difficult to carve out for herself. In the Life of the

39 All the saints in this book may be regarded as belonging to the category of the 'lay penitent', on which see Thompson, *Cities of God*, especially chapter 2.

Sienese Dominican Ambrogio Sansedoni (d. 1289) his work in this area
is summarised thus:

> He also instituted various confraternities of men, whom through his
> religious regulations he led to the observance of Catholic life and to the
> performance of penance for their sins. Women too, virgins and widows, he
> brought together into a religious mode of living, and this way of life too he
> subjected to discreet regulations, under the rule of the Friars Preachers.
> Married women too through his exhortations bound themselves to certain
> devout and pious observances, that is, serving the poor and sick to the best
> of their ability.[40]

The religious life, in both active and contemplative forms, was thus in
some measure opened to women who remained outside the cloister,
as the Beguines of northern Europe also demonstrated. The Franciscan Vito of Cortona argued that it was not God's intention that the
widowed Umiliana de' Cerchi should hide herself away as an enclosed
nun; under Franciscan directors of conscience, she attained the heights
of the contemplative life in her father's house.

In another Life of Ambrogio Sansedoni there is a more vivid description of his organisation of the laity:[41]

> In his own city of Siena, where he mostly lived, singular movements of the
> spirit of God occurred and societies of good men, including laity [were
> instituted]; some of these were established for the divine praises,[42] which
> were sung daily, even by small children, in religious places, especially in that
> of his own Friars Preachers. These people came together with wonderful
> devotion in these praises and [the institution] was exported to other cities.
> Others [came together] to give alms, which they obtained with marvellous
> fervour and distributed to the poor; others publicly subjected themselves
> to flagellation around the city, albeit with their faces concealed, among
> whom great men and once-famous sinners were included. All of these and
> many others elected a particular director for themselves and on certain days
> assembled, were counselled, examined, cautioned and corrected.

The friars could claim to be both saints themselves and the cause of
sanctity in others. Theirs was the visible and controlling initiative,

---

40 *AS*, March, 3, p. 192. On Ambrogio's importance in Sienese religious and civic life
see D. P. Waley, *Siena and the Sienese in the thirteenth century* (Cambridge, 1991), pp.
142–4. See also Giulio Sansedoni, *Vita del beato Ambrogio Sansedoni da Siena dell' ord.
de' Predicatori discepolo del beato Alberto Magno e condiscepolo di S. Tomaso d' Aquino*
(Venice, 1727).

41 *AS*, March, 3, p. 212.

42 *Laude* or hymns, several collections of which survive from the thirteenth century and
later. On the *laudesi* see Thompson, *Cities of God*, pp. 90–2.

and this inevitably bred some irritations, which were understandable enough if the attitudes espoused by the Franciscan Salimbene of Parma were in any way typical. Focusing on popular enthusiasm at Cremona and in its neighbourhood for the wine-porter Albert of Villa Ogna, Salimbene perceived that the populace and the secular clergy resented the mendicant claim to a monopoly of sanctity. The seculars openly declared to the friars, 'You believe that no one can do miracles except your saints, but you are deceived.' It was they who were deceived, for a relic of Albert's little toe turned out to be a clove of garlic. Salimbene also ridiculed the devotion of the Paduans to the obscure Antony the Pilgrim when they had a greater Antony, the Franciscan preacher, to venerate. In his view, 'the Lord came not only in his own person, but in blessed Francis and blessed Antony and Saint Dominic and their sons, in whom sinners must believe in order to merit salvation'. There were, he mused, many reasons for bogus devotions: the desire of the sick for cures and of the light-minded for novelties, clerical envy of the 'modern religious' and the appetite of bishops and canons for profit.[43]

It was not altogether surprising that such jealousies should arise. There were vexed issues of pastoral, burial and preaching rights and resentments created by mendicant involvement in the inquisition. Small though these cities were by modern standards, they were internally divided into quarters and neighbourhoods with their own local patriotism. To this day it is easy to see that the mendicant convents were typically founded in the 'suburbs' of the early thirteenth-century cities, often some way from one another and from the cathedral and other older churches. With the passage of time each acquired its own quasi-parochial identity. This sense of neighbourhood sometimes emerges from saints' Lives and miracles. It was assumed that Ambrogio Sansedoni had a special tenderness for the inhabitants of Camporeggio, where the Sienese Dominican church stood; only this could explain why he intervened unsolicited to rescue a boy in that neighbourhood from injury when a cellar fell in on him.[44] Pier Pettinaio used to live near the Dominicans in Camporeggio and was well known to the brethren there, but he later sold his house and moved to the vicinity of the Franciscans, with whom eventually he lived and died. The family that Zita served lived near, and were associated with, the regular canons of San Frediano of Lucca.

43 Salimbene de Adam, *Cronica*, ed. G. Scalia (2 vols, Turnhout, 1999) (*Corpus Christianorum, Continuatio Medievalis*, 125), 2, pp. 761–4; translated by J. Baird as *The chronicle of Salimbene de Adam* (Binghamton, NY, 1986), pp. 512–14.
44 *AS*, March, 3, p. 239.

The devout did not always plump wholeheartedly for either the regular or the secular clergy, and ill feeling and non-co-operation between churches and orders were not the invariable rule. The prior of San Frediano consulted with the Lucchese Franciscans and Dominicans before translating Zita's remains, and nearly half a century later the bishop of Treviso consulted with all the religious orders about the incipient veneration of Rigo. By this date no aspiring saint and no purveyor of pastoral care in the urban environment could remain unaffected by the ideals and values espoused by the mendicant orders, but the friars did not have a total monopoly. Traditionally partial to the Hohenstaufen emperors, Cremona was Ghibelline-dominated until 1275 and produced a number of non-mendicant holy men. After Homobonus there were the dubious Albert of Villa Ogna and the respectable Fazio (himself a Guelf), who was associated with the cathedral and buried there.[45] Just as Homobonus, Raimondo Palmario and others show lay charitable activism in being before the coming of the friars, Fazio's story reveals that lay confraternities involved in alms-gathering and other pious works were to be found, later in the thirteenth century, operating under the wing of the secular church.

After Homobonus, however, the exponents of this lay charitable activism did not attain official sanctity. There were several reasons for this, important among them the success with which the mendicants reaffirmed and even revitalised a clerical model of sanctity. This meant not only that monastic attributes – bodily austerities and suffering, prayer, visions and struggles with the devil – were confirmed in their central hagiographical importance, but that the virtues which were expressed in active service to mankind were mostly acknowledged in the forms in which the friars themselves represented them, such as preaching and teaching, which were clerical monopolies. Do the Lives translated in this book reflect a shift in the representation of sanctity between the thirteenth and the fourteenth centuries?[46]

The latest of them, Pietro da Baono's depiction of Rigo of Bolzano, was written perhaps in the 1360s. It is hard to know whether the author positively intended to portray this lay saint as a somewhat passive devout figure or simply lacked information about Rigo's early, more active, life. A generation earlier, the Life of Pier Pettinaio arguably hints at the suggested change and in the process reveals an ambivalence of

---

45 For Fazio and Cremonese politics, see Vauchez, 'Sainteté laïque', pp. 21–3.

46 Richard Kieckhefer, *Unquiet souls: fourteenth-century saints and their religious milieu* (Chicago, 1984) offers a profile of fourteenth-century sanctity and hagiography.

which its Franciscan author may not have been entirely conscious. Once the perfect godly businessman and the vigorous exponent of charity, Pier himself comes to believe that he can lead the spiritual life he wishes to lead only if he withdraws from active engagement with 'the world'. There is a contrast here with Raimondo Palmario, who is enjoined by Christ to go the other way, to embrace active charity in preference to pilgrimage. There was however no sudden, smooth or total transformation. Homobonus of Cremona is portrayed in different ways in the extant thirteenth-century Lives. In the one translated here there are no demons and no flagellation; but these elements are present in another Life and also in a fourteenth-century vernacular version.

For women, less capable of embodying the active virtues, the change would anyway be less striking. The Franciscan Vito of Cortona made it clear that Umiliana de' Cerchi was initially dedicated to works of active charity and that she was reluctant to abandon them and never totally did so. Yet Umiliana was unquestionably a 'suffering' saint, marked out by her endurance of illness and diabolical persecution as well as by prophetic, visionary and miraculous gifts and devotion to Christ's person. This was a model appropriate to the female saints whom the mendicant orders did so much to nurture, and one which was destined for a big future extending down to modern times. In its essentials, such a life could as well – or better – be lived by a nun. Vito insisted that God intended Umiliana to be a light to the world, not hidden away in a cloister, but her life equalled and indeed resembled that of the professed religious, which thus remained the standard.

Property, sanctity and gender

The saints relieved the necessities of others; by what means did they do this, and what were their attitudes to property and the secular occupations by which incomes were earned?[47] Answers to these questions are inseparable from the styles of life adopted by individuals in quest of perfection, but social status and inherited wealth were inevitably relevant. Some had little of their own to give. Raimondo, having signed his property away, relied on goading others into giving. Zita of Lucca and Rigo of Bolzano, the humblest in social standing of the saints included here, had limited means of doing charity. This did not prevent Zita

---

47 For some brief observations see D. M. Webb, 'A saint and his money: perceptions of urban wealth in the Lives of Italian saints', in W. J. Sheils and D. Wood (eds), *The church and wealth* (Oxford, 1987) (*Studies in Church History*, 24), pp. 61–73.

from mobilising the resources of the household she served, whether by raiding her master's store of beans to feed the poor during a famine or lending his warmest cloak to a shivering pauper whom she met in church one Christmas Eve. Others could draw in varying degrees on their own resources. We are not specifically told how Andrea Gallerani obtained the wherewithal to carry out his charities, but it seems reasonable to infer that, as he was 'noble', he was able to draw on family income and supplies. Umiliana used her own household stores (or her husband's). Repeatedly it is shown that urban households generated surpluses, not to say waste, which could and should be put to good use on behalf of the poor.

Although the Cerchi were described by the editor of Umiliana's Life as an old and noble family, they may not have looked like that to thirteenth-century observers. As Dante knew, and as his contemporary Dino Compagni made clear in his narrative of the bitter factional conflicts which Florence underwent at the end of the thirteenth century, the Cerchi were *nouveaux riches*,[48] and Umiliana's husband, father and other male kin are in varying ways made to exemplify the evils of that type. Saints apart, it was the women of these households who were regarded as most amenable to the demands of charity. Umiliana had support from her female relatives, and Zita was able to appeal to the benevolence of her mistress. Despite their differing rank, both saints spent part of their nights concocting dishes of leftovers for the indigent.

It would be rash to generalise about female sanctity on the basis of these two Lives, but it seems permissible to dwell for a moment on the relationship between gender and charity which they help to illuminate. *Avaritia*, like the other vices (and virtues), was usually personified as a female figure, if only because like the other words for moral attributes it was a feminine Latin noun, but actual practitioners of avarice were normally represented as male, for only males were perceived as acquiring and hoarding wealth. Women, however, were likely to embody vanity and *luxuria*, the attachment to material and fleshly pleasures which could well implicate the spending of money and therefore the desire for it. Both Umiliana and Zita, different though their social positions were, rejected all concern with self-adornment. Umiliana, once married, decided that she would not make up her face, and she cut up her own clothes, as well as the household linens, in order to make

---

48 The Cerchi were 'men of low estate, but good merchants and very rich; they dressed well, kept many servants and horses, and made a brave show': *Dino Compagni's chronicle of Florence*, translated by D. Bornstein (Philadelphia, 1986), I:20, p. 22.

charitable gifts; Zita had no concern at all for clothes and was fond of declaring that 'Christian perfection' did not reside in such things. We may be meant to understand that female servants usually spent as much as they could on dress.

Not only did Umiliana and Zita thus refrain in their own persons from self-indulgence and excessive consumption, but they rebuked avarice, which in their domestic worlds could be blamed on the men who were in charge. In the Life of Zita, this involves some rather delicate narrative manoeuvres. The author wanted to be complimentary to the Faitinelli family, who treated their servant by and large rather well, and the strictures he utters on the culpable failure of the rich to realise their duty to the poor are therefore couched in general terms and not specifically directed at the Faitinelli *paterfamilias*. The latter evidently knew his servant's predilections only too well and, when he loaned her his cloak so that she could go to church one freezing Christmas Eve, warned her not to give it to the first hard-luck case she came across. The author sails closest to the wind when he tells how during a famine Zita fed the poor from her master's stock of beans, completely without his knowledge. He is not directly blamed for hoarding, but the climax of the story (and the need for a miracle) comes when, unaware of Zita's depredations, he decides to sell the beans. The reader cannot but reflect that he too must have known there was a famine.

In her position as a housekeeper, Zita was able to disburse household surpluses by a variety of direct and indirect means. Marriage made Umiliana mistress of a household in her own right. Ambrogio Sansedoni displayed his charitable impulses as a young man in his father's aristocratic Sienese household; it was on her marriage that Umiliana suddenly both abjured personal self-adornment and embarked on a determined campaign of charitable activity. The men (as distinct from the religious) in her life, above all her father and her husband, were openly avaricious, and it may be that charity acquired a special meaning for Umiliana as a response to the vices of the men who to a large extent had control of her life. She longed to win her husband away from usury; after his death, her father, infuriated by her refusal to remarry, defrauded her of her dowry and thus deprived her of the means of doing charity. Umiliana's reported lament for this loss is almost as striking a statement of the supreme value of practical charity as Christ's injunction to Raimondo to eschew pilgrimage in its favour. It seems to have been by way of compensation, rather than as a first choice, that she turned to ascetic self-mortification.

Zita, a servant who attained sanctity in her own right, enjoyed greater mobility than her social superior Umiliana. She had to run errands (the mischief-making young ladies of the household amused themselves by sending her out in the rain), and her pilgrimages, albeit still local, probably took her further afield than Umiliana's did; we are asked to believe that she could walk to and from shrines some miles from Lucca alone but for divine protection. Other maidservants appear as supporting players and witnesses to sanctity. With their relative freedom of movement, they linked the members of Umiliana's network as well as performing other vital tasks (for example, assistance with the distribution of foodstuffs to the needy). The maid Piecilia was sent to forewarn Monna Ravenna of imminent tribulation (the death of her husband). Andrea Gallerani one night summoned his *famula* to carry on with the work of kneading the bread he wanted to make for distribution; he had heated the water, but did not want to miss matins and evidently left her to it. The unfortunate servant discovered that the grain he had brought home for the making yielded as much dough as three times the quantity would normally have done. She was a witness to several of his other marvels.

For Zita, the household in which she dwelt was by and large a favourable environment. She illuminated it by instruction and example, for the most part, it seems, enjoying the support of her masters and mistresses. Umiliana was under siege in her father's house, not only from her male kin, but from the demons who (like them) threatened her chastity and fixity of purpose. With her sister-in-law and other like-minded women, she reached out beyond the home and sometimes suffered disapproval and even punishment because of it. Although their activities are represented somewhat informally, as if they were entirely the products of private initiative, we can presume that they had the seal of Franciscan approval. The Dominican Ambrogio Sansedoni, as remarked earlier, organised groups of pious women to perform works of mercy. Pier Pettinaio, like his contemporary Fazio of Cremona, belonged to a similar male group. Pier had several named companions who shared with him the organisation and performance of a ministry to the poor. We also know the names of several of Fazio's associates in the *consortio* of the Holy Spirit at Cremona, some of whom also shared in his pilgrimages.[49] As these examples indicate, it would obviously be misleading to represent charity as in some way a distinctively feminine virtue. If a man, especially a head of household, decided to be charitable he possessed a greater initiative and a greater freedom, including

49 Vauchez, 'Sainteté laïque', pp. 26–8.

the simple freedom to move around the public space. Such a man's womenfolk may be portrayed performing a quite different stereotypical role. In the version of Homobonus's Life which is translated here, his wife opposes his charitable excesses and displays all the concern with social position and worldly advancement which was often attributed to women, to the extent that in order to preserve peace in the home Homobonus tries to conceal his benefactions from her.

Unlike Umiliana, several male saints perceived the ownership of property as a problem. Homobonus felt obliged to rid himself of virtually all his inherited property (to the exasperation of his wife); he retained only a small vineyard for his own sustenance and that of his poor. The possession of anything above the barest subsistence, although it made almsgiving possible, might seem an obstacle to personal holiness. Franciscan influence was bound to reinforce this already well-established principle and to that extent once again to confer a greater importance on what was good for the saint than on what was good for the potential beneficiaries of his charity. Pier Pettinaio dallied in his vineyard instead of attending vespers, so he got rid of it; here a parcel of land seems to have represented not so much superfluous wealth as distraction. A more interesting feature of Pier's Life, however, is the depiction of him as the perfect Christian businessman during the period of his life when he was actively engaged in the trade of making and selling combs. Homobonus and Raimondo are both described as making a living with total (and unusual) probity, but the treatment of this theme in Pier's Life is much more specific.[50] On the one hand he refused to use shoddy materials and always gave his clients accurate information about quality: on the other, he was not to be beaten down when all he was asking was the just price.

Although the chronology of Pier's life is far from clear, we are probably expected to see him progressing from being the married man, actively engaged in both trade and charity, to the chaste widower increasingly given up to contemplation. One day he was reproached for failing to engage personally in charitable activity when his reputation for holiness would have ensured big returns on his efforts. He replied that for him such activity counted as involvement in the world and would get in the way of devotion; for others (and he named one of his associates) this conflict did not exist and they could do both without detriment to

50 Vauchez comments on the uniqueness of the Life in this respect: 'the only one to reveal a desire to define a Christian ethic of professional and commercial activity' (*Sainthood*, p. 203).

their souls. Rigo of Bolzano we first encounter when he was too old to work any longer and himself needed alms, which, however, he always shared with other poor people. It is hinted, if only glancingly, that it was virtuous for him to work while he could; we see him only in the last phase of his life when he could no longer be anything but contemplative. Idleness, whether in the monk or the layman, was at all costs to be avoided. Fazio of Cremona was a craftsman, but his was a craft with special possibilities. As a goldsmith he could and did specialise in the making of liturgical vessels which he liked to bestow on favoured churches, and, as Vauchez has suggested, popular opinion may have awarded him, like other 'smiths', the reputation of 'good hands' which could confer a blessing.[51]

For the noble Andrea Gallerani, wealth and work were apparently not significant issues. Admittedly his extant Life is brief, but it gives the impression that for him generosity, rather than extremes of self-abnegation, sufficed and that he did not find the combination of the active and contemplative lives particularly problematical. It is probably significant that his sources of income were presumably unearned. Odd though it may seem to the modern observer, but conformably to a long tradition of thought derived from the ancient world, wealth derived from land was less troublesome to contemporaries than the money made by the craftsman or the merchant. The better the living made by the latter, the more likely it was to be tainted by greed, usury or sharp practice. For Andrea, as for others of his class, the master-vice which he had at all costs to avoid was pride or arrogance rather than avarice.

Fundamental for most of the saints considered here was the old question of the relation between action and contemplation, Leah and Rachel, Martha and Mary.[52] If the layman was going to become a saint, while remaining recognisably a layman, it followed almost inevitably that the corresponding hagiography would have to embody a positive evaluation of the *vita activa*. To an extent this did happen, as indeed it had already done in such earlier medieval Lives as that of Gerald of Aurillac. There was however no wholesale transformation of ideals of holiness; the service of one's neighbour, which anyway meant spiritual benefit as well as practical charity, was fundamental to sanctity in the view

---

51 *Ibid.*, p. 21.

52 On Martha and Mary as emblems of the active and contemplative lives, see G. Constable, *Three studies in medieval religious and social thought* (Cambridge, 1995), pp. 3–141.

of so imposing an authority as Gregory the Great.[53] The 'coming of the friars' was a crucial event. The friars made guidance and encouragement available to the layman and laywoman in pursuit of holiness, but, even more, they themselves produced saints who exemplified the perfect mixture of the active and the contemplative.

Chastity, suffering and demons

We are told little or nothing about the early lives of the saints included here, except that Raimondo Palmario as a child had aspirations to godliness. This silence may in part have been due to simple lack of information, but it was characteristic of these men and women that their sanctity was manifested in adulthood. As most of them were married they had no claim to virginity, and one frequent reason for describing a saint's childhood was to substantiate his or her claim to a lifelong purity, willed from earliest infancy. Zita was the only one of the saints included here of whose virginity we can be sure. Of her background and life before she entered the Faitinelli household we are however told nothing, apart from the names of her father and mother and of an uncle and a sister who are both credited with holy life. That is the only clue we have to the formation of a vocation which entailed the preservation of her virginity in the inauspicious conditions of domestic service, in which female servants were often expected to service the sexual needs of their employers.

The continuing power of quasi-monastic models of holiness can be perceived even today. The importance of chastity and physical suffering as means of imitating Christ is revealed in the number of modern saints who have claimed to have received the Stigmata and the many others who have suffered years of ill health. Christ-likeness is obtained by way of suffering rather than vigorous ethical activity. It is not perhaps surprising that the model was powerful in the medieval period. It was especially hard for an aspirant to sanctity to overcome the handicap of lost virginity. Sexual activity and procreation formed part of the expected role of laypeople, and ordinary men and women did not in practice have much opportunity to emulate the legendary St Cecilia and impose a spiritual brother–sister relationship on their spouses.[54] How

53 There is much reference to this aspect of Gregory's thought in Carole Straw, *Gregory the Great: perfection in imperfection* (Berkeley, 1988), for example pp. 93–5.

54 On this subject in general see D. Elliott, *Spiritual marriage: sexual abstinence in medieval wedlock* (Princeton, 1993).

did the saints included in this book cope with the intrusion of marriage and family on their spiritual ambitions?

Vito of Cortona effectively begins his Life of Umiliana de' Cerchi a month into her marriage, when her conversion began to manifest itself in abundant, not to say obsessive, works of charity. We are given no explicit indication that sexual revulsion played a part in this transformation, but there is one hint that up to this moment Umiliana had accepted the role of the 'normal' girl: now she did not want to adorn her face in the usual manner. It is not claimed that she had had religious aspirations before her marriage, although Vito emphasises that she had never been 'childish', and was always superior to the run of young girls. In one very important sense, marriage is represented not as an obstacle to the realisation of her ideals, but as an enabling device, for it gave her at least the limited disposal of material resources for charitable purposes.

Umiliana has been classified as a 'cruel mother', the aspiring saint who in order to achieve emancipation from fleshly concerns was at best indifferent to the deaths or illnesses of husband or children.[55] Admittedly she displayed no anxiety when her children were ill, thinking it no great shame if they were to die with their purity unsullied. The devil was on the wrong tack, therefore, when he tried to distract her from her divine meditations by showing her a vision of the corpses of two of her children. However, it does not seem that her children's existence, or even her husband's, seriously obstructed her spiritual life. She did not cut herself off from her children when she returned to her father's house as a widow, although they remained in the household of her late husband's family. One day her small daughter ran round to see her; Umiliana had no sooner let her in than the child fell down in some kind of fit. The feature of this story that has attracted attention is Umiliana's apparent concern that the family would hold her responsible and bring scandal upon her if the child died. However, it is also apparent that she took the usual steps to revive her (perhaps she had had fits before) and grew alarmed only when time passed and there were no signs of recovery. It is also worth observing that her children, or her surviving children, were girls. As Anna Benvenuti Papi has commented, Umiliana's distaste for the males of her family did not extend to the very young; when the dove of the Holy Spirit entered her chamber, she tried to catch it (before

55 B. Newman, '"Crueel Corage": child sacrifice and the maternal martyr in hagiography and romance', in *From virile woman to womanChrist* (Philadelphia, 1995), pp. 76–107. Later Italian examples of the type included Margaret of Cortona and Angela of Foligno.

she realised what it was) as a present for a little nephew.[56] Her longing to see Christ when he was three or four years old (shared by other holy women) may have sprung from deep personal roots.

Husband and family, then, were not in themselves insurmountable obstacles to the life that Umiliana most wanted to lead, or at least they are not so depicted in quite the way one might expect. It was as much circumstances as choice which made her take the path of austerity and bodily suffering, but once embarked on it she followed it assiduously until she died at the age of twenty-seven. We see her compensating as best she could for the loss of her virginity, and she certainly developed an extreme concern with bodily integrity. The devil on one occasion sought to compromise this, by first entering her tower-cell himself in the form of a phantasmal serpent, and then introducing a 'real' one, which pressed itself unpleasantly against her; she tried to keep her feet covered from it. The temptation to interpret this as a projection of specifically sexual temptations and anxieties may be irresistible to us, whether or not the hagiographer and his audience would so have understood it. When approaching death Umiliana was deeply distressed by the thought that her body might be exposed to the depredations of a relic-hunting mob; again she was specifically anxious that her feet should be kept covered. After her death she appeared, wearing a virginal crown, to a female religious friend who expressed surprise at seeing her so arrayed. Umiliana explained that God had granted it to her in consideration of the sorrow for her lost virginity which she had always carried in her heart.

It must of course be remembered that we see Umiliana, as we see all saints, only through a screen held up by her hagiographer. As already noted, it was not the latter's prime concern to depict a convincing or consistent character, except in the sense that everything she did after her change of mind as a young married woman must be shown to manifest holiness, from her charitable exertions while her husband still lived to her strivings to safeguard her physical purity as a widow. Brother Vito was bound to lay stress on her perfections rather than her imperfections, on her obsessive pursuit of chastity when she was her own mistress rather than on the unquestionably regrettable fact that she was no longer a virgin. She was above all intended to exemplify what could be achieved by women who did not seclude themselves in the cloister, some of whom had had the life-experiences, of marriage and motherhood, that she had had. Zita's dedication to virginity, while

56 Papi, 'Una santa vedova', in *'In castro poenitentiae'*, p. 67.

clearly unconditional and strenuously upheld, was a less painful issue; it seems that she preserved it by general consent. We are told how as a young woman in the Faitinelli household she vigorously defended herself against a bold young fellow-servant, to the extent of scratching his face. The young man would have got into trouble with the *paterfamilias* if his impudence had come to light, which Zita was anxious to avoid.

All the male saints included here could presumably have laid claim to mere chastity. If laymen, however exceptionally, were to be considered candidates for sainthood it was normal for them to have been married, if only because it was extremely unusual (and might even arouse suspicion) to have attained biological maturity without being married or known to be sexually active. Innocent III, canonising Homobonus, said nothing about his marital status, but all the extant Lives assert that he had a wife, and one of them credits him with children. We have no clue to the marital status of Andrea Gallerani, and nothing is said about his practice of chastity. As he did not have a wife to obstruct his religious aspirations, his brother is shown occasionally enacting this necessary role, for example by arrogantly trying to shoo away a poor pilgrim (Christ, of course, in disguise) to whom Andrea gives hospitality.

Pier Pettinaio was childless, but his hagiographer depicts an affectionate and chaste marital relationship, marked by Pier's consideration for his wife: he never kept her waiting for dinner. His wife does not obstruct his sanctity but she does not share or co-operate in it, except to afford him opportunities to show courtesy and devotion to her; she plays an entirely passive and domestic role and her death is experienced as an emancipation in that it frees Pier for a fuller devotion to the spiritual life. As a widower, he preserves exemplary chastity and severely rebukes some young men who flippantly ask him what he would do if he found himself alone in a locked room with a beautiful woman. Of the wife of Rigo of Bolzano we see nothing; she was presumably long dead when the story opens, and his son, elsewhere documented, is (perhaps significantly) ignored by his biographer.[57]

It is in the Life of Raimondo Palmario that real stress is laid on the negative implications of marriage and children for a male aspirant to sanctity. His hagiographer however manages to bring off a double. In accepting matrimony Raimondo implicitly accepts that it was divinely instituted and thus rebuts contemporary heretical condemnation of it;

57 See below, p. 243.

however, God clearly intends the whole business to be a trial to him. Certainly he seems to have felt more handicapped by family life than Umiliana did. He dreamed of continence within marriage but (obedient in this as in all things to the church's teaching) submitted to his wife's demands for her conjugal rights and obtained his wish only when she became ill, which is interpreted by Rufino as a punishment for her fleshly weakness. When she and all but one of their children were dead Raimondo had no compunction about leaving his one remaining son in the care of his parents-in-law and embarking on what he intended to be a lifelong pilgrimage.

Homobonus and Raimondo felt a tension between worldly callings and the Christian life they wanted to lead, and for both, albeit for slightly different reasons, their wives (or so we are told) were obstructive to their ideals; but the explicit tension between the active and the contemplative which later marks the Lives of Pier, Umiliana and Zita is absent from theirs. For Raimondo the question was only what form of pious physical activity he should embrace. He and Homobonus exemplified an activist model which seems to have lost its appeal, or at least to have been modified, in the course of the thirteenth century. Fazio, who represented a similar type of holiness somewhat later, also lived outside the mendicant ambience; he combined a devotion to strenuous charity with frequent pilgrimage to Compostela and elsewhere. Pilgrimage could however also be practised by less vigorous personalities such as Antony the Pilgrim of Padua (d. 1267), who sounds as if he was more in need of charity than able or inclined to give it.[58]

The contrast between Raimondo Palmario and Fazio's near-contemporary Pier Pettinaio suggests something subtler. No one could claim that Pier lacked spiritual or physical vigour, but the life that he aspired to lead and the way in which he was described were shaped by ideals, not in themselves by any means new, that were adapted and revivified under mendicant influence. The tension between the active and contemplative lives had an ancient and respectable ideological lineage. In addition, a layman or laywoman whose sanctity was going to be held up for public admiration had to enact two roles: on the one hand a choice spirit set apart for veneration like other saints, and on the other a model for imitation. Had Pier Pettinaio been a friar, he could have gone into ecstasies, talked with the Virgin and with angels, fought against demons, given

---

58 The Life by the fifteenth-century humanist Sicco Polenton was based on one composed around 1270 in support of an abortive attempt to secure Antony's canonisation: 'Vita beati Antonii Peregrini', *Analecta Bollandiana*, 13 (1894), pp. 417–25.

good counsel to friars and laymen alike, and demonstrated prophetic insights, all of which he did. He could not however have been the perfect husband, still less the perfect godly businessman and even taxpayer. The paradoxes, if not tensions, in his life are made more confusing by his biographer's narrative technique. At one moment we are told that he never ceased from charitable labours; at another he himself is quoted as saying that he has decided that he must abstain for the good of his soul from active charity because for him it leads to a damaging involvement in the world. This sort of mild anomaly is a result of the prismatic technique referred to earlier.

The brief treatment of Pier's bodily austerities suggests that, for all the richness of his interior life, they did not play the part in his sanctity (at least as far his hagiographer was concerned) that fasting and maceration of the flesh did in Umiliana's. Here one might simply suspect gender difference, but the issue is more complicated. As already noted, there is less emphasis on physical expressions of penitence in one Life of Homobonus (translated in this book) than in another, and these austerities are important also in the portrayal of Rigo as an old man no longer capable of strenuous activity. The alternative versions of Homobonus's Life also reveal the varying importance assigned to diabolical intervention. There are no demons in the one translated here, which mirrors the bull of canonisation in its simple emphasis on piety and charity. In an alternative version they are present alongside the saint's bodily austerities; different styles of sanctity are being evoked.[59]

The Franciscans who wrote the Lives of Umiliana and Pier Pettinaio believed that the quest for spiritual eminence embroiled their subjects with the devil. For Umiliana, at least, this might seem like part of a package of sufferings which she had to undergo in expiation of her earlier sexual relations, yet the virgin Dominican Ambrogio Sansedoni not only experienced raptures but had testing encounters with demons from time to time. These saints were being deliberately assimilated to a venerable tradition which derived ultimately from the model supplied by St Athanasius in his life of St Antony: he who seeks God in the real or metaphorical desert must expect to find the devil along the way, challenging the saint's invasion of his domain. Yet Zita, Andrea Gallerani and Rigo are differently described. All experienced ecstasies and heavenly visitations without (apparently) having to put up with demons. Only for Zita could this have been the reward of virginity. If a demon had ever tried to bother Raimondo Palmario, unquestion-

59 See further below pp. 49–53.

ably both husband and father, he would probably have been too busy to notice; he was not treading the risky, lonely path of contemplation.

Both Zita and Rigo possessed (but rarely used) uncomfortable hard beds, and both went in for breast-beating, quite literally, sometimes using a special stone for the purpose. Zita tied a cord tightly around herself which ate into her flesh (so too did Homobonus in the more 'penitential' version of his Life), and Rigo wore a hair-shirt. Umiliana, Zita and Pier were in the habit of keeping their eyes cast down when walking along the road. This too belonged in the monastic tradition: it was a ritualisation of humility, of detachment from the world and the avoidance of distracting or unseemly sights. Rigo insisted on confessing such trifles as that he had observed the flight of a bird with pleasure. For Umiliana lowering her eyes was also a defence of her embattled chastity, and she was deeply distressed when she was forced one day to look up to avoid a rearing horse and chanced to see its rider.

It was clearly necessary, for the sake of 'final perseverance', that the saint should make, and be seen to make, a good end, and the deathbed provided an obvious opportunity for the display of extreme fortitude or of gifts of prophecy, or simply for improving farewell utterances. Homobonus's death, prostrated before the Cross at matins in the church of Sant' Egidio, summed up and exemplified his piety. It had been his custom to prostrate himself in this manner, and it was not until he failed to rise for the gospel reading that the bystanders realised he must be dead. Umiliana's death is narrated in painful detail; it crowns her expiatory suffering. Sometimes however the notice of the death is brief, and more stress is laid on what happened next: the crowds flocking as rumour of the death spreads, the lamentations of the poor deprived of their patron, the first miracles, the launching of the cult. Pietro da Baono's eye-witness reminiscence of the morning of Rigo's death is not of the death itself but of the frenzied crowds following the corpse to the cathedral, where he, then a young canon, happened to be standing. The account of Zita's exequies, possibly written by an eye-witness, follows a not dissimilar pattern. The special value of these narrations is that they illuminate, if not the actuality of popular, spontaneous reactions to the saints, then at least the ways in which those reactions were managed, encouraged and presented by the clergy.

A saint's life is not primarily a portrait of the saint as an individual, but one of his or her sanctity. To the extent that it mirrors contemporary conceptions of what sanctity was we may be justified in treating it also as a 'portrait of the age', but we must be aware that traditional models were and remained powerful shaping influences. A saint could not be a saint (or, perhaps more properly, described as a saint) unless in certain significant particulars he or she resembled the saints of all and other times. We cannot be confident that we can deduce the biography of saints from their hagiography, and in seeking to glean materials for social history from it, we must always bear in mind that it was not the hagiographer's conscious intention to provide them. Yet it is equally obvious that the Lives translated in this book were written in a specific historical environment and that they have interesting and important things to tell us about the Christian life as it was lived in that setting.

It has seemed preferable here to give a few *Lives* in their entirety rather than to compile a collection of extracts chosen for their presumed interest to the social historian. Pressure of space has meant that in order to provide the most generous selection of complete translations they have been only sparingly annotated. The innumerable scriptural quotations and allusions which are woven into all these texts, sometimes signposted, sometimes not, have not all been identified. The reader should be aware that the likeness of the saints to Christ and the Apostles is constantly being affirmed and illustrated by means of such references.[60]

60 Biblical quotations follow the Vulgate text and numeration, which would have been familiar to medieval authors and readers. Modern translations such as the New Revised Standard Version sometimes differ slightly.

I: HOMOBONUS OF CREMONA (d. 1197)

Pope Innocent III proclaimed the canonisation of Homobonus of Cremona on 11 January 1199, in the bull *Quia pietas*.[1] This was within fifteen months of the saint's death in November 1197 and a year of Innocent's own accession to the papacy. The canonisation was promoted by Sicard, bishop of Cremona since 1185, who commemorated the event in his chronicle: 'Also at this time there was a certain simple man of Cremona called Homobonus, faithful and devout to a degree; after whose death and at whose intercession God manifested many miracles to this [world]. Wherefore I went as a pilgrim to Rome, to the presence of the supreme pontiff, and obtained the canonisation which I sought.'[2]

Cremona was one of many northern and central Italian cities around 1200 to be afflicted by the presence of heretics, probably (although not necessarily solely) Cathars. In an epitaph for his predecessor Offredus, Sicard called him 'the goad of heretics' (*stimulus hereticorum*) as well as the soul of charity and lover of peace.[3] These were traditional attributes of the good bishop, whose turbulent urban flock was much in need of both. Sicard's chronicle suggests that he also saw the cult of saints as central to episcopal concerns. He carefully collected references to the translations effected by earlier bishops. Cremona lacked native saints of note, but the martyr Archelaus had been brought from Rome by Bishop Lando in 875, and Himerius, a fifth-century bishop of Amelia in Umbria, had arrived in the time of Otto the Great; Bishop Odericus was responsible for constructing his shrine in 994.[4] Himerius was submerged in the ruins of the cathedral as a result of an earthquake in 1116; solemnly 'invented' and re-enshrined by Bishop Oberto in 1129, he performed many miracles in 1174.[5] In 1196, with immense pomp, Sicard performed a fresh translation of Archelaus and Himerius to 'a stone shrine'. A rhymed hymn in honour of Himerius, possibly Sicard's own work, lays great stress on his patronage of his

---

1 O. Hageneder and A. Haidacher (eds), *Die Register Innocenz' III*, 1 (Cologne and Vienna, 1964), pp. 761–4. André Vauchez has written extensively on Homobonus: see most recently *Omobono di Cremona († 1197) laico e santo* (Cremona, 2001). He is also preparing a critical edition of the Lives.

2 On Sicard's writings, see E. Brocchieri, 'Sicardo di Cremona e la sua opera letteraria', *Annali della Biblioteca Governativa e Libreria Civica di Cremona*, 9 (1956). The chronicle was edited, with related Cremonese chronicle materials, by O. Holder-Egger in *MGH Scriptores*, 31; the present quotation is on p. 177.

3 Brocchieri, 'Sicardo di Cremona', p. 109.

4 *MGH Scriptores*, 31, pp. 156, 158, 159.

5 *Ibid.*, pp. 162, 164, 167.

adopted city and on the miracles, including the healing of a blind man, which accompanied the translation.[6]

It is hard to know precisely what effect such ceremonies were expected to have on the lay populace, and there is no real justification for supposing that Homobonus was simply conjured into existence by a desire to improve Cremona's saintly stock. Certainly there is little evidence that pride in the possession of him made the Cremonese less discordant in the early thirteenth century. Violent internal conflicts erupted in 1210–11 when the 'old' and 'new' cities elected competing *podestà* and there was fighting, some of it around the church of Sant' Egidio, where Homobonus had worshipped and died. In 1210 Sicard was involved in negotiating a settlement, evidently without total success.[7] By this time, Homobonus had lain for some years in the cathedral, brought there in June 1202 and exhibited to the public on the high altar on his feast-day, 13 November.[8] Over four years after his canonisation the saint was thus affirmed to belong not to a neighbourhood, new or old, but to the bishopric and the entire city. In the course of time he and Himerius were represented in stone as joint patrons of Cremona, flanking the Virgin on the façade of the cathedral.

In 1197–8 there was certainly every reason for Sicard to bring this opportune holy man to the pope's attention as promptly as possible. Innocent for his part doubtless sympathised with local concerns but added to them a global anxiety about the political loyalties of the Italian cities. After the unexpected death of Henry VI in 1197 the pope had hopes of exerting a greater degree of control over the destinies of the Empire and establishing a firmer hold on the territories to which the papacy laid claim in central Italy. Of course he had no time for heresy, but his conciliatory approach to lay religious enthusiasts whom he judged to be inoffensive was consistent with a desire not to aggravate causes of resentment against the official church in societies where lay religious enthusiasm, if thwarted, could all too easily merge with hostility to ecclesiastical jurisdiction and property. A few years later Innocent would welcome (as the bishop of Assisi also did) the appearance of an unusually charismatic lay preacher in an area of central Italy – the vale of Spoleto – which was badly infected with Catharism.[9]

As near-neighbours and old enemies of the Milanese, implacable enemies of the Hohenstaufen emperors, the Cremonese were rather inclined to favour the Hohenstaufen: Frederick Barbarossa had visited the city in 1184 and had

6 *Ibid.*, pp. 174–5; F. Zanoni, 'Vita metrica dei SS Imerio e Omobono secondo gli uffici rimati dei corali della cattedrale', *Annali della Biblioteca Governativa e Libreria Civica di Cremona*, 9 (1956), pp. 22–5.

7 *MGH Scriptores*, 31, pp. 12–13, 188.

8 *Ibid.*, p. 187. Sicard himself himself was absent from the city, in the Holy Land and at Constantinople, for three years from late 1202.

9 See in general and for further references D. Webb, 'The pope and the cities: heresy and anticlericalism in Innocent III's Italy', in D. Wood (ed.), *The church and sovereignty c. 590–1918: essays in honour of Michael Wilks* (Oxford, 1991), pp. 135–52.

been magnificently enthroned in the cathedral square.[10] A few weeks before he proclaimed the canonisation of Homobonus, Innocent III wrote to the people of Cremona urging them to give no aid or comfort to Markward of Anweiler, the German adventurer who was seeking to carve out a power-base in Italy, ostensibly in the name of the young Frederick of Sicily. In his chronicle, Sicard noted Innocent's election and his conflict with Markward just before he recorded the canonisation of Homobonus.[11] For both bishop and pope Homobonus may have seemed to have an immediate and practical value in the current situation. While this may help to account for the alacrity with which the bishop promoted the cause and Innocent responded, Homobonus's qualifications and style of sanctity must also have made a very positive appeal to the pope, given his spiritual agenda. Here was a model layman, characterised on the one hand by his 'good works', on the other by his obedience to the church and punctilious observance of its rituals. These are the features of his sanctity which are highlighted in *Quia pietas*.

The Pope declares that Sicard and his delegation had 'humbly opened to us the life and deeds and the mode of passing' of the holy man. Although not unequivocal, this may imply that a written Life had been submitted to him, perhaps the one which Sicard himself is known to have composed but has been presumed lost. Several very different versions of the saint's life, all anonymous, are extant,[12] and it seems quite possible that Sicard's Life is in fact among them, albeit cloaked in anonymity. In 1301 the Lives were collected into a quasi-official dossier, which survives in an early sixteenth-century copy.[13] This must surely have included Sicard's work, unless it had mysteriously vanished during the preceding century. The bishop's 'autograph' is supposed to have been in the cathedral library of Cremona in the eighteenth century and was apparently still in Cremona around 1880, when a canon of the cathedral, Paolo Lombardini, was reproached by a colleague for having sold it to 'a canon of Oxford'. The colleague may have got hold of a half-truth. A liturgical manuscript now in the Bodleian Library, Oxford, which is however of fifteenth-century date, contains a Life entitled *Cum orbita solis*, which Vauchez believes can be identified as Sicard's.[14]

Cum orbita solis is a 'liturgical' Life, that is, one divided into nine readings for service use. It is first attested in a Venetian copy of the first half of the thirteenth century, which is the oldest hagiographical monument to Homobonus.[15]

10 *MGH Scriptores* 31, p. 6.

11 *Ibid.*, p. 176; J. Böhmer, *Acta imperii selecta* (Innsbruck, 1870), p. 627 n. 906.

12 As already noted, Vauchez is preparing a critical edition of the Lives. In the meantime they are all to be found in D. Piazzi, *Omobono di Cremona: biografie dal XIII al XVI secolo* (Cremona, 1991). For an unpublished text which may be a fragment of another Life, see Vauchez, *Omobono*, pp. 49–50.

13 Munich, Bayerische Staatsbibliothek, MS Lat. 434.

14 Brocchieri, 'Sicardo di Cremona', pp. 103–4. For a description of Bodleian MS Can. Liturg. 165 (19295), see Piazzi, *Omobono*, pp. 27–8.

15 Venice, Biblioteca Marciana, MS. Lat. 2798; Piazzi, *Omobono*, pp. 30–42.

It was partly on the grounds of this manuscript priority that Vauchez judged that *Cum orbita solis* was 'in all probability' Sicard's work, composed before the canonisation.[16] Piazzi agrees, suggesting that Sicard's hand is to be seen at least in the first six *lectiones*, that is, those devoted to the saint's life; the last three concern the miracles.[17] *Cum orbita solis* is largely eulogistic and theological in character, containing very little biographical or anecdotal material apart from a brief description of the saint's charities and an account of his death. Even if it was presented to Innocent by the Cremonese delegation, there is much in the bull of canonisation that must have come from elsewhere. Another possible occasion for its composition may have been the translation of Homobonus from Sant' Egidio to the cathedral of Cremona in 1202.[18]

The deficiencies of *Cum orbita solis* inspired another hagiographer to produce the Life known as *Quoniam historiae*, which is contained in the same Venetian manuscript.[19] According to this second hagiographer the author of *Cum orbita solis* had omitted certain things 'out of negligence or ignorance and because they had not been revealed before the canonisation', a remark which might seem slightly disrespectful if Sicard was known to be the author in question. *Quoniam historiae* was written 'out of love for those who want to follow in this saint's footsteps'. This did not mean providing a biography of Homobonus but illustrating his virtues in action. *Quoniam historiae* begins with a detailed account of his fasts and of how he confessed weekly and flagellated himself (sometimes naked, sometimes not) when he went to his vineyard to pray; he also bound himself so tightly with a belt that the flesh around it putrefied. All this was exceedingly displeasing to the devil. Homobonus was comforted in his tribulations by the archangel Michael, who gave him a rod with which to ward off unclean spirits, as he subsequently confided to his wife. After his death, his son Monacus conversed at his tomb with a demon who admitted that Michael's rod had been effective protection.

Quoniam historiae describes the saint's physique (tall and thin, dark in colouring) and the sober dress he assumed after his conversion. He lived to be eighty, spending fifty years in worldly occupations and fifteen 'in religion' (*in spiritualibus*); presumably the first fifteen years of his life are reckoned to childhood. He had several children and was a widower for ten years. His wife prophesied his future spiritual fame to their son and exhorted him to make money, because his father would leave him poor. Homobonus had to contend with his whole

16 Vauchez, *Omobono*, pp. 39–41. Vauchez had not arrived at this opinion when he wrote *Sainthood*, in which he stated that Sicard's Life had 'disappeared without trace' (p. 202 n. 157).

17 Piazzi, *Omobono*, p. 46. The ninth *lectio* appears differently in different manuscripts. A copy of *Cum orbita solis* in Milan, Biblioteca Braidense, Gerli 26, fols 159r–161r, contains only the first six *lectiones* and ends with the saint's death: cf. Vauchez, *Omobono*, p. 43. *Quoniam historiae* follows on fols 161r–163v.

18 *MGH Scriptores*, 31, p. 187.

19 Piazzi, *Omobono* pp. 50–4. In the Marciana manuscript *Quoniam historiae* is inserted between the sixth and seventh *lectiones* of *Cum orbita solis* (*ibid.*, p. 27).

household in his efforts to be charitable: the *familia* went to the lengths of locking his possessions away, so that he had to steal the key. They also objected to his habit of giving his clothes to the poor. One day on the way to his vineyard he gave his cloak to a naked pauper, and on his way home he borrowed one from a hospital; when asked where his own cloak was, he said he had been robbed.

If *Cum orbita solis* and *Quoniam historiae* had no other value, they would strikingly exemplify contrasting hagiographical idioms and purposes. The purpose of *Quoniam historiae* was clearly homiletic. It suggests the uses that a preacher could make of the outline of a saint's life and the kinds of stories that were deemed to be entertaining and improving. A later Italian-language version goes still further in the same direction, relating how Homobonus crossed the road to avoid disturbing a bird which had settled in his path and how once, after he gave up his trade, his hands were indelibly blackened by a sum of money which was brought to him.[20] These details have a somewhat Franciscan flavour.

The introduction of demons into *Quoniam historiae* (and its vernacular sequel) seems particularly significant. It has been suggested that these are code for heretics, or at least enemies of the church, with whom Homobonus clashed.[21] To be singled out for demonic attentions was, however, a distinction appropriate to the especially holy man from St Antony onwards; it instantly assimilated Homobonus to the company of the great saints. To what extent (if at all) he was an active participant in faction-fighting at Cremona seems fated to remain unclear. Like many Lives, *Quoniam historiae* may tell us as much about hagiography as it does about Homobonus.

That it was possible to describe his life and spirituality in a rather different style is demonstrated by the Life (translated here) known as *Labentibus annis*.[22] That this is absent from the Venetian manuscript which contains *Cum orbita solis* and *Quoniam historiae* has been taken to show that it must be later in date. It was included in the 1301 Cremonese compendium already mentioned; otherwise the earliest manuscript testimony comes not from Cremona but from Reggio Emilia, in two manuscripts which also contain *Cum orbita solis* (but not *Quoniam historiae*).[23] By the late fifteenth century *Labentibus annis* was in liturgical use at

---

20 *Ibid.*, pp. 72–7. This work survives in a fourteenth century manuscript in the Estense library at Modena and was first published in G. Bertoni, 'Di una Vita di S. Omobono del secolo XIV', *Bollettino Storico Cremonese*, 8 (1938), pp. 161–76.

21 Vauchez, *Omobono*, p. 25, citing U. Gualazzini, 'Delle prime affermazioni dal "populus" di Cremona', *Archivio Storico Lombardo*, new series 2 (1937), pp. 44–5.

22 Piazzi, *Omobono*, pp. 59–66. For earlier editions, see F. S. Gatta, 'Un antico codice su S. Omobono', *Bollettino Storico Cremonese*, 12 (1942), pp. 96–115; L. Maini, *Sancti Homoboni civis Cremonensis Mutine patroni minoris Vita antiquior* (Modena, 1857). The phrase *Vita antiquior* indicates that it was recognised to be older than the sixteenth century *Authentica*, discussed below.

23 A copy in the Archivio di Stato of Reggio (published by Gatta) is dated to the thirteenth century by Piazzi (*Omobono*, p. 27), to the mid-fourteenth by Vauchez (*Omobono*, p. 42). The copy in the capitular library of San Prospero in Reggio (published by Maini) is fourteenth-century.

Cremona and was printed, again with *Cum orbita solis*, in an incunabulum now in Cambridge University Library.[24] Perhaps this suggests that (whatever its date of composition) *Labentibus annis* gradually supplanted *Quoniam historiae* in general estimation.

Labentibus annis begins with a sketch of the lamentable spiritual state of Cremona at the time of Homobonus's death: God raised him up like a rose among the thorns of the heretics. There is a faint resemblance here to *Quia pietas*, in which Innocent (echoing the *Song of Solomon*, 2:2) likens the saint to a lily among the thorns of 'worldly men'. The saint's family, place of residence and birth and trade are described; he enters into a marriage, arranged by his kin, but there is no mention of children. He turns his back on the world after the death of his father, to the irritation of his more worldly wife. Apart from the charities which earn him the title of 'father of the poor', his piety centres on church visiting, prayer and fasting; by marked contrast with *Quoniam historiae*, the fasting is mentioned in a single word. The priest Osbert opens the doors of the church of Sant' Egidio every night to admit him for matins; once when the saint is early the doors miraculously open by themselves. Homobonus performs two classic miracles of replenishment of bread and wine, in both instances trying to avoid his wife's complaints of his improvidence. The Life ends with a description of his death and of his miracles. The poor and the sick flock to the tomb and cures of all types occur, five of which are recounted in more detail. The last of these tells how a possessed woman, who some think is not truly possessed, is tested with holy water and consecrated hosts, which proves that she is. This was the miracle selected by Innocent III for inclusion in *Quia pietas*.

In 1570 *Labentibus annis* received an additional lease of life when it was taken as the model for the *Vita authentica*, presented by the canons of Cremona to their bishop, Niccolò Sfrondrato, in 1570, specifically to update and correct the older Lives according to a more modern taste.[25] It displays a perfect similarity to *Labentibus annis* in the essentials of the saint's life-story, although it considerably abbreviates the introductory account of his background. Otherwise, it deals with the same topics in the same order, including no incident and virtually no detail which is not present in its prototype. The miraculously opened church doors and the two replenishment miracles appear in their sequence. There is some elaboration: when the saint's wife rebukes him for giving away their substance, the *Authentica* inserts a little homily in which Homobonus explains to her why she is wrong. To the account of how he habitually prostrated himself before the crucifix in the church of Sant' Egidio, the *Authentica* adds 'and the image of the most Blessed Virgin'. Like its prototype, it ends with a brief description of Sicard's mission to the pope and a note that the documents of the canonisation were preserved in the cathedral of Cremona.

---

24 Piazzi, *Omobono*, pp. 59–60. The incunabulum is Inc. 5 B 20.5 (2170). It does not include *Quoniam historiae*.

25 *Divi Homoboni Vita* (Cremona, 1570), reprinted in Piazzi, *Omobono*, pp. 82–90. Sfondrato was appointed to the see in 1560 and later reigned briefly (1590–1) as Pope Gregory XIV. The *Authentica* superseded *Cum orbita solis* in liturgical use in 1617.

If the redactors of the *Authentica* consciously sidelined *Quoniam historiae* as a source for the saint's life, it was presumably because they found the relative sobriety of *Labentibus annis* more to their liking. However, they used the last three *lectiones* of *Cum orbita solis* extensively in their treatment of the miracles. The author of these *lectiones* may well have drawn on the *libellus* ('booklet') of miracles which was in all probability submitted for Innocent's consideration, but he omitted the pope's choice, the miracle of the demoniac woman. The *Authentica* too omits this miracle, presumably because the bull of canonisation was transcribed as an appendix to it. It gives pride of place instead to the cure of an erstwhile crusader who had been unable to speak for fully ten years since he received a neck wound in a 'battle at Jerusalem'.[26] This miracle is present in *Cum orbita solis* but not in *Labentibus annis* and is one of several that were taken from the former into the *Authentica*. Piazzi supposes that the author of *Labentibus annis* drew on *Cum orbita solis* for his description of the saint's death and for the miracles which the two Lives have in common. On this view, the miracle of the demoniac woman came from the bull of canonisation. That the borrowings went this way of course depends on the assumption that *Labentibus annis* is indeed later than *Cum orbita solis* and *Quia pietas*; it is well to remember that we do not in fact know its date of composition, except that it must fall within the thirteenth century.

The bull includes a few particulars not found in any of the extant Lives, such as the saint's burial of the dead and the fact that he took the indigent into his own home. Innocent could have obtained these details from a number of sources: Sicard himself, his Life (if that was not in fact identical with *Cum orbita solis*) or witnesses such as the priest Osbert, whom the pope personally interviewed, noting that he had heard the saint's confession for over twenty years. Osbert is not mentioned in either *Cum orbita solis* or *Quoniam historiae*, but in *Labentibus annis* he is credited with twenty-six years in charge of the church of Sant' Egidio and is the source for the miracle of the opened doors. *Labentibus annis* gives Homobonus a wife but no children, thus differing from the bull on the one hand and *Quoniam historiae* on the other. The pope did not mention the saint's trade, wife or children. There is a great deal in *Labentibus annis* that cannot have come either from the bull, close though it is to it at several points, or from *Cum orbita solis* or *Quoniam historiae*, including the historical and biographical preliminaries, the miracle of the church doors and the two replenishment miracles.

Piazzi has suggested that the author of *Labentibus annis* downplayed the authentically penitential character of Homobonus's spirituality as portrayed in *Quoniam historiae*. Thanks to the perpetuation of his work by the compilers of the *Authentica* he distorted posterity's understanding of the saint.[27] Certainly the author has nothing to say about the saint's demonic tribulations and self-mortification or about the details of his fasting, clearly intended by the author

---

26 Piazzi, *Omobono*, pp. 40, 88. This could be a reference to the battle of Hattin (4 July 1187), at which Jerusalem was lost to Christendom; certainly the date, ten years before the death of Homobonus, would fit very neatly.

27 See e.g. Piazzi, *Omobono*, pp. 69, 91–2.

of *Quoniam historiae* to elicit admiration and (perhaps) to provide a model for imitation. The point at issue, however, is arguably not what Homobonus was really like, but how he was represented by different hagiographers.

A sideways glance at his contemporary Raimondo Palmario of Piacenza is instructive. As will be seen later in this volume, Raimondo was a charitable saint in whose Life (written in 1212 by one who had known him) there is little of the penitential culture which characterises the Homobonus of *Quoniam historiae*. Raimondo's hallmark was sheer tireless activity; his aversion from 'the world' expressed itself straightforwardly in a desire to reject his worldly calling and sexual relations, in an appetite for pilgrimage and prayer and finally in a dedication to charity and peacemaking. If he indulged in flagellation or extremes of fasting, his hagiographer felt no need to tell us about it. Here was a possible saintly model in a milieu geographically and chronologically very close to the Cremona of Homobonus and Sicard. In May 1209 Sicard was involved in the attestation of a couple of miracles that Raimondo had performed on behalf of inhabitants of Cremona; how much, if anything, had he known about Raimondo before his death in 1200?[28]

If the Homobonus of *Quoniam historiae* differs almost totally from Raimondo, the Homobonus of *Labentibus annis* differs from him primarily in performing wonders in his lifetime. Other Lives of charitable saints display a similar activist emphasis. Gualtiero of Lodi (d. 1233) was supposed to have performed miracles both before and after death, but his hagiographer was interested almost solely in his hospital foundations.[29] Later in the century Fazio of Cremona was described with a strong emphasis on his pilgrimages, his good works and his wonder-working while alive (*in vita*).[30] Andrea Gallerani of Siena was tireless in the service of the sick and was also a modest wonder-worker; once again we are told nothing about either austerities or demonic tribulations.[31] As far as Homobonus is concerned, the choice may therefore be not between more or less biographically accurate accounts but between styles of hagiographical representation, all of which have something to tell us about the spiritual and cultural context. I have chosen to translate *Labentibus annis* alongside the bull of canonisation, aware that it tells only one possible hagiographical story and making no presumptions about its relationship to the other Lives.

28 *AS*, July 6, pp. 657–8.

29 Caretta, 'La Vita di S. Gualtiero di Lodi'.

30 See Vauchez, 'Sainteté laïque'.

31 This Life is translated below, pp. 144–59.

Innocent III's bull of canonisation of Homobonus of Cremona: *Quia pietas* (11 January 1199)

To the whole clergy and people of Cremona.

Because piety is promised both the life that now is and that which is to come, God the just and merciful frequently glorifies his faithful (whom he has predestined to life) in this life and always crowns them in the future life. To them he has also promised through the prophet, 'I shall give you for praise, honour and glory among all peoples'; and he has himself promised, ' The just shall shine like the sun in the kingdom of their Father.' Marvellous in himself is the Lord, marvellous in his saints, marvellous in all his works, and truly he demonstrates his power, kindles the cooling spark of charity in many by the signs of his wonders, and, taking up into his glory those who have fought truly in the world, instigates signs in memory of them and, according to the prophet, creates marvels, so that he who is a saint with him shall be held to be a saint by men also. Thus especially shall the perversity of heretics be confounded, when they see wonders multiply at the tombs of Catholics. For although, according to the witness of the truth, only final perseverance is required for the sanctity of the soul in the Church Triumphant, since he who perseveres to the end will be saved, two things, namely the virtue of life and the virtue of signs, that is works of piety in life and miracles after death, are required for someone to be reputed a saint in the Church Militant. For because frequently an angel of Satan takes on the appearance of an angel of light and certain people do good works, as they seem to men, some also are renowned for miracles whose life is reprehensible (as we read of the mages of Pharaoh), and Antichrist would lead even the elect into error, if he could, by means of his miracles. For this purpose neither works nor miracles alone suffice, but when the latter follow on the former, they provide us with a true indication of sanctity. These two things may be more fully gleaned from the words of the Evangelist, where speaking of the Apostles he says, 'They went forth preaching everywhere with the co-operation of God, who confirmed their words with subsequent signs.' In that he says 'co-operation' he shows that they themselves 'operated', and that 'subsequent signs' follows shows that God illuminated them in his miracles. This God does still today in his saints, and manifests his power in evident signs, curing the ills of men in memory of the dead and showing that the dead who die in the Lord live more fully and more happily than those who live in the world.

But, coming to the present, our venerable brother your bishop, S[icard], accompanied by many religious men and other honourable persons of his diocese, has humbly expounded in our presence the life and deeds and also the manner of dying of a certain blessed man, in name and in fact Homobonus,[32] in all of which we have scented the odour of his holy comportment and in faith have recognised and proclaimed the marvellous God and all his works. For this holy man, like a tree planted near a watercourse which gives its fruit in its season (as both the verbal declaration of these same people and the letters of many other honourable persons have made plain to us), so meditated on the law of God, both by day and by night, that seeking him in fear, and in the words of the prophet rising at midnight to confess to him, he was always present at the office of matins. He frequented the office of the mass and the other hours with the utmost devotion, attending with such assiduous prayers that at certain hours he either prayed without ceasing or sometimes anticipated the hours themselves; unless perchance the concern which as a man of peace he showed for peacemaking throughout the city, or the opportunity of acquiring alms for the poor, or some other just cause among the other works of mercy, detained him. He customarily prostrated himself before the Cross of the Lord and, whatever work he did, standing, sitting or lying down, his lips seemed to move continually in prayer. He was zealous in the works of charity which he undertook, both among the poor, whom he kept with him in his own house, looked after and provided for, and among other unfortunates, for whom while they lived he was accustomed to perform devoutly the duties of humanity, and when dead the office of burial. He held himself aloof from the society of worldly men, among whom he bloomed like a lily among thorns, and sternly spurned the heretics whose poison infects those parts. When the course of his life was run, he rose for the matin office, it is said, on the feast of San Brizio, and about the time of the beginning of mass prostrated himself in his accustomed manner in prayer before the Cross; and while the angelic hymn was being sung, he quietly entered into his rest.

As it would be a lengthy business to enumerate one by one what miracles, how many and how great, followed, and what gifts of healing were bestowed on those who came to his tomb, we think that one among the rest is to be noted in detail for the strengthening of the Catholic faith. A certain woman possessed by a demon was brought to his tomb and, lest any fraud should go undetected, she was first sprinkled with

32 The Latin means 'good man'.

unblessed water. Patiently submitting to be sprinkled, she then spat out holy water. So that the case should be still clearer, without any fore-knowledge she accepted an unconsecrated host that was presented to her, but then rejected with horror the consecrated Eucharist. She went away freed by the merits of the saint.

So that the virtue of life, as expounded above, should be manifested still more clearly to us, although all doubt seemed to have been removed by the succession of signs by divine judgement, and lest the virtue of the miracles should depend on any fraud or delusion, we thought that the truth of the matter was to be more carefully investigated. Confidence about his manner of life, which, without any fraudulent delusion of hypocrisy, the divine judgement seemed to have clearly shown, we strengthened by the testimony of our beloved son Osbert, priest of the church of Sant' Egidio at Cremona, exacting an oath from him. On which oath he, who, as his spiritual father[33] for twenty years and more had often received his confession, with the bishop and the others afore-said on oath, affirmed that what we have previously stated about his holy conversation was true, and informed us further about the obedi-ence which he showed in prayers, vigils and other fruits of penitence, more than fulfilling what was laid upon him. What we had been told about his miracles, we confirmed by the oath of all the aforesaid who had come on this business, obtaining the assurance of the bishop on the virtue of obedience, so that following both divine and human judge-ment we could proceed with greater security.

Since therefore we seemed agreed on everything, concerning both the probity of his life and the validity of the miracles, in favour of the petition for which the aforesaid bishop and the others mentioned on your behalf fervently pressed us, after much deliberation with the arch-bishops and bishops whom for this purpose we had summoned to our council, trusting in the divine mercy and the merits of the saint, we decreed that he was to be inscribed in the catalogue of saints; resolving that on the day of his death, his feast should be devoutly celebrated henceforth each year by you and the other faithful of Christ. Hence we ask and instruct all of you in God, commanding by the apostolic writing that venerating the memory of this saint, as has been said, with due solemnity, you should humbly seek his intercession with God; through whose merits may you attain to the eternal joys.

---

33 *Patrinus* can mean 'godfather' but Piazzi, *Omobono* (p. 19) take it here to mean 'spiri-tual guide'.

The Life of Homobonus: *Labentibus annis*

When 1,197 years had elapsed from the Incarnation and Cremona was blinded by the great falsehoods of heretics, which like thorns often tore the souls even of the good, God produced a rose on the thorns, to inflame not only the city of Cremona but the neighbouring region with its fragrance and lead it from the stench of sin to the sweet smell of virtue and the minds of men from vice to a decent and blessed life in the knowledge of their Creator, spurning the falsehoods which disturb the fickle minds of almost all men.

At that time in that city, near the basilica of the renowned confessor Giles, the citizens had created a not inconsiderable area both in terms of the number of citizens and the amount of building. There, among other citizens and families of middling popular rank, lived the family then called de' Tucenghi, whose ancestors practised a variety of trades at different times, and also lived by making clothes, the sort of people we usually call 'tailors'. An old man of this Tucenghi family lived there with his wife on the produce of his labours, in a house which his forefathers had owned; they also obtained the necessaries of life from a sufficient landholding, not far from the walls of the city. This man had by his wife a son, whom he called Homobonus, hoping that the name would be an augury of good to him, and indeed the name was not inappropriate to the young man, for he was no less good in reality than in name.

This Homobonus dedicated himself to his parents' trade, and having been instructed in it so conducted himself that to the utmost of his ability he preserved faith and equity in his dealings (a rare event). As a youth his virtues inspired the good will of all the citizens towards him, and at his parents' wish he was joined in marriage to a virgin of suitable age. He lived with his wife for several years while his father still lived, obedient in all things to his parents. When the time came for his father to die and he was his own master, he began to reflect on the brevity of human life, the falsity of the world and its fleeting goods, and that there could be nothing holier than to do what the gospel says, ' Store up for yourself treasures in heaven, where neither rust nor moth destroys.' When he had considered this for several days, his previous great preoccupation with increasing his fortune began to cool; he was already assiduous in attending church, in prayer and fasting, and the wealth he acquired by his trade he gave with his own hands to the poor and needy. He bestowed assistance upon the sick and pious gifts on those in want, succouring the afflicted by his own efforts, and was so completely devoted to pious works of mercy that he was popularly known as 'Homobonus the father of the poor'.

When his wife saw that his ideas had so changed that he had abandoned his accustomed trade and had dedicated himself to a life lived in contempt of worldly men, she was greatly perturbed, and said, 'What madness has seized you, Homobonus? You used to be a prudent man, and now you no longer attend to the trade by which you used to live honourably, but abandoning it you are eating up all our substance, giving it to wretched people from whom we cannot ever expect the least service!' She poured out reproaches and insults on the holy man, which he took patiently, telling her that fleeting earthly goods were like a flow of water and that he was a happy man who stored up treasure in heaven by aiding the poor of Christ. Accepting the various trials of his wife with patience and humility, he always prevailed.

It was this holy man's custom to go every night to his church and always to be present at matins. A certain priest called Osbert, who was then in charge of the church, himself a good and God-fearing man, observed Homobonus's devotion and every night, when he had rung the bell for matins, came to open the door and let him into the church. On one occasion, Homobonus came before the bell had rung and stood waiting for some time in front of the church doors, when, by God's will, they opened of themselves before the saint's eyes. When the priest saw him standing in the church, he marvelled, asking who had let him in. He replied, 'I found the church doors open.' The priest knew that he himself had closed them in the evening. A few days later, the same thing happened again: the doors stood open for him when he came before the hour of matins. The priest knew that this was the work of God and that this was a holy man, for in the twenty-six years during which the priest governed the church this happened several times as has been narrated above. God's saint always observed the canonical hours; always present at matins, he did not leave when it was over, but waited for daybreak and the time of mass, praying continuously before a certain old Cross. He persisted in prayer and often remained in contemplation, prostrated full-length before the Cross.

One day, during a time of famine, the baker delivered a quantity of bread, as usual, to the holy man's house. Many of the poor and needy realised that this bread was for Homobonus, the father of the poor, and followed him as he took it to the house of the man of God. Finding him at home they begged him to give them alms from this bread in his usual manner. He yielded to them and, so that his wife, who happened to be out, should not suspect, gave them the greater part of the bread. His wife returned, and when the time came for dinner she went to the cupboard and found two types of bread there. Loaves of an incomparable fineness and quality, as many in number as Homobonus had given away, were there with the rest. His wife asked how they came to be there, and the holy man himself marvelled, seeing that this was God's work, and told the housemaid, who had seen what had happened, but instructed her not to say anything.

What happened with the bread happened similarly with some wine. He was having the little vineyard tended which was all he had retained for the support of himself and his many paupers (for he had sold everything else and distributed the proceeds to the poor), and he was carrying a jug full of wine to the workmen. Some poor people begged him to let them have a drink from this jug. He gave it to them, and it was almost completely emptied of wine. He didn't dare return home to fill it for fear of his wife's reproaches, so he filled it with water, signed it [with the Cross], covered it and took it to the workmen, whom he found very thirsty. When they tasted it, they found it was the most delightful and exquisite wine; they had never tasted any so good. The man of God heard this and thought they were mocking him, but when he tasted it, he recognised the work of God and rendered him abundant thanks. Some people who had seen him put the water into the jug and knew what had happened reported the great miracle. He showed many other signs of his sanctity while he lived, but no fewer after he died; and the bad faith and incredulity of many heretics were overcome by the signs, the virtue and the words of the man of God.

Thus he devoted himself to abstinence and good works. One day, when he was an old man, that is, on 13 November when the feast of the great confessor St Brice is celebrated, he was present at matins in his usual church, well and untroubled. After the office he knelt in prayer before the cross, as he usually did, and there remained until the hour of mass. When the priest began the mass with *Gloria in excelsis Deo* he prostrated himself before the Cross, debasing himself in reverence to God like a knight before a king, a slave before his lord, his hands extended in the form of a cross on the earth, and without a motion or sign of death rendered his soul to the Creator. No one suspected his death until the time came for the reading of the gospel; when he didn't get up, some thought he was asleep, and going to arouse him they found his body was lifeless.

At once his glorious body was raised up, washed and prepared for burial with solemn rites. The poor heard that their father was dead and rushed to his funeral, lamenting the death of Homobonus, the father of the poor. And behold, when they came to the place where he lay buried, God shone forth in his saint with innumerable great miracles. Among these paupers there were lame people who were cured when they came to lament their benefactor, for their legs and feet were strengthened; the blind received light, the deformed were straightened, and people oppressed by various infirmities were at once restored to health at the tomb which was built in the church of Sant' Egidio. Many with withered and distorted limbs were cured. People flocked there carrying invalids on litters and on stretchers; those who could brought themselves, even on sticks. All God cured when they invoked his saint, by his intercession. One woman who for many years had been bent double so that her face touched her knees had herself brought there on a stretcher; many laughed at her, thinking she could never be cured. When she had been placed before the tomb, she prayed and was cured, and rose up well and steady, giving thanks to God.

As the fame of the miracles grew, someone began to say stupid things about the saint; all at once, by God's will, his tongue so swelled in his mouth that he couldn't speak at all. He feared for his life and repented in his conscience, and having made a vow to God was at once cured. There were several born dumb for whom their parents made vows, and by the intercession of the saint they received the use of their tongues; he also miraculously cured one born both blind and dumb. Many demoniacs were healed. Before his death a demon had been afflicting a young girl of Bergamo; when he was constrained by conjuration and exorcism the demon said he would never leave her, unless Homobonus of Cremona expelled him. The parents did not know who this Homobonus was and thought the spirit was mocking them; but when she was brought devoutly to the tomb, there she was healed. There was another demoniac woman, but some thought she was not really possessed. So they secretly brought holy water, and put into one container a consecrated host and into another an unconsecrated one. First they sprinkled her with water that had not been blessed, and she made no sign, but remained quiet. When however they sprinkled her with holy water she at once cried out in horror and showed her distress; the same thing happened with the hosts, so they knew that she was truly possessed, and brought her devoutly before the tomb of the saint, where she was cured.

The bishop of Cremona and the wise men of the city, observing these and many other miracles, decided to apply to the supreme pontiff with an account of the miracles, so that he could examine them and see whether the man of God deserved to be canonised, that is, inscribed in the catalogue of saints. So they sent the bishop, whose name was Sicard, to Rome to Innocent IV[34] with a large embassy. He listened to and examined everything, and said that he had dreamed the day before their arrival that he was canonising a saint of Cremona, and by bull and apostolic letters he canonised St Homobonus with solemn rites. Given at the Lateran in the first year of his pontificate. These bulls are in the sacristy of the cathedral of Cremona, with the aid of our Lord Jesus Christ.

34 This is of course a mistake for Innocent III and might suggest that the work was composed after 1254 (the death of Innocent IV), but Piazzi (*ibid.*, p. 66 n. 44) suggests that the author may have accepted the Lombard antipope Lando di Sezza (1179–80), who took the name of Innocent III. This seems even stranger, but if true might suggest an early date for the Life.

II: RAIMONDO PALMARIO OF PIACENZA (d. 1200)

The Life of Raimondo, called 'the Palmer' (Palmario), was written in 1212 by Master Rufino, a canon of the church of the Twelve Apostles adjacent to the hospital which Raimondo himself had founded in Piacenza.[1] Although Rufino seems to have been personally acquainted with Raimondo only late in the saint's life, he claims to have drawn on the testimony of not only Raimondo's only surviving son, Gerardo (at whose urgent request he wrote the Life), but the whole community of those who had known and worked with him. The result, as published in *Acta sanctorum* in 1729, has accordingly been accepted as authentic and trustworthy both by Vauchez and by Luigi Canetti in his study of the cult of the saints at Piacenza.[2]

The text as we have it is not however the one Rufino wrote but the outcome of a double process of translation. Its Bollandist editor, Peter Bosch, explained how his search for a Life of Raimondo revealed that Rufino's work had been translated in 1525 by an anonymous Dominican friar for the use of the nuns who by that date occupied the site of Raimondo's original foundation. Evidently they could not read the Latin text, which was in their possession, and they made it available to the friar, who subsequently retained it. By the time Bosch appeared upon the scene two hundred years later this manuscript had perished or vanished along with others which had once belonged to the Dominicans of Piacenza. The nuns however still preserved the Italian translation, and Bosch set about retranslating it into Latin. The result is what we now have.[3]

Even if it was a faithful rendering of the Italian, Bosch's Latin would not have been that of a north Italian cleric of the early thirteenth century. With this reservation, can we believe that he has preserved the substance of Rufino's Life? Here we are largely dependent on the sixteenth-century Dominican, who seems to claim that he simply translated his original. In September 1525, writing to the nuns to introduce his work, he described Rufino's legend as 'written in an obscure and somewhat fanciful style'. Out of religious affection for the nuns he had turned 'the whole thing into the vernacular idiom'. He did not claim – or admit – that he had revised the text more extensively. Did he have any reason to do so, to alter the facts or the sentiments contained in the Life? Bosch judged that the Italian version was 'barbaric' and very different from modern Italian,

---

1 *AS*, July, 6, pp. 645–57.

2 Vauchez's opinion is in *Biblioteca sanctorum*, 11, cols 26–9; L. Canetti, *Gloriosa civitas: culto dei santi e società cittadina a Piacenza nel medioevo* (Bologna, 1993), p. 169 n. 6, judges the present text 'più che ragionevolmente affidabile'.

3 *AS*, July, 6, p. 644. The manuscript of the Italian translation was among several stolen from the Biblioteca Comunale of Piacenza in 1985.

but he was convinced of the probity and sincerity of the translator. Without Rufino's original text before him he may simply have been wrong, but he was at least able to measure the difference between the Dominican's translation and a version published in 1618 by the Piacentine hagiographer Pietro Mario Campi. The former, he thought, had taken pains to translate 'faithfully rather than elaborately' whereas Campi 'throughout freely wanders from the sentiments and brevity of his prototype'.[4]

There seems in fact to be little in the present text that is not acceptable as a product of Rufino's time and place; the concerns revealed in it are well documented around 1200. It is plausible, for example, that when Raimondo's kin, knowing his piety, urge him to take a wife, for the married too can practise their religion and find salvation, they are to be understood as upholding the orthodox view of marriage in face of the rejection of it by contemporary heretics, notably Cathars. Innocent III felt it necessary to deal explicitly with this issue (among others, such as heretical dietary taboos) in a letter of admonition written to the people of Treviso in April 1207.[5] Raimondo's careful limitation of his preaching activities also makes sense in this context. On the other hand, there is little sign in the Life of the improving sentiments or pious elaborations which a sixteenth-century translator might well have felt tempted to inject for the benefit of an audience of nuns.

There are admittedly a few anomalies. The author is uncertain about the saint's family name and trade, although Rufino, writing in 1212, would surely have known, or could have found out, what these were. Possibly he omitted them as of no interest or importance, whereas the translator, three hundred years later, may have thought that his readers would be curious about such particulars. To remark that 'the verses of St Maurice' were 'at that time' believed to have power over demons also seems strange for an author writing so very close to the date of the miracle concerned.[6] There is a double difficulty here, for this oddity occurs in the account of a miracle which cannot have been known to Rufino in 1212. According to the notarial records which Bosch printed as an appendix to the Life it took place on 28 May 1217 and was attested on 7 June at the church of the Twelve Apostles. Among the witnesses were not only Raimondo's son Gerardo but two canons of the church named Rufino; so it is not impossible that Rufino himself later inserted it into the Life.[7] It could not simply have been inserted by the Dominican translator from the notarial record, for the account in the Life contains several details not given by the notary, including the names of the bothersome demons and the mention of the verses of St Maurice. The

---

4 *Ibid.*, p. 643. On Campi, see Simon Ditchfield, *Liturgy, sanctity and history in Tridentine Italy* (Cambridge, 1995), pp. 198–203.

5 Webb, 'The pope and the cities', p. 149. There is nothing comparable in Innocent's letters to Piacenza, but (at a very similar date) he referred to the city as 'seduced by heretical fallacies': *ibid.*, p. 137.

6 *AS*, July, 6, p. 656.

7 *Ibid.*, pp. 661–2. Noting the difficulty with the date, Bosch proposed correcting the year to 1206, in which the days and dates matched; but 1206 (mccvi) for 1217 (mccxvii), though possible, is not an obvious copyist's error.

translator might however have inserted the phrase 'at that time' if he thought that his audience had never heard of the verses.

Compared with much hagiography, the Life is a remarkably straightforward account of a practical saint. Raimondo is not represented as a wonder-worker during his lifetime, and supernatural interventions in the narrative are few, although one is pivotal: the appearance of Christ himself to Raimondo in the portico of St Peter's prompts him to abandon a life of pilgrimage and to dedicate himself to works of charity in his native city. While insisting on some obvious saintly characteristics such as aversion to sexual relations, Rufino feels no need to credit his hero with visions (apart from that crucial visitation from Christ), ecstasies or ascetic practices such as flagellation. As a married man he is simply 'sparing in his food, assiduous in almsgiving, fasting and prayer and tireless in attendance at the divine office'. Nothing is said to suggest that he adopted more extreme penitential measures before or after the death of his wife. Whether as pilgrim or as charity worker, Raimondo is essentially an exponent of the active life.[8]

Perhaps this modesty reflects the limited concerns of the author and his audience. They remembered Raimondo for his pilgrimages and for the qualities he displayed in the service of the poor and sick. He was, first and foremost, their saint. Although the recording of the miracles may suggest the flickering of wider ambitions, especially when we find testimony being gathered from citizens of Cremona and elsewhere, there is no evidence of a serious intention to take the matter further. Without promotion and influential support a canonisation process could not even begin. Certain lay saints of a later epoch lived under the wing of the mendicants, who professionally nurtured the memory of all their saints, canonised or not, and publicised them as examples and objects of veneration to the faithful. Raimondo seems most obviously comparable with Homobonus, who like him lived before the coming of the friars. We may wonder whether the vital difference between them was not the style or magnitude of their sanctity but the initative that Sicard of Cremona decided to take on behalf of Homobonus.

As was the custom of *Acta sanctorum*, Bosch divided his retranslation into long chapters, but he listed the chapter divisions which he found in the Italian translation, which were probably those of the original Latin Life. I have divided the text at the places which seem to be thus indicated but have abbreviated the rather lengthy chapter headings which Bosch transcribed. He also printed as appendices the notarial records of several miracles which he found preserved in the archive of the nunnery of San Raimondo, of which the latest is dated 1247. These are not translated here, but some of them, including the one noticed above, correspond to miracles recorded by Rufino in the last chapter of the Life.

8 The account of his pilgrimages in the Holy Land and elsewhere is of some interest if it is indeed a contemporary record: D. M. Webb, 'Raimondo and the Magdalen: a twelfth-century Italian pilgrim in Provence', *Journal of Medieval History*, 26 (2000), pp. 1–18.

The Life of Raimondo 'Palmario' of Piacenza, written by Master Rufino

Preface

To the humble servants of Jesus Christ, the poor of the hospital of our most blessed father Raimondo Palmario, I Rufino, least of masters in the canonry of the Twelve Apostles, greeting.

Dearest sons in the precious blood of the only-begotten Son of the most pure Virgin, I cannot sufficiently commend your desire and the ardent prayers with which you have for a long time incited and almost compelled me to compile the origins, the career, the happy and admirable end, the wonderful virtues, the amazing miracles of Raimondo, your and my most holy father, and put them into writing; the more so, because my own eyes have seen how gloriously the most merciful Lord God has revealed himself in this our blessed father; and many of you, dearest sons, as intimates of his, have given me abundant testimony of the piety, the inexpressible toil, the harsh travails which our most devoted father day and night sustained in the support of the poor and sick of his beloved hospital.

Even though all these incentives should have broken down my lukewarmness and tardiness, I thought myself unworthy to undertake such a task and said to myself: how could this be a eulogy worthy of so holy a father, as my command of writing is so poor and especially as I am a sinner? So I did nothing until this moment, nor would I have dared to begin even now, had it not been for the urgent promptings and effective arguments of our beloved brother and spiritual son, Brother Gerardo, subdeacon in our canonry and the sole surviving son of our blessed father Raimondo.

I would have you know, dearest sons, that I was for a while kept in bed by an acute fever, and the aforementioned son of your father Raimondo came into my little room in a perturbed frame of mind, as if he was uneasy about my sickness. Flinging himself down in tears before my couch, he said, 'Alas, dear master, if you should happen to die now, what written testimony would remain of the life of my dear father? As you well know he was, for this our city of Piacenza, the shining mirror of all virtues, an unwearied refuge for the poor of the hospital, and for those who were to come after him the most diligent provider; the example, in short, of all goodness, and above all of patience, humility and perseverance. I beg you, my dear master, not to put it off any longer.

Think, perhaps the divine justice has afflicted you with this illness so that you may realise your negligence. Do not reject my warning, which stems from filial love; but, for the ardent love you bear towards God, towards my blessed father, towards me his unworthy son, I beg you to resolve to set your hand seriously to this holy work as soon as you are cured of this sickness; and I am sure that the accumulated merits of my most holy father will assist you.'

Overcome by so just a speech, I raised up my mind to the Lord and to the blessed father Raimondo, resolving within myself that if the heat of the fever should leave me I would put the holy project into execution without delay. I was restored to health after three days and confirmed my resolve. Receive, therefore, what I have written, by means of which I have set out to make the blessed father Raimondo known to all. Lest I should be accused of audacity because I have dared to write things that are all but incredible about a man like the blessed Raimondo, who was simple, open and illiterate, I have mentioned only facts of which either I myself was a living witness or to which you, or others, have sworn on the sacred Gospels. Let us therefore begin in the name of the Lord and what we write let us divide up under suitable headings. Amen.

Of his origins and early life

By nationality the blessed Raimondo was a Piacentine, born in the city of Piacenza. His family were not of illustrious origin, but nor were they lowly: if you consider their domestic circumstances, they were private citizens, neither poor nor wealthy. The blessed father was of medium height, with a graceful body; nimble and quick in action, although thin. He was intelligent and endowed with an innate prudence, tempered however with a wonderful openness which one might call dove-like simplicity. He abhorred all suspicion and scoffing and never indulged in sharp practice or deceit in his dealings with anyone; he was a man of good and honest faith, such as the gospel rightly describes: 'Here is a true Israelite, in whom there is no guile'. He spoke little and seriously; he was loving and charitable; he had an immense fellow-feeling for the afflicted and the poor, to whom he opened the bowels of compassion to the utmost of his powers, as will be related.

His mother brought him up at home when he was an infant. When he came to the age of about twelve, his father placed him with a certain craftsman, not to learn letters, but to practise his servile and ignoble trade and learn how to do business in it. (What this trade was is not entirely clear: there are those who say it was shoe-mending, but this is opinion, not knowledge.) What however is true is that, whatever the craft was, it was not a little displeasing to this excellent youth, as one who was born for bigger and better things, as will become apparent later. Meanwhile, being still a boy and under his father's authority, he had to put up with it, thus obeying the Lord's command which directs us to honour our parents and obey the divine law.

How he went to Jerusalem on the death of his father

The blessed Raimondo had already attained the age of puberty, or adolescence, which begins with the fourteenth year, when his father passed from this brief life into the heavenly homeland. Then the holy youth considered himself at liberty to say farewell to that lowly trade, not in order to pursue idleness or give himself over to vice but to cleave more closely to his Saviour in a life wholeheartedly consecrated to the divine service. Wherefore, so as to burn entirely with the love of the blessed Jesus Christ, he decided to go on pilgrimage to his Holy Sepulchre and to visit the holy places both at Jerusalem and round about. He did not want to set out, however, until he had told his mother and obtained her permission.

He chose his day, went into her room when she was alone, and addressed her thus: 'My dear and most beloved mother, I thank my Creator endlessly that he has put it into my mind to leave these tedious worldly trades to worldly men and to embrace the Cross of sweet Jesus, my Saviour and yours, and to leave my homeland; I will say goodbye to all my friends and kinsfolk and visit the Lord's Sepulchre as a pilgrim. It is only anxiety for you, my dearest parent, that bothers me, for you are alone and a widow, and you have no comfort or refuge besides me, your only son. But consider, I beg you, what it says in the holy gospel: "He who loves his father or mother more than me, is not worthy of my grace." Do not therefore, mother, I beg you, be the reason why I lose my Saviour's grace; but let me go with your good will and blessing.'

Hearing this, his pious mother burst into floods of tears, embraced her son and exclaimed: 'O my one dear light! O support of your wretched widowed mother! Do not torment yourself on my account. You could have said nothing more pleasing to me, especially at this time; for now that I am released from the bonds of matrimony, and have no other child but you, who are grown up and no longer a child, and now that I am well on in years, I had decided to spend whatever life is left to me in

the divine service and in visiting holy places; I want the Creator only
to grant me the grace to imitate that most holy widow Anna, who did
not leave the Lord's temple at Jerusalem even at night. Be of good cheer,
my son; we will go together to the most Holy Sepulchre, from which
only death will tear me.'

Who can match the joy of the mother and the youthful son, when they
realised that they were of one mind in so pious an intention? Each gave
all the thanks they could to the Lord God who had set them apart from
worldly loves and attachments and inflamed them with spiritual longing.
Then, to fulfil their vows, they made the necessary arrangements for
their pilgrimage; and when they had taken leave, as was proper, of their
friends and kin, they went to the most venerable bishop of the city of
Piacenza and said to him: 'Most reverend father and pastor, we have
decided to go hence on pilgrimage to the Holy Sepulchre; therefore,
with our hands crosswise, we ask what such pilgrims are accustomed
to ask.' When the holy bishop understood the mutual request of the
mother and son, he fixed a red cross on their breasts, and said, 'This is
the sign which will guard you from all danger. May the most merciful
Saviour lead you and bring you back safely. When you pray, be mindful
of your homeland.'

When everything was in readiness, they left, not without many tears
on the part of their kinsfolk, neighbours and friends, and, partly by sea,
partly by land, and experiencing great toil and many dangers, they
finally reached the desired harbour. When they beheld the most holy
city of Jerusalem both wept abundantly out of a most tender sense of
devotion, reflecting upon the obdurate cruelty of the treacherous Jews,
who were so blinded that they put the author of life to death. They
meditated on the immense love of the eternal Father, who to redeem
his sinful servants permitted his and the most pure Virgin's Son to be
crucified. When they came to the Holy Sepulchre, and saw the place of
the most holy Cross, they prayed thus, most fervently and with abundant tears: 'Behold us, Lord, who for our crimes died and was buried in
this place. We beg you, sweet Saviour, that you will receive our souls in
peace, and do not permit us to be detained longer in this vale of miseries;
this whole world is as smoke to us, nor can anything in it delight our
senses any more, now that we have with eyes and mind received this
sweet and spiritual consolation which the glorious place of your death,
burial and divine Resurrection has bestowed upon us.'

When they had thus visited the holy places of Jerusalem as suppliants, and had kissed them a thousand and more times, they went to the

town of Bethlehem, to venerate the palace of the Son of the most chaste Virgin, that is the holy crib; at the sight of such a religious and beautiful place they were overcome with an inward sweetness of the spirit, and all the splendid places which are on show throughout the world they esteemed as nothing; they were entirely taken up in contemplation of the goodness of the Lord of all, who thought fit there to abase himself. Then they went to the most holy and precious tomb of the Virgin, nearby in the valley of Josaphat; and from there to Bethany, to the house of the beloved Magdalen, who thought herself so blessed because, sitting at the feet of her sweet Master, she had heard his divine and supremely wise words. After several days, when they had toured all the holy places, they thought about returning home, so that they could share all the marvels they had seen with pious and religious men and inflame the cold hearts of worldly men and women with divine love. Therefore when they had once again visited the holy sights and sprinkled them with flowing tears, they returned to the sea, to return to Italy by ship and at last see once again their native soil.

How Raimondo almost died on the voyage home

The blessed Raimondo had suffered a great deal, during his long pilgrimage, from problems with food and drink, from protracted vigils, from the effort of travelling and weariness, from heat and cold. Two further miseries were added to these on the ship on which they were returning to their homeland, which at length made him gravely ill. The first arose from the bilges, which emitted such an intolerable and putrid stench that they infected all the air round about. The second was brought by the rain, which fell in enormous quantities on the long-suffering father, who had no protection. These evils, added to the previous ones, and also divine providence which desired to put the patience of its servant to the test, brought him a violent and continual fever, which in a few days so weakened him that he seemed to be at his last gasp. The sailors, when they saw him all but dead, decided to throw him into the sea lest he should die on the ship and they should all be drowned and the ship itself founder (for they believe, superstitiously, that if anyone dies on ship, the voyage must be imperilled). Having taken this resolution, they were about to perform the cruel deed when the poor widowed pilgrim mother perceived it and flung herself on her son's body, exclaiming, not without bitter tears, 'O cruel ones, do not deprive this wretched widow of her one light; don't take the prop of my life away from me; do not tear the bowels out of me and out of my womb. Either leave me my child, or throw me with him into the deep. If you want to lighten the ship, start with me, because I am weighing it down with these laments. Don't you see that my eyes have become a fountain of the bitterest tears? My sons, put your trust in sweetest Jesu, for whose love I and my son have borne such burdens, and pour out trustful prayers along with me; for I hope that we will be heard by the divine goodness.'

The mariners were moved to pity by these tears and persuasive words, and prostrating themselves they prayed thus: 'You, Lord, are the protector of poor pilgrims, the consolation of widows, the salvation of the sick; we beg you, O Lord, to accept our vows, and restore your servant Raimondo to health, so that we commit no such cruelty against his unhappy mother.' Scarcely had they finished their prayer, when the good father began to speak and said, weeping, 'The Lord God has punished me with this sickness, and has given death no power over me.' Hearing these words his mother and the sailors praised the Lord, saying, 'Blessed be thy name; blessed our preserver, who does not desert those who call upon you with sincere faith.' After a few more days the good father was completely well again.

How his mother died before reaching home

When this difficult and dangerous voyage was over, and they had disembarked in Italy, they had not yet reached Piacenza when the unhappy parent, so buffeted by care, so worn out by effort, fell ill. When she realised that the end of her miserable life was not far away, she summoned her son. 'Dear Raimondo,' she said, 'my sweetest son, I see that the time is near when my Creator will call me to my rest and the longed-for reward of the hardships I have borne. I therefore beg you not to take it sadly; for you know that to live, for me, has been Jesus, the only-blessed; to die will be eternal reward. I am not deserting you, my son; but I go to prepare a blessed place for you.'

The excellent Raimondo lowered his eyes and repressed his grief, hiding his tears, both lest he should sadden his mother's happy departure and lest he should offend the divine goodness; for he knew that in all things it worked for the good of those it loved. He made this reply: 'My sweetest mother, the Lord God was our companion in all our pilgrimage; we have fulfilled our vows; now, if it pleases his majesty to separate us, what else can we say, but "May his most just will be done"?

But I beg you, O holy parent, when you come before your Saviour and mine, that you tell him on my behalf that I am already sated by this life; but to live without you, dear mother, is to me an intolerable punishment. Pray the Lord, therefore, that he will soon gather my spirit to him in peace.' Then his mother, having received the sacraments of the church, within a few days ceased to live. The devoted son closed his beloved parent's eyes, and with many tears devoutly attended to her funeral rites.

How Raimondo came to Piacenza and was called 'Palmer'

When he had buried his dear mother, the excellent Raimondo, considering himself now alone, turned his mind to the Lord God, and weeping said, 'Woe is me, for my father and my mother have left me! But I hope that you, Lord, will take charge of me. I beg you, Lord, be to me my father and my mother; for I have no hope in anything, except that which I place in you; and putting my faith in that, I will now return to my homeland.' So the good Raimondo went on his way, clad in the habit of a pilgrim, that is, with a red cross on his breast, and in his hand a branch of palm, from which he got the surname of 'Palmer'. (There are those who say his family name was Palmario, but I have found no clear evidence of this.) At length he reached Piacenza, and before he went to his own home, he visited the cathedral and presented himself, with the signs just described, to the most reverend bishop. Having then given thanks to the Creator for benefits received, and having received the bishop's blessing, he went home, with an escort of friends and kinsmen and a very kindly reception.

How Raimondo was married and exercised his trade

When a few days had elapsed after his return to his homeland his kinsfolk began to say to him, 'Brother Raimondo, if you are going to live unmarried and alone, you will have a hard life; for you will have no one to take care of things for you. Let us help you to find a wife, and reflect that married people too can serve God; for matrimony was instituted by him.' Raimondo allowed himself to be persuaded, the divine goodness permitting it, so that his servant should experience what trials those joined in marriage undergo, in feeding and bringing up children and looking after a household.

When he was married, he realised that his patrimony did not suffice to support a family, and returned to that first trade (cobbling, as it is thought) which he had learned at his father's direction. He practised it without fraud and without avarice, solely in order to feed himself, his wife and their children, and to give alms to the poor. This trade, however, was not pleasing to him, because it distracted him from his spiritual purposes. In the hours which he could set aside from pursuing his work, and especially on feast-days, as he was enthusiastic for the knowledge of the divine law and the study of scripture, he devoted himself to conversation with religious men, distinguished by their good character and learning. From this he derived such profit that, even without knowledge of letters, though not without the gift of divine wisdom, he seemed most knowledgeable about those things which had to do with God and the Catholic religion. Furthermore, so as to divert worldly men, and especially those who followed the same trade as he did, from frivolous gatherings and idle games, he chose a particular workshop on a feast-day, where with great warmth and love he could preach the true knowledge of the holy law of God to his fellows in a homely fashion, and instruct them in the works necessary to fulfil the divine commands and the way to follow the virtues above all and avoid the vices.

It did not take long for Raimondo's fame to reach the point at which on feast-days many people, as soon as they found out in which house or workshop he was performing, flocked there, eager to hear his fervent words. Some people urged him to hold meetings in public places, even in the main piazza. But the humble servant of God refused to do this, saying that that was the office of priests and learned men; error could creep up on him, because he was not instructed in letters. He was unwilling to follow this advice, because he possessed self-knowledge; but so effective were his humble domestic exhortations among his companions in his trade that they formed a sort of religious order and had recourse to the good Raimondo as to their spiritual father and guide.

Of his life after marriage; the birth and death of his children

The servant of God ordered his life and works on the model of holy Tobit: sparing in his food, assiduous in almsgiving, fasting and prayer and tireless in attendance at the divine office. He sought the frequent confession of his sins in a thoroughly contrite spirit, and also the Holy Communion, which he accompanied with floods of tears. Although he lived on earth in the body, his whole mind was turned to the heavens. He wore modest clothes. His wife he corrected and taught like a daughter, loved like a sister, revered like a mother. He had several children by her. These he was accustomed to offer to the Lord, the author of all good things, as each one was dipped in the sacred font, saying, 'Lord, these bear your image; you have given them to me; I hold them for you, as created by you; in your hands are their life and death.' But the benign Creator of all things, as he knew that his servant could not devote himself with all his heart to the pursuit of the spiritual life while he was bound to servitude by the conjugal yoke and the care of children, took pity on him and decided to give him some liberty; he took all the children from this life within a year. This afflicted the parent somewhat at first, because of natural love; but soon, reflecting that he must bear the divine will, he acquiesced in it entirely, appropriating that saying of holy Job, 'The Lord gave; the Lord has taken away; blessed be the name of the Lord. Henceforth I shall be more easily freed from worldly cares.'

How he exhorted his wife to continence and offered his last child to Christ

The deaths of his children extinguished all the desires of this life in blessed Raimondo. Desiring to consecrate himself to God, he began to exhort his wife to maintain continence between them in future. It was now the time for them both to transfer all their love to God, and not to try any longer to produce children. But she was little attached to heavenly things, and rather harshly said, 'When I become a nun, then I shall heed your warnings; now, since I was taken by you as a wife, I am certainly going to behave like a wife, not like a widow or a nun.' The prudent servant of God, perceiving his wife's imperfection and peril, was unwilling to press her more insistently, wishing that they should live peaceably and without sin between themselves.

Thus it came about, by divine providence, that he begot one more child. One day, seeing that he was reduced to servitude, the good Raimondo lifted the child from his cradle while his wife was away, and taking him in his arms carried him to the church of St Brigid in Piacenza, to the place where he was accustomed to attend the divine office, before the image of the crucified Christ; and lifting him up as high as he could, he uttered this prayer: 'My Lord and Saviour, who receives all who fly to you, reach out your arms I pray thee, so that just as you have taken five of my children to yourself at a tender age, making them co-heirs of eternal beatitude, deign likewise to accept this my little child, given by

you to me beyond my hopes. I beg you, my Saviour, do not separate him
from his brothers. If you have decreed a longer life for him, preserve
him chaste and pure for the life of holy religion, in which I wish him to
be at some time enrolled, and I now offer and dedicate him.' When he
had finished his prayer, he covertly returned the child to his cradle, so
that his wife would have no clue to what he had done.

How he again sought to embrace continence; his wife's illness

After he offered his little child to the sweetest Saviour, the longing to
embrace perpetual continence became ever more deeply implanted in
Raimondo's breast, but he was unwilling to coerce his wife, who he
did not think would agree. The Lord in his wisdom however opened
another path to his desire. He allowed his wife to become so afflicted
with an incurable disease that she was incapable of performing the
marital act; and so the servant of God, without doing any injury to
his wife and without sin, was able to accomplish his vow. This severe
illness lasted for many days and months, and caused Raimondo no little
inconvenience. Nevertheless he tried to support his wife with constant
sympathy, groaning, 'This evil has befallen you, my sister, on my
account; I would willingly bear it for you.'

At last it pleased God to relieve his servant from servitude and transfer
him to nobler and more useful occupations, and at the same time to
release his wife, who was almost worn out by long sickness, from her
torments. He therefore brought it about that she passed from this life,
with a mind rightly prepared and subdued by perfect patience. Thus
the good Raimondo, emancipated from the marital yoke, confirmed his
resolution of perpetual chastity and continence.

How he left his little son in the care of his wife's parents

When the servant of God saw that he was without father, mother, spouse
and children, that last little one excepted, he immediately decided that
he would entirely abandon all concern with temporal things. He was
however aware that only the upbringing of the child could get in his
way, and by divine inspiration he approached his wife's parents, bearing
the child in his arms. Handing it to them he said, 'To you, dear father-
in-law, and you, my honoured mother in law, I consign this child, born
to me and your daughter. See to it, I beg you, that he is rightly brought

up and educated, and instructed in good letters, and that he turns out at last religious, upright and useful; to this end I have dedicated him to the blessed Jesus Christ. I am making over all my property into your hands; use it for the benefit of yourself and the child. It is my fixed purpose to abandon the world, and to go post-haste to those places where the relics of the saints are venerated, first of all to Rome, to the church of St James in Galicia, and to St Antony, and to other famous places. I shall not come back here again, nor will you see me more. I will not let myself be detained any longer; but I shall set out to spend the rest of my life in continual pilgrimage. One boon I beg of my Saviour, that he will permit me to complete my course there where his most holy body, born of the most pure Virgin, was buried.'

When his parents-in-law heard this, they both rushed to embrace him and not without tears thus replied: 'Dear son-in-law, it is entirely pleasing to us that you should bring the little boy here and commit him to our care; for you have no one at home who can take care of him, and he will be more easily brought up and educated here. But we cannot bear that you should leave us, and your homeland, and lead a miserable life, like ill-starred and desperate men who have no place of refuge, wandering hither and yon;[9] this would be both grievous to us and shameful for you. Better to come here and live with us; leave us the charge of the child; you will be free to devote yourself to your pious duties, and it would be much more agreeable to us. Can you not serve your Creator in your own land, which is so richly endowed with relics?'

The blessed Raimondo responded to all this with heartfelt gratitude, but he totally rejected any idea of remaining at home, saying that he had not been restored by the Lord God to his liberty in order to stay; in this he was divinely inspired, and he would be of more benefit to their souls absent than present. After a very few days he arranged all his affairs as if he was about to die and left secretly, well knowing that the counsels of his kinsfolk and worldly friends were not for the good of his soul.

How he visited the most celebrated shrines of the West and was divinely warned to return to Piacenza to undertake the care of the poor

Having set out from Piacenza the blessed Raimondo did not hesitate, but went to St James in Galicia, living by begging, with great patience

9 A disapproving view which may well have been typical of the settled householder and quite probably embraced perpetual pilgrims.

and submission of spirit. When he had seen the relics of the most holy Apostle, on his way back to Italy he turned aside to the relics of the most holy Magdalen and the harsh site of her penance, not far from Marseille. Then he crossed Provence, and visited the relics of the Three Maries and St Lazarus. Then he went to St Antony and then to St Bernard.[10] When he re-entered Italy he venerated the holy places of that region, first of all the relics of St Augustine at Pavia. In this way he came at last to Rome. When he had spent several days visiting the relics of the chief Apostles and of the holy martyrs and virgins, he decided once again to visit Jerusalem and in so holy a place to meet his death. But while he was awaiting an opportunity to take ship he received a warning from our Saviour, as we are about to narrate.

The blessed Raimondo was at Rome, clad as a pilgrim and sleeping with other poor folk under a portico of St Peter's. The blessed Jesus Christ, in the guise of a pilgrim, as he appeared to the two disciples he accompanied to Emmaus, appeared to him and addressed him thus: 'My servant Raimondo, your prayers have been so acceptable to me that up to now I have satisfied your pious longing for pilgrimage, and for this reason I have freed you from the slavery of wife and children. Already you have seen all the holy places which you most wanted to, and there is now no vow remaining but that you should go once again to my most Holy Sepulchre. But I do not approve of this intention. I want you to engage in occupations more pleasing to me and more beneficial to you: I mean works of mercy. You are not to think that I shall be thinking principally of pilgimage, and works of piety of that kind, when at the time of Judgement I say, 'Come, O blessed of my Father, take possession of the kingdom of Heaven: for I was hungry and you gave me food; I was thirsty, and you gave me to drink; I was naked and you clothed me; I was sick and you visited me; I was in prison and you ransomed me. I do not want you, my son, to wander any more around the world, but to return to your homeland, Piacenza, where there are so many poor people, so many abandoned widows, so many sick and overcome by various misfortunes who call upon my mercy, and there is no one to help them. You shall go, and I will be with you, and I shall give you grace so

10 For observations on Raimondo's pilgrim itinerary see Webb, 'Raimondo and the Magdalen'. To be noted is his concentration on the saints associated with Bethany, which so much moved him on his pilgrimage to the Holy Land, and the fact that he is apparently the earliest recorded Italian pilgrim to the shrine of St Antony of Egypt at La Mothe in the Dauphiné. The 'St Bernard' mentioned was almost certainly not Bernard of Clairvaux, as Peter Bosch assumed, but Bernard of Vienne, venerated at Romans-sur-Isère, on Raimondo's likely return route to Italy and not far from St Antony's shrine.

lead the rich to almsgiving, the unquiet to peace, and erring and sinful women to a right way of living.'

The faithful servant of God replied in a humble voice, 'Lord, I am not equal to such an undertaking; I am a simple man, unlettered, without experience of affairs, and sinful. Do not bind me to my fellow-citizens, I beg you, Lord; you see how bitterly divided they are among themselves, how strife-torn. They will not listen to me; I shall labour in vain; I know what they are like. Then, did you not yourself declare, Lord, that a man is not received in his own country?' To which the Saviour replied, 'There is no reason, Raimondo, for you to be afraid; for the hearts of men are in my hand, and I shall sway them wheresoever I please. I shall give such force to your words, such spirit, such grace, such prudence in your dealings, that no one may contradict you. You shall return therefore to Piacenza, and take up your pious duties in this guise: wear a garment blue in colour, down to the middle calf, with loose sleeves and no hood. Always carry my Cross on your shoulders, and in its name and virtue carry out all your works of piety. A holy place will be established for the needy and for pilgrims; known by your name, this will stand as a permanent memorial to its founder. Rise up, get started; abandon your doubts; leave Rome, where you are wasting time and energy, and set out for your homeland. I will ensure that you are accepted as my servant and my messenger. Before you enter your city, put on those garments and raise my Cross upon your shoulders. Go to the bishop and explain to him the duties which in my name you have resolved to carry out. I will in the meantime make him favourably disposed to you.'

When the blessed Raimondo realised that this was his Saviour's mind, he added only, 'You are my Lord, and I am your servant; let your will be done.' And thus the heavenly vision disappeared.

How he returned to Piacenza

Raimondo set out from Rome to Piacenza, and when he came to Vico di Taro[11] he put on the garments he had been commanded to wear. Then he made himself a cross of wood, two cubits long and wide in proportion. On his head he wore only the *galera* [broad-brimmed hat] used by travellers. He put over his shoulder the holy Cross and a large bag in which to put the alms intended for the poor. Thus at last he entered Piacenza. The onlookers were all dumbstruck by this amazing sight, and

11 On the outskirts of Piacenza.

a huge number of them accompanied him all the way to the cathedral. In the meantime he spoke to no one and replied to no one, but kept his voice and eyes modestly downturned until he came to the bishop. When he had sought his blessing he said, 'Most venerable father, although I had it in mind not to return to my homeland, my Saviour has exhorted me to come back and, with your approval and in his name and that of the most holy Cross, to devote myself totally to collecting alms for the needy, gathering up poor pilgrims, reconciling those in conflict. But I can do none of this without your good will; wherefore I beg you, most reverend father, according to the command and the words of the Saviour, that you extend helping hands in such a holy enterprise, to which, I confess, I am altogether unequal.'

The holy bishop received the servant of God with the utmost joy, and said, 'Blessed for ever be our Saviour, who has sent you hither! I shall help you, and protect you by whatever means I can.' On leaving the bishop, he did not want to go to his own house as if he was still its master, for he had previously made over all his property to his parents-in-law for the support of his child. Many people offered him hospitality, but he did not want to go to any of them. He went to his parents-in-law and greeted them thus: 'I went away a poor man, and as a poor man I return, not by my own will but my Saviour's; I wish to lead the life of the poor and to serve the poor.' Then he explained his intentions fully to them. They did not dare to persuade him otherwise, lest they should be resisting the divine will.

How he made his dwelling near the church of the Twelve Apostles

It was necessary to find some pious and adequate place to carry out his task, and he decided to make his headquarters near the canonry of the Twelve Apostles. This site the canons granted to him; it was both big enough for the storage of alms and highly suitable for a hospice for the poor of both sexes, whether they were pilgrims or invalids. When he had got possession of this place, the good Raimondo began to seek out the needy around the city, those whom shame or disease prevented from begging;[12] and having duly found out about several of them, he began openly to seek donations for them all over the city, carrying the Cross on his shoulder and shouting earnestly, 'Woe to thee, O avaricious rich, for the supreme sentence will be pronounced against you!' The good

12 For the *verecundi pauperes* see above, p. 26.

and generous were inspired by these words and the avaricious and hard-hearted were terrified; so he obtained generous alms from both. However, he accepted nothing that was not voluntarily given, for he wanted them to acquire merit from their giving. He took the proceeds to the house and with the utmost equity divided them between the poor, the sick and the decent poor, keeping a tiny portion for himself.

A huge crowd of beggars flocked there begging for a share of these alms, but the good servant of God said to them, 'Go and beg openly as you usually do: for you're not sick and you know no shame.' They objected, 'Yes, we beg; but we don't get anything.' When he heard this the blessed Raimondo was inflamed with love and stirred up against the harshness of the affluent. He put the holy Cross on his shoulder and ordered the wretches to follow him; going around the thoroughfares, he called out, 'Help, help, hard and cruel Christians, for I am dying of hunger while you have plenty.' The citizens, especially the women, were struck by these sounds; some came to the windows and some opened their doors and ran into the piazza, saying, 'Come, Raimondo, come and eat, don't distress yourself so.' But he went on, saying, 'I don't have just one mouth, for I could suffer hunger not unwillingly; but there are as many mouths as you see here, perishing for want of food. I beg you, by the most holy Cross, have pity on the poor of Jesus Christ.' And so saying he lifted the blessed Cross up on high. Seeing the charity of the servant of God, everyone was moved to pity and gave generous assistance to the unhappy flock of beggars.

How Raimondo separated the women in his care from the men

In a short space of time blessed Raimondo's reputation grew to such an extent that all the afflicted, the sick, the poor both public and private, regarded him as their father and defender. In addition, several pious men left their homes and joined him, so that they could lend assistance in his godly work, collecting alms and ministering to the sick and especially the pilgrims who were received there. However, when blessed Raimondo saw that it was necessary not just to dispense relief but so to arrange the reception of men and women that there was no chance either of overcrowding or of sin and scandal, he decided to separate their accommodation. This he did, assigning to the women a special dwelling, rather better appointed but more secluded, near the canonry of the Twelve Apostles. Here he admitted not only foreign women, but poor citizens who were bereft of any resources. Furthermore, if any

women emerged from the haunts of vice, provided they were repen-
tant and wanted to lead a chaste life henceforth, blessed Raimondo did
not hesitate to receive them and, putting them in the care of the most
respectable matrons, guided them by the best and most considered
example. Then, when he judged that sufficient time had elapsed, he
asked them what sort of life they would choose. Many said that they
preferred the married state, so that they could persevere with greater
security in their intention of leading a decent life. He respected their
desires and obtained dowries for them from upright men. Others said
they wanted to maintain chastity as long as they lived, and these he
had admitted to reputable enclosed convents, being well aware of how
difficult it would be to preserve this virtue untarnished in the world,
especially for those who had long been accustomed to vice.

There were those who relapsed from their chaste intentions into their
previous immorality. As soon as he saw this, the excellent servant of God
reproved them with the kindliest words and fervently exhorted them to
respectability: ' Think,' he said, 'daughters, how unhappy your condition is: if you return to uncleanness and totally prostitute your honour,
you forfeit your souls, you become the servants of evil men, and at the
last you die miserably. I beg you, daughters, by this most holy Cross, by
the most pure Virgin, by him who deigned to die for you, Jesus Christ,
have pity on your own souls, and don't be unmindful of his benevolence.'
Some of them yielded to these fervent promptings, but others remained
stubborn, and these he quietly expelled, lest they should infect the more
virtuous with the contagion of their bad example.

How he defended the cause of the poor against the powerful

Blessed Raimondo's genuine holiness earned him such a reputation
that poor widows, orphans and others who were unjustly oppressed by
others, and could not obtain justice from the judges and the magnates,
flocked to him as to the common father and guardian of all the wretched,
crying, 'Servant of God, help us; we can't afford to go to law and struggle
in the courts with our enemies.' When he was informed about this sort
of injustice, he was inflamed in spirit, like another Elijah, and thus
addressed them in their distress: 'Remember, my children, that they are
blessed who for the love of their Creator put up with adversity. Be of
good hope and courage; you will have my help.' And then, prostrating
himself before the most holy Cross, he would pray thus: 'You know,
Lord, that the poor man is left to you; you have promised to be his future

helper; by the most holy Cross, I beg you, O my Saviour, that you supply me with the power to protect your poor against unjust judges.'[13]

Then, rising from prayer and taking the Cross on his shoulder, absorbed wholeheartedly in God, he would go to the court, where, taking the Cross in his hand, he addressed the unjust judges thus: 'Love and do justice to the poor, O you judges who judge the earth; remember that with that judgement with which you have judged, you too will be judged, by him who died on the Cross for you; and remember that after this life you will no longer judge, but be judged.' The holiness of his life added such force and weight to his words that he was readily listened to both by the magnates and by the *podestà* of the city; and when he was heard, he was often successful in getting cases settled according to his advice. Indeed, if any danger or difficulty occurred for the city, they consulted the blessed Raimondo as if he were a prophet; and often they followed his judgement in deciding what was to be done.

How he reconciled those in conflict and how he was imprisoned at Cremona

Because he knew that without peace nothing could be preserved, he held it in such high estimation that when he realised that there was conflict or hatred between people, he did not rest until he had restored them to concord. This was his usual speech: 'Do you not know, my sons, that the Son of God himself came down to earth, and laid down his life on the Cross, to reconcile man to God? Then why do you want to be enemies to one another? Those who know enmity know no rest; they are in continual danger, and, while they lay traps for one another, they are deprived of the Saviour's grace, for he has commanded them to love one another.' Not a few were moved by these pious warnings to remit the cause of their conflict to the good Raimondo for settlement; and because he was endowed with the gift of prudent counsel he soon restored them to a state of grace.

He could not by any means tolerate the factions and parties in which he saw his city on all sides distracted and divided. In order to remove them, he poured out constant prayers to God and spared no efforts with the most reverend bishop, to whom he made this suggestion: 'Do you not see, father, how your flock is scattered? Take action, show yourself to be a good shepherd; bring them back into oneness, so that there may

13 For the *pauperes* and the *potentes*, see above, Introduction, p. 27.

be just one flock, and truly one city.' The venerable bishop replied, 'My son, the wound is an old one; only God's omnipotence can restore that harmony.' When he saw these accursed factions rioting and fighting among themselves in public places, the good Raimondo, carrying his Cross, would shout out, weeping, 'Woe to thee, rebellious Piacenza! Already God has prepared the scourge with which he will strike you. You will be flayed and you will burn; you will lose life and fortune; because you are a dismembered body, and you do not fear God.' How true this prophecy was, the Piacentines learned by experience after his death.[14]

In the blessed Raimondo's time, Piacenza was not just torn apart by internal hatreds; the cities were in arms in external warfare, to their mutual destruction. First of all the Cremonese attacked the Piacentines.[15] When Raimondo first learned that armies had been assembled, he left Piacenza and sped to Cremona, armed with the most holy Cross, and coming up with both forces, he cried out in a voice of grief, 'Brothers, think of him who consented to die so that you should not die. Why are you rushing either to suffer death or to inflict it on your neighbours and all because of transient wealth or fleeting injuries? Alas, remember you are Christians, and imitate your Saviour. Think, think, and make peace. Put the whole thing in my hands; appoint a most just arbitrator.'

In this manner, rushing back and forth between the armies, he struggled to achieve agreement, which was not displeasing to the Piacentine leaders; but the Cremonese drove the servant of God away with threats and sometimes blows. He bore these patiently, but rebuked them mildly, saying, 'Because I seek peace, you repay me with abuse; but my Saviour will judge my case and yours.' The Cremonese were the more enraged by these words, and lest he should annoy them any further they took him to Cremona and imprisoned him. There Raimondo raised shouts to heaven which no one passing by could fail to hear, saying,

---

14 The *Annales placentini guelfi* (*MGH Scriptores*, 18, p. 422) record disturbances (*seditio*) between the commune and the bishop and clergy in 1203, which provoked papal intervention and threats of commercial embargo and loss of episcopal status: Webb, 'The pope and the cities', p. 137. In 1198, according to the *Annales* (p. 419), party conflict between nobles and non-nobles at Piacenza prevented a military expedition.

15 There was ongoing conflict, provoked by the contested possession of Borgo San Donnino, which ranged Piacenza and other cities against Parma, Cremona and their allies. Peace was made in 1202. According to the *Annales* (p. 416), a defeat was inflicted on Piacenza by Parma and Cremona in 1186, but Bosch (*AS*, July, 7, p. 653), thought that the attack by Cremona mentioned in the Life took place in 1190. See also W. F. Butler, *The Lombard communes* (London, 1906), pp. 202–3.

'O my Saviour, I commend my poor to you; I fear that they will die of hunger while I am kept here in bondage. As far as I am concerned, I am prepared not just to put up with the sufferings of prison, but to meet death, if only you will compose the hostile spirits of this people in peace. Consider the Cremonese, O Lord, who have thrown me into this place; they don't know what is good for them.' Scarcely had the citizens of Cremona heard this when they recognised the great sanctity of the blessed Raimondo and took steps to send him back free to his own people, begging pardon for the harm they had done, for they feared the imminent vengeance of God. This fear of divine judgement, because they had thrown him into prison was so enduring that when the blessed Raimondo died they came as suppliants to his tomb to beg for forgiveness. They feared him more dead than they had done alive, not unaware that God is marvellous and terrible in his saints.

How he tried to prevent dangerous games

Whenever it happened that the blessed Raimondo saw a crowd of horsemen gathered together or preparing to play the Trojan game,[16] or other gladiatorial sports of that kind, in which brawls and woundings and homicides are by no means rare, he was greatly moved in spirit, being totally averse to these futile sports, and he reproved them thus: 'Our Saviour does not want you to exert yourselves like wild beasts in games which arouse fury, but in ones which are honourable, peaceful, civilised and apt to restore weary spirits; nor does he want life to be endangered in the vain desire for some sort of glory, but only if it is for the sake of the welfare of the country or the upholding of the divine law. If the love of your Saviour means anything to you, if you have any care for preservation of body and soul, abandon these pernicious contests.'

This is what he said; but because these gatherings consisted almost entirely of young men, who are driven by hot blood and eagerness for glory, his warnings were in vain. He used to go to the venerable bishop and the urban magistrates, and would not give up until he had taken them with him to the place of the contest and by their intervention broken up the game and dispersed it; caring little that he offended the giddy and unthinking youth, if he had averted both sin against God and opportunities for sin.

---

16 The mention of *equites* ('horsemen') suggests that this 'game' was little less than a pitched battle.

How he visited the imprisoned and sought mercy for them

The blessed Raimondo was also assiduous in visiting prisoners, taking with him things which he had collected to give bodily comfort to them in their misery, so that he might thus prepare them to accept comfort for their souls. When he had given them refreshment, he used to add these words: 'My sons, the end of this life is not the same for everyone. One man dies in his bed, another in battle, another at sea, another in the wilderness; one person dies a natural death, another a violent one. Don't for this reason lose heart and hope, and don't be afraid of things which kill the body, which have no power to do anything more afterwards; but do fear the thing which, as my Saviour says who was sacrificed for you on that most cruel tree, has the power to send you to hell after it has killed. Make the decison, my sons, to change your life and your ways for the future, placing your sure hope in the Saviour's mercy; and I, as best I can, will not allow you to be abandoned.' The power of these words, coming from the most burning charity, was such that none of these criminals was so hardened spiritually in his crimes that he was not moved to piety and patience.

With God's inspiration Raimondo knew that the repentance of some of them was so sincere, and their good intentions so firmly grounded, that they would in future be useful to the people of God, both as shining examples and for their good works. For these he sought pardon from the judges and governors, saying, 'Lord Judge, I have borne a spiritual son, who will bring great profit to the Christian republic; I beg you by this most holy Cross, which the Son of the most pure Virgin adorned with his death so that he might give true life to us, that you will pardon him for me. Just leave it to me; I promise you will not regret it; rather it will be a consolation to this whole city.' The judges, moved both by the man's known holiness and by the voice of God speaking through him, acceded to his demands without difficulty. Several were pardoned in this way who, constant in virtue and carefully weighing up the dangers of the secular life, with the blessed Raimondo's encouragement embraced the religious life in the canonry of the Twelve Apostles and there faithfully served God.

How the Lord brought an end to his servant's labours and granted him a happy end

But if I wanted to follow one by one the virtues of the blessed Raimondo, all his labours, all his works of piety, the whole year would not suffice.

Wherefore I think it sufficient to have plucked out these things, by way of summary, to the glory of God and his saint and as an example both to those who are now living and to those who are to come. I could not say, for example, how many bastard children, secretly abandoned here and there, he found and, so that they should not perish miserably, brought them back to the hospital to be looked after by his efforts, often two at a time with one on each arm, weeping for pity. Or how many sick people, especially foreigners and pilgrims,[17] he found destitute in the public squares, and carried them himself on his shoulders; these, I say, I omit, and come to the description of his blessed and laudable death.

When the time approached for the divine goodness to put an end to his servant's troubles and strivings and to give him his ample reward, lo, a violent fever seized him, which day by day got worse, and the holy man realised that his end was near. He asked for the last sacraments to be given him, which he received from the hands of worthy priests. Thus fortified, he resigned the whole care and responsibility for the hospice to his associates, who for twenty-two years without interruption had faithfully assisted him in his pious work of nurturing the poor of Jesus Christ. Summoning them to his chamber he addressed them thus: 'Brothers and companions in my pious works, place my most holy Cross before my eyes and listen to me. First I thank you, my Saviour, and you, O holy Cross, that I see that my pilgrimage and the course of my weary life have at last reached their longed-for end. Next I thank you, my faithful companions, who have done and borne so much with me in feeding and preserving the poor to whom, in the spirit of charity, I have given birth. I beg you, by that most holy Cross in which I have always put all my hope, do not become lukewarm now and let youselves be worn down by the labours you have undertaken. I leave my place and position to you, and commend to you also my poor, and this most holy Cross; put your faith in that; and let no one flag in their holy efforts. The time is near when I shall return to my Saviour, from whom I hope for an eternal reward, not relying on my own merits but on his infinite goodness.'

At this sad news his faithful companions shed tears. 'Holy father,' they said, 'do not desert us wretches; without you we are nothing; however hard we try, we cannot long sustain so pious a duty. You are our leader,

17 There were probably numerous pilgrims in Piacenza. The city was at an important crossing of the Po; it was also the ancient terminus of the Roman consular road, the Via Emilia, which remained (and remains) the major road across the north Italian plain and formed part of the Via Francigena, the principal route from north-western Europe to Rome. See Webb, 'Raimondo and the Magdalen', p. 15.

our support, our counsel. Holy father, do not abandon your poor. You see how unrighteous men are, how hard, how stubborn; as soon as you have gone, we will be cast out and your poor dispersed.' These words moved the blessed Raimondo deeply, and he replied, 'I beg you, do not distress yourselves at my departure, which I have longed for. Have faith, because I overcame the world, although it was unmerciful; and have no doubt that I shall be of more value to you, and to my poor, after my death than if I went on living; so you may look after them not only more easily but even more generously.' His cherished companions accepted this reply as if it were a divine oracle, although they grieved bitterly that so great a father was torn from them.

Then the blessed Raimondo turned his thoughts to his son, who was present, and said, 'Come hither, my son; give your father your hand and the kiss which is his due; and promise to do what I shall tell you.' He did so and with his eyes full of tears kissed his father. Then the blessed Raimondo said: 'If you want me to die contented, renounce the world and embrace the religious life to which I once offered you in the church of St Brigid, before the image of the Saviour, when I took you from the cradle. I have often reminded you; but you have not yet fulfilled my desire. Don't put it off any longer, my son. Consider, the image of this world passes and death approaches at no tardy pace. Do not trust the blandishments and riches of the world; think rather about the riches in which they abound who follow voluntary poverty; here whoever is rich and avaricious is the real beggar. My son, may our Lord bless you; you close my eyes.' Having spoken, he turned to the most holy Cross with a peaceful countenance and said, ' In your arms, in your name and strength, I pass from this world to my Saviour and Creator.' And thus that most holy soul departed, escorted by holy angels.

When his son saw this he fell on his knees and with the utmost reverence closed his blessed father's eyes; the other companions who were present fell down and kissed that holy body, which emitted an odour not of this earth but of heaven. Then they began to lament, 'Alas that we poor wretches must now live without our father! Remember your faithful servants, O holy soul, remember what you have promised.' Such was the happy death of the blessed Raimondo Palmario of Piacenza, in the year 1200, on the twenty-seventh[18] day of July, in the sixtieth year of his age.

---

18 Raimondo is in fact traditionally celebrated on 28 July.

How the whole city flocked to see his holy body and his son embraced
the life of a canon of the Twelve Apostles

Scarcely had that most holy soul departed, when the news spread
that the blessed Raimondo had died. The leading men of the city, the
nobles, the worthy matrons rushed to his dwelling, not to mourn, but
to venerate the departed and to commend themselves to the servant of
God, who was already in their opinion blessed and possessed of great
merit with the Saviour. It was a spectacle beyond imagination to see
the leaders of that city, counts and nobles, humbling themselves before
the body of this poor man. Everyone competed, in a wonderful spirit
of devotion, one to touch and kiss his hand, another his feet, another
to obtain a piece from his clothing. This concourse lasted for all of
three days, when the rulers of the city at last decreed that he should be
placed in a precious sarcophagus and laid to rest in the canonry of the
Twelve Apostles, a honourable location where he could be venerated
and approached in supplication by the faithful; for they had no doubt
but that our Creator would reveal the merits of his servant in immense
wonders, as indeed was the case.

Before he was removed, however, the poor inmates and those of both
sexes who had been brought up in the household presented a spectacle which merited commiseration; they groaned miserably, weeping
and wringing their hands before the holy corpse and crying out, 'O
holy father! O our shepherd and governor! What is to become of us
wretches? Who will feed us, who will instruct us in virtue? Do not
forget us or cease to care for us, holy father, for we have no hope save in
you.' The women whom he had first converted to an honest life, some of
them married, some, as we said above, who had become nuns, came and
lay prostrate on the ground in such strength of feeling that they could
not express their praise of their father, but with unbearable sorrow that
they were not permitted to remain in the place where his holy corpse
was to be buried, not at least to guard and serve him.

When everything was ready for the exequies, the venerable bishop came
with all the clergy and, transferring the most holy body with great
solemnity to the canonry aforementioned, buried it there, so that all
might conveniently venerate on bended knee the tomb that was made
there. When the befitting funeral rites were completed, Raimondo's son
stood before the venerable bishop and the reverend prior of the *canonica*,
in the presence of the whole clergy and the leading men of the city.
Kneeling on the ground, he said, 'Most reverend father, at last it is time

that I kept my promise to my blessed father (although my vices prove me unworthy of his name); I am seeking the religious habit, and I pray that I may be admitted to this holy canonry and also be custodian of my father's tomb. It is my one desire that some day I may by his merits achieve eternal happiness.' Both requests were granted; for he was clad in the religious habit and designated guardian of the holy relics, and was given the name Brother Gerardo, as we said in the preface. It was he by whose counsel and pressing entreaties I undertook to compile and write down this rough legend, which is totally inadequate to the sanctity which radiates from the blessed Raimondo.

How pilgrims came to the tomb and miracles began

When the holy body had been placed in the canonry, as we have just related, a huge crowd of Christians, citizens and foreigners, lamenting diseases and other evils, flocked there, and there was no lack of the most evident miracles, by means of which the Lord demonstrated the sanctity of his servant. Such an amazing abundance of objects, coins, images, were offered every day that the rulers of the city appointed worthy and pious men, especially those who had been close companions of the blessed Raimondo, and charged them to expend these offerings on the support of the poor of the hospital; which was done. They were so numerous and so great that they were sufficient by themselves for the purpose. Then it was remembered that blessed Raimondo had lately said that he would be of more assistance to his poor when he was dead than when alive.

After some days, the urban magistrates took note that the devotion and the enormous flow of goods continued, and decreed that the hospital he had founded should henceforth be named the Hospital of San Raimondo (the name it still preserves). This was both to gratify the poor by assigning them a patron and guardian, and an eternal memorial of the servant of God. Many Cremonese flocked to the tomb. As was said before, they had punished the servant of God, when he urged them to make peace, with insults, blows and imprisonment; now, equipped with generous offerings and beating their breasts with their fists, they implored pardon, fearing that the saint might invoke the avenging hand of God upon them, saying, 'Avenge O Lord the injuries and oppressions of your servant.'

Some miracles which confirm blessed Raimondo's sanctity

The divine power performed so many signs and marvels through the merits of its servant Raimondo: healing the sick, liberating the possessed, rescuing those in peril at sea, in rivers, in war, in prison, on journeys, and in all the various calamities to which this life is exposed, that it would be impossible to relate them all, given anyone's utmost efforts, let alone mine. I think I will have done enough if I recall a few things, both to affirm the blessed Raimondo's sanctity and to foster and gratify the devotion of the faithful, so that they can publicise the sanctity of the servant of God to their successors. But I would like anyone who examines this legend in future to know that I have not described any miracle which has not been attested, on oath, by responsible and reliable men.

In the furthest parts of Italy, which they call Piedmont, there was a certain German called Ogier, who at Christmas was eating cabbage cooked with beef. Unfortunately it happened that he ingested a fragment of bone which was mixed in with the brassica, which he was devouring so greedily than he swallowed the bone together with the cabbage. It descended into his chest and stuck there, and for many days inflicted torments on him, the cause of which escaped the doctors. It happened while he was suffering this pain that a certain neighbour of his went to Piacenza and saw the tomb of the blessed Raimondo and his incredible marvels. When he returned to Piedmont, he told Ogier what he had heard and seen. Ogier immediately made a vow that, if only he was cured, he would go to Piacenza and visit the tomb, not without a devout offering. Scarcely had he made the promise when he vomited the bone into his hand, and brought it here with him; when he had paid the proper reverence to the sacred tomb, he ordered it to be hung up on high, as proof of such a noteworthy miracle.[19]

In the *contado* of Lavagna, in the diocese of Genoa, a woman whose mother was called Sophia and her father Hugo was plagued with a demon.[20] Her parents took her to the exorcists to get rid of it. They could get nothing out of her, except these words from her infernal guest: 'Raimondo will easily expel me.' When the demon was asked who and where this Raimondo was, it replied, 'A new saint at Piacenza.' Learning

19 Ogier swore to this miracle in the bishop's chamber on 29 April 1202: *AS*, July, 7, p. 659.

20 This miracle and the following one were attested before Otto, archbishop of Genoa (*ibid.*, p. 658).

this, her parents soon and with great difficulty brought their daughter to the glorious sepulchre. As soon as she touched it, the demon began to yell, 'Raimondo, Raimondo, may you be accursed for forcing me to come out.' And so, having so much troubled her, it left her free.

A certain noble in the same territory, Bernardo della Torre, and his wife Gelasia had a daughter called Mabilina. A contraction of all her nerves had for two years so completely deprived her of the use of her limbs that she could not raise her body up unaided or stand upright on her feet. It happened that it became known to her mother how the blessed Raimondo had restored the possessed girl whom we have just mentioned to herself. She therefore vowed on behalf of her daughter that she would send a wax image to his tomb if her vow was answered. On the fifth day following, her daughter felt active and well; she got up, she stood, she walked, as if she had never been crippled or handicapped. The mother fulfilled what she had promised with an offering appropriate to her status.

Berta, a woman of Pavia who was well known to the whole city, by divine judgement was subjected to the power of demons who invaded her body, often shouting out, one saying, 'I am Tralinus', another 'I am Capicius', and yet another 'And I'm Carincius'. The poor woman was so tormented by them that she was often thought to be dead, for there was no sense or movement or any sign of life in her, to the extent that some people inserted bits of twig between her fingers and her nails, and she felt nothing, or they poured burning liquid wax over her face and she didn't stir. Sometimes the demons so agitated her that only two strong youths could restrain her; sometimes they threw her as much as six cubits into the air; sometimes they flung her down headlong like a corpse; sometimes they inflated her so that she swelled into the shape of a jar. Certain learned men came to her to chant over her what they call the verses of St Maurice. (It was believed at that time that these verses had the power of expelling demons from afflicted bodies when they were chanted and that they had often done so.) She, being ignorant of letters, repeated these verses, but derived no benefit. She was taken by her sister and other neighbours to various churches and monasteries which were particularly celebrated for saintly relics, but did not obtain there what she hoped. Of course divine providence had reserved this marvel for the blessed Raimondo, so that his glory might shine forth over people both near and far. At last she was brought, not without immense force, to his tomb. She had scarcely knelt down when the demons began to howl like dogs, saying, 'Accursed Raimondo! We are coming to no good.' Thus, by the merits of our saint, the body of this woman was cleansed of all diabolical filth, and was henceforth the abode of honour.[21]

In the *contado* of Piacenza, and the place which is called Riva, a certain Geraldo Vitale was afflicted with what we commonly call a hernia, so that his intestines were swollen as if they had spilled out into a sack and did not permit the man to move or perform any task. His wife urged him to have recourse to the blessed Raimondo by making a vow, but he refused to do so, nor could he be convinced that Raimondo was a saint. Then his wife did it herself, with the most earnest faith, secretly and without betraying anything to her husband. She promised she would take a wax taper to Raimondo's tomb, with some money, and have the divine office solemnly performed. When she had made the vow, she asked her husband if he would at least accompany her to the saint's tomb. He consented, not expecting any benefit. His wife's devotion and trust were so great that, when they came to the church and her husband was able to kneel there as a suppliant, he at once felt better and his bowels were restored to their original place. After a few days he was sufficiently well that he could perform any labour. Then at last his wife revealed to him the vow she had made; when he heard this he endorsed it, and henceforth held the saint in particular devotion, every year sending two measures of wine to the poor of the hospital, choosing that time to send them when the overseers were accustomed to go around soliciting gifts of wine.[22]

A woman of Venice called Maria had for thirty years been so bent or, as is commonly said, gibbous, that she would not walk without sticks nor raise her head sufficiently to look at the sky; she carried it so low that you could have called her a quadruped. When she heard about the blessed Raimondo's miracles, she went to his tomb, not without considerable fatigue; there at last she prayed the blessed Raimondo with tears to free her from this misery; at last she was heard and, leaving her crutches as evidence of the miracle, returned home upright and without anyone's assistance. Seeing this, those who had known her praised the Lord in his saint.[23]

In the territory of Aqua a certain man called Lomello was suffering from such a troublesome hernia that his intestines were kept in by an

---

21 For certain difficulties raised by this miracle, see above, p. 63 and n. 7.

22 Reported in the bishop's palace at Piacenza, 26 September 1208 (*AS*, July, 7, p. 656).

23 Reported in the bishop's palace, 4 October 1208 (*ibid.*, pp. 656–7).

iron girdle. Learning of the famous miracles of blessed Raimondo, he vowed, if he was cured, to go on foot to the saint's tomb. As soon as he made the vow, the vow was answered; so that there should be no doubt of the miracle the iron girdle fell to the ground and broke into many pieces. His wife beheld this wondrous event; she had been confined to her bed for a whole year with contraction of the nerves and limbs. She at once promised to go with her husband to the holy tomb, and she was cured. They both came hither with gifts in proportion to their resources, to testify to their respective miracles.[24]

I select these few marvels to recount in confirmation of the powers and merits of the blessed Raimondo; the others, which are well known to all Lombardy, my eloquence cannot relate, nor my memory encompass, nor my hand and pen suffice to write down. I have decided therefore to leave them, because they exceed my powers, to other more accomplished authors, among whom I am the least.

The author's epilogue

I have composed this little work on your account, dear brothers. I beg you to receive what I have written in charity; and to pray our father, and God's servant, that he will intercede for us and the whole city with the blessed Jesus Christ, to whom is honour and glory with the Father and the Holy Spirit for ever and ever. Amen.

Here ends the tractate of the life and miracles of the blessed Raimondo Palmario of Piacenza, composed and summarised by Master Rufino, canon of the Twelve Apostles, in the Year of Grace 1212.

---

24 Reported before the bishop of Piacenza, 14 March 1207 (*ibid.*, p. 660).

III: UMILIANA DE' CERCHI OF FLORENCE (d. 1246)

The Life of Umiliana de' Cerchi was written by the Franciscan Vito of Cortona, ostensibly in 1246, the year of the saint's death.[1] However, it contains references to several later events, for example a vision of the saint which another member of the Florentine Franciscan community, Fra Buonamico, experienced in July 1247. This is recounted in full among the *apparitiones* (posthumous appearances) which Umiliana's devotees reported in the two or three years after her death.[2] Some of the earliest of these are related at the end of the Life, while others were collected as a kind of appendix to it, probably by the Fra Ippolito who states that he collected the miracles in 1249. If at the same time he edited the rest of the dossier this would account for the references in the Life to the expulsion of the Guelfs from Florence, which seems most likely to be the one which occurred in early 1248,[3] and also for a reference to Bishop Ardingo, who died in 1249, as 'of happy memory'.

The miracles and *apparitiones* were evidently recorded as the result of purposeful enquiry, for in several instances there is a considerable time-lag between the date of the supernatural event and the date on which it was formally sworn to before witnesses (usually including Fra Ippolito himself) at Santa Croce, the Florentine Franciscan church. It is not clear that the friars intended to seek Umiliana's formal canonisation and there is no evidence that they actually did so, but this may have been the intention at the moment when the dossier was compiled.[4] Their attention may have been more narrowly focused on one or both of two objectives. First, the commemoration of Umiliana may have been seen as a contribution to the formation of a Franciscan hagiography: Vauchez connects the production of the Life with a current trend among the Italian Franciscans 'to exalt the memory of all the members of the "triple militia" who had shown signs of sanctity during their lifetime'.[5] Secondly, Ippolito may have had his eye on the Florentine public. He introduced the miracles aggressively, attacking those who, like dogs, 'howled' their opposition to Umiliana's sanctity. It is not clear from whom this canine hostility was coming, but neither Umiliana's Franciscan and nor her family associations may have encouraged instant or universal popularity in Florence.

Both the friars and the styles of lay piety they were promoting were relatively novel. To many people, Umiliana would have looked first and foremost like

---

1 *AS*, May, 4, pp. 385–401.

2 *Ibid.*, p. 403.

3 Below, p. 111 n. 32.

4 A canonisation process took place in 1804: Vauchez, *Sainthood*, pp. 239–40.

5 *Ibid.*, p. 117.

one of the Cerchi, a family which later in the century stood at the head of one of the principal political factions in the city. She was, furthermore, a young woman who was known to have been married, had children and died young as so many others did. Over a century later, the pious Franco Sacchetti named Umiliana among the suspect 'saints' of local origin who, in his view, usurped popular favour at the expense of older and greater saints.[6] That the friars seemed disposed to encourage women such as Umiliana in behaviour which cut across family marriage strategies presumably did not increase their popularity in certain quarters.[7] To establish her sanctity beyond cavil was therefore not merely to do her memory a pious service but also to strengthen the claims of the Franciscans to public devotion during what was still a relatively early phase of their establishment at Florence.[8] It gave them a saint who rested bodily in their conventual church, while the visions and miracles constituted an impressive succession of marvellous events which were reported and attested at Santa Croce and some of which actually took place there.

Pressure of space has prevented the inclusion here of all the components of Umiliana's hagiographical dossier. Several of the miracle stories implicate individuals – especially women – who are mentioned among Umiliana's associates in the Life. They thus amplify the picture of the pious network of which the saint formed a part during her lifetime. The witness-list which prefaces the Life is headed by the names of three Franciscans: Fra Michele, Umiliana's confessor and confidant; Vigor, another friar of Cortona; and Buonamico of Florence. The rest consists of a large number of women, including relatives and servants of the saint who make their appearance from time to time in the body of the narrative. Fra Buonamico is among the witnesses to Umiliana's posthumous apparitions, and other friars figure as witnesses to the miracles recorded in the first three years after her death.

It has been asserted that 'in the contemporary accounts of her holy life and miracles all the witnesses were women; Umiliana's story was quintessentially a woman's'.[9] In fact there were ordinary Florentine laymen among the witnesses as well as among the beneficiaries of the miracles, which might be regarded as indispensable if the cult were actually to make headway in local society. Many of the miracles were performed for the benefit of children of both genders; such cures, important to fathers and mothers alike, were central to the posthumous activity of many saints. While it is true that women predominate among the dramatis personae, Umiliana's story is not simply that of a woman, or women, against the world; it is (implicitly) a story of women and Franciscans against the world, a document of the important relationships which mendicant friars

6 Franco Sacchetti, *Opere*, ed. A. Borlenghi, 1 (Milan, 1957), p. 115.

7 Carole Lansing, *The Florentine magnates: lineage and faction in a medieval commune* (Princeton, 1991), pp. 110–20; the chapter is significantly entitled 'Disaffection from the lineage'.

8 On the Florentine background to the Franciscan promotion of Umiliana's cult see A. Benvenuta Papi, 'Una santa vedova', in *'In castro poenitentiae'*, pp. 59–98.

9 D. Weinstein and R. Bell, *Saints and society: the two worlds of western Christendom, 1000–1700* (Chicago, 1982), p. 53.

formed with urban women and of their disposition to recognise and promote lay sanctity in a female form.[10]

Sometimes there is a glimpse of the friars at work as a social service agency. After Umiliana's death, Monna Fresca was left destitute with her children when the family was plunged into poverty and her husband left the city (perhaps to try to repair his fortunes). A rascal who, it seems, was linked to her by spiritual kinship tried to exploit her predicament by offering her material support in return for sexual favours. In a first encouraging vision Umiliana told her that help was coming from a woman who was already known to her. The rascal then threatened to take Fresca to court; Umiliana again appeared to tell her to ignore the summons and to go instead to Santa Croce, where Fra Ippolito and Monna Argenta (elsewhere described as a 'religious woman') would help her. Fresca swore to her visions of Umiliana there in January 1248, before Ippolito and Fra Daniele. Precisely how the situation was resolved is not explained; perhaps the friars interceded with the city officials on her behalf.[11]

Here the villain of the piece was a man who threatened to use the public authorities, a shadowy masculine collectivity, to achieve his dastardly ends. Ordinary men play only negative roles in the Life. Umiliana's husband is a usurer; her father cheats her out of her dowry. Her brothers, her father's allies in the effort to get her to remarry, are described as her 'fleshly brothers' (fratres carnales) in implicit contrast to her spiritual brothers in the Franciscan order. They are caricatures, who cannot tell the difference between ecstasy and death (or epilepsy); Umiliana herself laughs at them. She prays for her male kin, but rejects them. Her dying wish is that no member of her father's house shall be present at her death, and at the last, without comment or explanation, the friars come and take her body for burial to the Franciscan church.

Umiliana left the world under Franciscan escort, but precisely how the order entered her life is not explained. The one clue as to what precipitated her conversion is the importance given to Monna Ravenna (perhaps the wife of her husband's elder brother), who was almost certainly older than Umiliana and both encouraged her in her new cavalier attitude to dress and shared in her works of charity. It is hinted that, like Umiliana, she was punished for her absences from home on pious errands. Umiliana thought she was likely to grieve for the imminent death of her husband, but that may have been because of his likely damnation; it is implied that this was why Umiliana lamented her own husband. Umiliana and Ravenna, married women of some social standing, formed a network with their friends among religious women and the friars which had a certain impregnability. Not only Umiliana's own sisters and other kinswomen, but her stepmother – her father's wife – were prepared to speak as witnesses to her holiness.

The Life is a manifesto for a particular way of life which was to the friars' liking. Umiliana had wished, in her widowhood, to become a nun, but this

---

10 Papi, 'I frati e le donne', in 'In castro poenitentiae', pp. 119–40; J. Coakley, 'Friars, sanctity and gender: mendicant encounters with saints, 1250–1325', in C. Lees (ed.), Medieval masculinities: regarding men in the middle ages (Minneapolis, 1994), pp. 91–110.

11 AS, May, 4, p. 402.

was not God's will, although it might have been more instantly intelligible to some of her contemporaries, including her father. Umiliana lived the feminine version of the Franciscan life to perfection, but the important thing was precisely that she did so, not enclosed in a convent, but living in a room in her father's tower. In fact, as the narrative makes plain, she remained to some degree open to the world. For all the insistence on her ceaseless application to prayer and contemplation, she did not altogether cease from pious and charitable visits, although they became less frequent. Thus her life demonstrated the ancient and indissoluble association between the perfection of the knowledge of God and the love of one's neighbour, dear to the mendicants although hardly their discovery. A charitable visit to a sick boy, which ends in her taking his sufferings upon herself, leads to the vision of the infant Christ for which she has so much longed. Umiliana loved to meditate on the childhood of Christ; we can imagine her much enjoying the elaborations on this theme in the *Meditations on the life of Christ* which a Tuscan Franciscan later in the century wrote for a nun of his order and which, misattributed to St Bonaventure, became a widely popular manual of devotion.[12]

There are other sources of ambivalence or tension between ideals. Umiliana exemplifies not just feminine, but Franciscan, values, especially the love of 'poverty', just as Pier Pettinaio did later in the century. Yet while she was able to do so, she made use of her property in order to perform works of charity. After her husband's death and her return to her parental home, she let her father do what he would in the matter of reclaiming her dowry, out of a principled indifference to worldly and legal business. It seems clear, however, that she was not expecting him actually to defraud her and that this came as an unpleasant surprise. Had she retained control of her property she might well have given it all away and embraced voluntary poverty, as Pier Pettinaio did later in his life, but in fact her hand was forced, and at least initially she felt her loss of means as a severe deprivation because it restricted her charitable activities. She was, so to speak, driven back upon herself, and it was in these circumstances that she began to explore the possibilities of ascetic self-mortification. Umiliana is in effect shown as seizing, or even creating, one initiative as another is taken from her. The friars are there in the shadows of the narrative, guiding her course.

The translation offered here is a hybrid inasmuch as the chapter divisions have been imported into the Latin text from a fourteenth-century Italian version of the Life, which may well have followed the layout of the original; at all events, it gives an idea of how the Life might have been divided for reading or reference. The fourteenth-century translator slightly abbreviated his version by omitting the whole of Brother Vito's prologue and certain other references to people who were important contemporary witnesses to Umiliana's sanctity, but whose names would have meant nothing to an audience a hundred years later.[13]

12 Translated by U. Ragusa and R. B. Green as *Meditations on the life of Christ: an illustrated manuscript of the fourteenth century* (Princeton, 1961).
13 'Leggenda della Beata Umiliana de' Cerchi', in Giuseppe de Luca (ed.), *Prosatori minori del Trecento, 1: Scrittori di religione* (Milan, 1954), pp. 724–68.

The Life of Umiliana de' Cerchi by Vito of Cortona

Prologue

These are the witnesses to the life of the blessed Umiliana: brother Michele, a Florentine by birth, and Brother Vito, a native of Cortona, both Friars Minor; Brother Buonamico of the same order, a native of Florence; Monna[14] Ravenna, a kinswoman of the blessed Umiliana, a woman thoroughly religious and honourable, and very well known in the aforesaid city; Monna Gisla, who watched over the blessed Umiliana in her illness, a woman of holy life and conduct; Sister Gisla of Mugello, a thoroughly religious and honourable woman and of holy conversation; Sister Benvenuta, the companion of the aforesaid, of holy life and conversation; Monna Luciana, wife of Raniero of the parish[15] of San Procolo in the city of Florence; Diana, of the parish of Santa Margarita in the same city, a woman of holy life and coversation; Monna Sobilia, a recluse in Sasso above the monastery of Camaldoli, of the aforesaid city, a woman of holy conversation and honourable life; Monna Dialta, of the parish of San Lorenzo of the aforesaid city, wife of Ugalotto, a woman of good life and conduct; Monna Altabene, wife of Bonaiunta, of the parish of Santa Cecilia of the aforesaid city, of honourable life and conversation; Monna Jacoba, wife of Bene of the parish of San Martino aforesaid; Monna Bonitia, wife of Buonaccorso, of the aforesaid parish of San Martino; Monna Diana, wife of Mainetto Giudice, of the parish of San Pietro di Buonconsglio in the aforesaid city; Monna Scotta, wife of Bernardino the dyer, of the parish of San Pancrazio in the said city; Monna Compiuta, wife of Tedaldo, of the parish of San Pietro Maggore in the aforesaid city; Monna Tabbaria, wife of Torsello, of the aforesaid parish of San Martino, and her daughter, named Geminiana, the wife of Consio, of the same parish; the two sisters of the blessed Umiliana, that is to say Monna Cecilia, and Monna Guittonbella; three of her kinswomen, that is Monna Cecilia, Monna Guittonesca and Monna Gasdia; Monna Ermellina, the stepmother of the blessed Umiliana; three maidservants of the aforesaid saint, that is Piecilia, Mellior and Gisla; Monna Ricevuta, of the parish of San Martino in the above-mentioned city; and Monna Scotta, her kinswoman, wife of Racio, of the same parish.

---

14 In the Latin, *domina.*

15 The word translated here as 'parish' is *populus,* a literal equivalent of *plebs,* from which the Italian *pieve* is derived.

A certain lady, Umiliana by name, the daughter of Oliviero Cerchi, citizen of Florence, was given in marriage by her parents when she was sixteen years old; and as if inspired by God, a month after she went to her husband she began to reject the pomps and adornments of the world. So she did not make up her face, and the fine clothes which she wore out of respect for her husband were a source not of joy but of torment to her. A certain lady, her kinswoman, who herself feared God and was daily practised in his ways, urged her to do this.[16] It would take a long time to recount everything about her life and actions and therefore, like one who gathers flowers in a field, let us bring together a few things out of many, for the honour of God and for our own profit and the edification of our hearers.[17]

Of her works of piety

In the first year of her conversion she had masses celebrated every day for sin, and we could not possibly say what a quantity of alms she distributed during that year in clothing the naked, strengthening the weak, visiting the sick, comforting the afflicted and [other] works of piety. Who can tell how often that blessed soul covertly took scraps of bread from her husband's table and hid them, before giving them to the poor! She would collect a large number of these scraps, and filling her bosom (which was wounded by pious compassion) she bore them to the poor and needy, together with the kinswoman who has been mentioned. And who could reckon up the works of piety, in which she was ceaselessly engaged, which she performed in the five years which she spent with her husband? how she laboured with her own hands to fulfil the vow which she had made, that is to assist the poor as best she could?

The abundant resources of her husband's household did not satisfy her passion for almsgiving. Let us not relate (because it would take too long) how many naked persons she clothed and how much cloth she gave to the poor, including bed-linen. This she often cut up, keeping part for herself and giving part to the poor. When cloth was given to her for them she took out a small amount and sewed shorter sheets; a silken mantle which she possessed she sold, and she gave [the proceeds] to the poor. While she was under her husband's authority, she gave away

---

16 It seems that Monna Ravenna is meant here, as probably in later references to a 'kinswoman'.

17 This paragraph constitutes the prologue of the vernacular version (*Prosatori*, p. 723).

all her headbands, only keeping one of linen and part of another, made of silk, which was cut down; this, like St Martin, she divided, giving the larger part to a certain poor lady, and keeping a small part for herself with which to cover the linen one. A new tunic of scarlet which her husband bought for her she took in at the sides and cut a considerable part off the hem; she made sleeves from this and sold them and spent the money on food for the wretched poor.

She took her husband's old woollen clothes and her own and sold them, giving the money to the poor. She secretly collected what other linen cloth she could, new and old, and sent it to a certain confidante of hers to give to the poor and needy in accordance with her vow. One day she cut up the headband she was wearing and, keeping part herself, gave the other part to a leper whom she found in the street suffering acute head pains. All the linen which she found in her husband's chamber, and her own when she had any, she gave to the poor; and whatever else she could acquire, she gave in large measure to the poor. When the resources of her husband's chamber and her own were exhausted she had linen cloth made, by her own hands and others', and sold it, and she also bought woollen cloth, which she cut up and distributed as clothes to the poor, according to her assessment of their individual needs. On one occasion, together with her kinswoman, she made up a couch from the furnishings of her own bed and gave it to the sick at the house of the Poor Nuns of Ripoli.

Of her reverence for the divine cult

From the work of her own hands she provided altar hangings and adorned the altars themselves with clean cloths. If she knew that there was a new chalice to be made, or an ecclesiastical book, or any furnishing for the altar or other holy purpose, she never failed to put her pious hand to the task. How great was her reverence for divine things and the alms which supplied them! One day she was asked for flour to make hosts; out of reverence for the Body of Christ, she gave a measure of one bushel of flour, taken from a supply of eight.[18]

18 An approximate translation of the Italianate Latin *staio*, from the classical *sextarium*.

Of her piety towards holy men and sisters

With her own hands she made dainty foodstuffs for holy men and sisters, the daintiest for the more frail and the more robust for the stronger, in kindly fashion. In addition, she collected together the leftover food from the household, which was often a considerable quantity, and made it up to be more palatable and tempting and set it aside to give to the healthier poor. She withdrew a lot of good food secretly from her own mouth and reseasoned it to give to the poor. For herself she was contented with coarse food and, receiving it, she gave thanks to the Almighty for his benefits. Thanks to the various affairs of the household, and the number of servants and people rushing around, she was not able to prepare the food during the day, but did it in the stillness of the night. Alas! What are the pleasure-seekers in the streets to say, when this tender creature, concerned for her salvation, often passed the great part of the night without sleep in such labour? At dawn, she took with her the kinswoman who was her partner and confidante in all this, and they went about the town to distribute the food to the poor, both sick and healthy; not conceitedly seeking worldly honour and pride, but, like handmaids of God, not afraid to put up with taunts for the sake of Jesus Christ. The more liquid cooked foods were carried by their maidservants to feed the indigent in their absence.

They also visited holy places according to the Florentine custom, that is the nuns of Monticello and the poor [hospital] of San Gallo, and other places where there were indulgences for the remission of sin, so that they might become sharers in all good things; disregarding the threats of their husbands and the ill-treatment they received from them because of the time they spent in their lengthy visits. How great was her fervour, and the compassion for the wretched which had taken possession of her heart! A holy fervour overcame all ill-treatment, all lethargy, all fear or enticements of the flesh. With what injuries she was afflicted, and with what insults belaboured, by high and low in the household! She was sometimes beaten because of the works of piety with which she humbly served the needy, but continued unheeding, affable and docile, towards them.

Of her compassion for the sick

She ministered to the sick with pious compassion like a pious mother, busy about their necessities, prepared in all things to help as best she could. She was moved by a special compassion towards the sick, knowing how great were their needs, because she herself was often very ill; and she understood, in the words of the gospel, 'What you have done for one of the least of these, you have done for me', that what you give to the creature, you do for the Creator. She went often to confession and did not receive the sacrament of the Body of Christ unless she had made a good confession; she frequented the church of Christ and gladly heard the divine office. She was of such great humility and patience that she bore all inconveniences without complaint and with patience, because she carried the fear of God in her breast. Never, like other under-age girls, was she frivolous; but both under age and of age she was the model of honour, a lover of peace, loving all; never childish, but old, not in years but in behaviour and honour.

In the illnesses which she suffered, she displayed such patience that no sound of complaint was ever heard from her lips. Often, in her husband's house, she suffered severe pains in her stomach and womb, to the extent that she seemed not merely to be in agony but to be experiencing child-birth. Always she burst forth in the praise of God, not in complaint, blessing and praising God. If any of her little children were ill, she was not greatly concerned, nor did she fear their dying, but said, 'How blessed they would be if they were to depart thus without spot, taking their virginity with them! I would rather that they should die, if it is the will of God, and enter into glory, than they should live, lest it should happen that at some time they offend God and lose a part of his supreme love and eternal inheritance.'

It is said that when her husband was close to death, she was willing to give up her dowry for the love of God if he would truly repent and according to the instructions of God's priest restore the usury which he possessed. After her husband's death, to the extent that she was freer than before, she displayed her generosity more liberally in his house; she often had poor people at her table and devoted herself more to prayer. In her husband's house God consoled her with many visions and revelations, showing her the glory which she would obtain in future. She saw herself gloriously clad in white garments amid ranks of children who were clothed in white, which signified purity of life in the present, and in the future that she would be surrounded by ranks of angels.

Of her return to her father's house after her husband's death and how
she was urged to remarry, and of her immense constancy

After spending some time in the house of her dead husband, she returned
to her father's house and came under his authority. Her father, brothers
and kinsfolk wearied her over a lengthy period with threats and persecutions to contract a second marriage, and she was so buffeted by their
importunities that she would have succumbed, had she not founded her
house on the firm rock of Christ. When they threatened her because she
would not accept a husband, she was moved to laughter and showed her
contempt of her persecutors.

One day her maternal aunt,[19] on behalf of her kin, took her on one
side and gently tried to persuade her to take a husband. When she
mentioned her youth (for she was then only twenty-two years old) and
the fragility of womankind, this is what she heard: 'My dear aunt, you
may know for certain that I possess the worthiest of husbands, whom
I shall never have to mourn, nor shall I be perpetually widowed by his
damnation. But enough of this; if you please, like a good Christian, give
something for the love of God to the enclosed sisters, because today I
have been around the town to gather alms for them.' And although she
was firmly resolved to continue in chastity, she did not place reliance on
herself, but had recourse to Our Lady in frequent prayer.

One day, wanting to know God's will in this matter, she sped to the
tower where God enlightened her, and there she prayed before an image
of Our Lady which she had then, painted on a sheet of parchment, asking
God fully to reveal to her his will.[20] In the course of this prayer she was
so infused with grace that she seemed as if drunk, and she received such
an inner determination not to marry, and was so fully assured of the
will of her true Spouse, that she was prepared to give her body to the
flames rather than to a husband. The next time she heard a word about
accepting a husband she firmly replied: 'Why do you torment me every
day about a husband? Bring me him to whom you want to give me, and

19 *Matertera*. This was probably the Monna Luciana, also called *matertera*, who received
   some angelic bread from Umiliana; see below, p. 118.

20 The image was painted on *carta*, either parchment or paper: see H. B. J. Maginnis,
   'Images, devotion and the Beata Umiliana de' Cerchi', in A. Ladis and S. Zuraw (eds),
   Visions of holiness: art and devotion in renaissance Italy (Athens, GA, 2001), pp. 13–20.
   I am most grateful to Dr Joanna Cannon for drawing my attention to this essay.
   Maginnis takes it from later references to a *tabula* that Umiliana possessed both this
   image on *carta* and a panel painting of the Virgin and Child; in another essay in the
   same collection, Victor Schmidt suggests that the former was later *replaced* by a panel
   painting (*ibid.*, p. 32).

light a furnace for me on the other side, so that, standing between them, I can choose which I prefer.' At these words her kinsfolk were much disturbed and did not dare to bother her further on the subject. From that day forth they allocated to her and her maidservant four bushels of grain for her table, and other things in moderation.[21]

How her dowry was taken by her father and how she bore this patiently

Because she remained immovable in her determination on continence, her father waited and one day assembled a number of unknown foreigners,[22] that is, the judge of the commune and certain other people, for the purpose, and summoned Umiliana to him. When she came, he said, 'My daughter Umiliana, I am negotiating with your dead husband's family, so that you can have the dowry back which I gave for you. Because of this it is necessary that you make your rights over to me in a public deed.' The humble Umiliana, not paying any attention to this, said, 'Father, it is not necessary to do this; let your will be done, so long as I do not have to take an oath.' She did not say this because she believed oaths were illicit, but she did not want to swear on a temporal matter.[23]

Then, by deed, her dowry was extorted from her by her father. When, afterwards, she realised this, she said, 'I did not perceive that my father was acting fraudulently against me. So he has deprived me of the dowry which he had given me, blessed be God.' Not complaining, but bearing it patiently, the lover of poverty said: 'As I see, there is no faith on earth: the father deprives his daughter and denies the truth, and the daughter her father. Henceforth my father will have me in his house not as a daughter but as a servant and handmaid.'

Loving the divine law, she desired in all things to follow Christ and to possess nothing of her own in this world. She bore the word of Christ in her breast, where it is said, 'Unless someone gives up everything which he possesses, he cannot be my disciple'; and 'If someone seeks your tunic from you, give him also your cloak.' Of the wrong which had been done

21 It is not made clear whether this was an annual allocation.

22 The *podestà* and other temporary officers of the commune were non-Florentine.

23 On the refusal of oath-taking by professed lay penitents, see Thompson, *Cities of God*, p. 85; on Umiliana in particular, p. 144. Brother Vito seems to portray Umiliana's reluctance as personal and wants to make it clear that it had nothing to do with objections to oath-taking as such, which might be deemed heretical.

to her in the matter of her dowry for the sake of Christ she cared little
or nothing; she wanted to achieve the heights of perfection and, as far
as it is possible for human weakness, to be raised on high in the love of
God; therefore she walked fearlessly in the way of counsel, and did not
deviate at all to the left or the right.

Henceforth she did not possess the means to extend her hands in
generosity to the poor as she had done before; wherefore she abated her
almsgiving to no small degree. She did not however totally abandon
her previous ways but to the best of her ability was conscientious and
concerned in visiting the poor. Often, as the companions of her journeys
declare, she carried six loaves at one and the same time in her bosom for
the needy, and she visited holy places as before, not fearing the threats,
and certainly the bodily sufferings, this brought upon her.

With what solicitude she sought alms to assist the poor and needy

She did not fear foul weather, not heat, not rain, but conscientiously and
with eagerness of spirit assiduously visited holy places. Her companion
often complained of the heat, but she said, 'Our gracious God will send
us a friendly wind which will mercifully temper the heat.' Wonderful
to relate, the pleasant breeze which she had foretold immediately
sprang up which, as she wished, mitigated the heat for herself and her
companion.

O God! With what zeal she sought you in your poor members,[24] going
so swiftly along the road with her companion in search of you, that a
multitude of other strong women could not keep up with her rapid steps;
nor did this seem to tire her, for often, because of the distances involved,
she continued fasting until nones,[25] because she did not want to return
home until she had completed her visits. And since the almsgiving
of her own hands could not satisfy her fervour, she visited noble and
discreet and God-fearing ladies of the city of Florence, humbly seeking
alms from them for the love of Jesus Christ for poor enclosed nuns;
what she received she put with much devotion in a little bag specially
made for the purpose and carefully took to the poor sisters. She was
afflicted by a special compassion for the decent poor, and showed great

---

24 That is, the needy both lay and clerical.

25 The 'ninth hour' of the day, one of the liturgical 'hours' for prayer, originally fell in
   mid-afternoon but later moved towards midday (hence 'noon'); this shift had taken
   place in thirteenth-century Florence.

concern for their support, giving them such necessaries as she could. A certain lady who was in great poverty (and who without assistance would perhaps have resorted to prostitution to support herself) she personally supported for as long as she lived, and while she lived she helped not just her but many others as much as she could.

Every day, for the whole of the first year after she returned to her father's house, she heard the divine office without fail and devoted herself to works of piety. In the morning, when she had heard the office, she returned to her cell, and on a day when she was not fasting was continuously engaged in prayer. When however she was fasting, she persisted in prayer until nones and, having eaten, engaged for a while on works of charity for the poor and at once returned to prayer so that no hour should be wasted in idleness. When evening came, she spent the greater part of the night in prayer, slept a little, and then rose, spurning somnolence, and spent the rest of the night in her devotions. This manner of keeping vigil she maintained until God increased his grace in her; then she adopted another path, so that when evening came she rested for a little, and spent the whole of the night, after her rest, in prayer.

How she led an ordered life and spent her time in prayer, work and fasting

In the second year she gave up long visits and reached unbelievable heights. Because she did not have the means to look after the poor, she made this vow, saying, 'Lord, you know that while I could I served you generously; now I have been deprived of my income, and I give my soul and body totally to you.' From that moment, inflamed by the divine love, she burned to achieve the solitary life, desiring to fulfil her intention and lovingly to give herself to God as she had promised, so that, having long thirsted, she might taste the fountain of life as she wished.

She wanted to enter the house of the enclosed poor ladies of Santa Maria of Monticello,[26] but God, who had other plans for her, did not permit it. God did not want her light any longer to be hid under a bushel, and therefore placed her high up on a candelabrum of life and example, so that she might give light to those in the house, that is in the Church Militant; for she was the chosen vessel of the Lord, on

26 A house of Poor Clares, founded in the Arno valley near Florence in 1221 and placed by St Francis under the direction of Agnes, St Clare's sister.

whom the edifice of the heavenly Jerusalem, the holy city of celestial citizens, was to be raised. While the divine wisdom, building himself a house in which he hewed out seven columns, sent its handmaidens, that is the various founders of orders, to issue summons to the citadel (that is the height of life in the way of grace) and to the walls of the city (that is to the glory of the eternal rewards), he also sent this wondrous foundress of a new way of holy life. The others, under the guidance of the Holy Spirit, hastening in new forms of life to the single kingdom of life, distinguished their own orders each by different customs and honourable habit; she, retaining the honourable habit of the Third Order, soared to that same kingdom, and holding to the form of other religions,[27] laboured mightily at those things by which God is most nearly approached, that is the love of God.

What did she lack of the monastic life, who lived in such continuous silence and observance? What less did she possess than the holy hermits, who found for herself a solitude in the midst of the city and converted her bedchamber into a prison-cell? What austerities did she sustain less than the holy sisters of San Damiano,[28] exercising such sobriety in food and drink? Refreshed by a little sleep, she spent the whole night in prayer; and what grace was poured out upon her, they can say who saw it, insofar as they were able to perceive it. With what tears she flooded her cheeks and breast, which seemed not tears but streams flowing from her eyes! Who could have more completely fulfilled the life of the Friars Minor than she who so perfectly observed Christ's gospel? For when everything which she could have possessed was taken away, she gave all of herself to the poor and bestowed her body and soul faithfully on God. Some leave the world and their paternal home and fleeing into the desert fight for the Lord; she brought the desert into her father's house, and fighting nobly defeated the world and vice in the midst of worldly things.

Of her ecstasies and tears

How often did she soar higher than others in her mind? Rising above herself and miraculously united with God in contemplation, she was so often ravished in her senses in the sweetness of God that sweetly savouring God she slept, not a sleep of the body, but one of ecstasy, of

---

27 That is, other religious orders: Vito emphasises the equivalent validity of the Franciscan tertiary's way of life.

28 St Clare's own house, on the side of Mount Subasio near Assisi.

which Christ speaks in the Canticle of his Bride: 'I adjure you, daughters of Sion, by the goats and stags of the fields, do not disturb or awake my beloved until she wishes.'[29] On this level of ecstasy Umiliana tasted that secret manna of which it is said in the Apocalypse that no one knows it who does not receive it; and therefore no one can adequately treat of the grace she received unless he or she has tasted what she was privileged to taste.

What about her preaching, in which she preached more by deeds than by words and does not cease to preach, now the body is dead, and will preach in perpetuity? If she did not abandon her father's home and her widow's weeds, it was not her own doing, since all that is under heaven she freely abandoned in her mind, but God did not permit it. He wanted to attract the sluggish of this world by her example, those who, held back by idle curiosity or timidity or being unable to find a religion after their own hearts in which they might be received, wallow in the depths of vice; so that no one from the lowest to the highest might have the excuse that they could not serve God to the best of their ability in their own home and in the secular habit, no one hide themselves from the warmth of her charity. What then? Having established her little cell, her prison rather, in her father's tower, she transformed that prison into an oratory, as far as she could, and was content there to exert herself to do the best she could. Instructed in the commands of salvation by God and the Friars Minor, especially by Brother Michele, who was her teacher in the way of devotion, she abandoned all cares and almost putting an end to the cares of Martha, she aspired with Rachel to run to the closer embraces of the Creator.

But God wanted to reveal her fervour and did not give himself, whom she awaited with such longing, to her so quickly; rather he showed her a certain hardness, for she was unable to weep at her devotions. She couldn't bear this and applied lime to her own eyes, so that she thought she had blinded herself. She did this so that God, moved by pity, would grant her pious tears, and, well knowing herself, feared that this had happened because of the vice of her eyes.[30] And because she sometimes lamented the death of her kin, she vowed to God that she would never weep in future unless because of the memory of her own sins, or because of the grace of God or the Passion of the Lord. After a few days, God

29 Song of Solomon (in the Vulgate, *Canticum canticorum*) 3:5. Brother Vito inserts a lengthy quotation, omitted here, from St Gregory's exposition of this text.

30 The phrase *vitium oculi* presumably refers to Umiliana's obsessive fear of seeing things she deemed improper.

poured out on her such a great grace of tears that they seemed not tears but rivers.

How a dove appeared miraculously to her

Once, in the silence of the night, while she was silently saying the Lord's Prayer as devoutly as she could, and was meditating carefully and subtly on the words of the prayer, the light of the lamp in her cell, which she kept alight all night by the image of the mighty Mother of God, suddenly went out. This annoyed her, but out of humility she did not want to wake the servant for this reason. She wanted to have light, but couldn't see how she was to have it, unless God provided. Suddenly, while she was thinking about this, a dove of pure whiteness, carrying in its beak a new red rose of marvellous beauty and brilliance, flew through the cell and rested on the ceiling; by its radiance the cell was illuminated as if it were day. Seeing the dove, she wanted to catch it as if it were an external reality, not realising what it was (she had decided, so she said, to send it to a little nephew of hers). As she put her hand near it, the dove hopped a little further up the beam, seemingly to avoid her pursuit. As she pursued it with more determination, she drove it from the beam, and it began to fly around the cell near the panel of the Blessed Virgin. The devout Umiliana approached the panel in pursuit of the dove, which turned into a sort of brilliant sun in front of the painting and merging into the image disappeared, together with the light. Praising God who had deigned to do this for her, she returned to her original meditation on the Lord's Prayer and meditated on it all night; so in that whole night she said just one Paternoster, and savoured much of the sweetness of God.

How the lamp in her cell was lit miraculously by the hand of an angel

Another night, when the lamp in her cell went out and she had no other light and didn't want to rouse the maidservant for the same reason, she humbly asked the Lord to provide her with some light. Hearkening to her prayer the most gracious God miraculously gave her light by the hand of an angel. For a youthful hand appeared near the lamp, carrying a brilliant light with which it ignited the dead lamp. On yet another night, when there was no oil in the lamp or in the cell, she took a lamp and filled it with water, putting a wick into it in the usual way. When

she had done this, she said, 'Most holy and almighty Love, it is as easy
for you to change water into oil as it is for you to produce oil from hard
wood.' And thereupon she lit it; and wondrously the water nourished
the flame like oil, gently and without hissing, and gave light until it was
consumed.

How the devil wearied her with many temptations and tribulations

Observing her abundant grace, the enemy of the human race, who
envies our salvation, the malignant besieger of all good, was violently
enraged, and after a short while began to weary her with temptations
and tribulations so that she would cease from her devotions out of fear.
Who could enumerate how often he appeared visibly to her and struck
her, as the divine power permitted him to do? We will speak of all these
things in a moment.

How the devil appeared to her in the semblance of Our Lady with her child Jesus and how he struck her

In the second year of her incarceration, during Lent, which she spent
in continuous silence and prayer, a demon appeared to her, carrying
dead bodies, and said, 'Speak to your kinsfolk, whom you see placed
before you.' She remained silent, thinking nothing of the illusions of the
devil. The devil however removed these images and after a little while
made ready something else: he produced certain shapes in the likeness
of two of her daughters, who were living in her husband's home, and
showing them to her, as if just dead and in the grave, he said, 'Do you
say nothing to your daughters whom you see newly dead before you?'
She ignored this in silence. But the crafty devil, understanding her
desires, showed her the figure of Our Lady and the child Jesus, radiant
of face and raiment, saying, 'Why don't you speak to your Lady and
her Son who are standing near you, who have come to you, who are
thus visibly and miraculously visiting you?' After a little while, since
she spurned this illusion, he produced the image of Monna Ravenna,
saying, 'Speak to your dear kinswoman, who has so faithfully visited
you.' All of this she ignored because under the guidance of the Holy
Spirit she knew them to be demonic illusions, and the devil disappeared
with his figments, striking her such a heavy blow in the kidneys that her
teeth were violently clashed together. For about fifteen days she could

not chew her food properly for the pain in her teeth.

On another day the deceiver appeared to her visibly, bearing with him the bodies of dead people, men and women as if recently killed, their limbs torn and cruelly lacerated, caked with blood, saying, 'Bah! You want to converse with the sisters of the monasteries of Monticello and Ripoli – and because of them and their disputes about their lovers, all these horrors that you see here are laid before you, when you could be well and honourably married to a noble and prudent man.' She ignored him in silence, attributing no importance to what she was seeing, but the devil, vexed that he was ignored, struck her hard on the shoulder-blades and vanished noisily, saying, 'I commend you to all the devils of hell.'

One day a certain Friar Minor visited her with his companion, a priest. Lent was over, which she had spent in silent prayer and devotion; and he asked her in friendly fashion, because he was a close friend of hers, what she had been doing and how she had been in respect of God during Lent and if she had prayed for him (this brother had frequently commended himself to her prayers). Because of his insistence on an answer she replied reluctantly, 'I have been well, blessed be God. And I have often prayed for you, but the devil has often besieged me with much suffering and tribulation.' She told one story out of many.

How the devil appeared to her in the form of a certain abbot

'Yesterday, at the time of prayer and silence, the enemy of the human race stood in front of me and suddenly burst out in these words: "I am an exiled abbot, expelled from a certain monastery, and I have come to you to obtain some comfort." When I didn't answer him, the demon paused for a little while and said, "Rise and go to meet Brother Michele, open the door to him, he is coming; he has arrived, he's here." I spurned his illusions and closed my eyes; I didn't interrupt my silence and concentrated on my own concerns. He couldn't bear this and impatiently added, "Open your eyes and see your Lady coming to you and carrying her own Son in her hands, whom you so much long for." When I said to him, "Whoever has sinned mortally, and does not do penance for that sin, is condemned and eternally punished", he vanished at high speed.'

When the friar said, 'Have you asked anything for me?' she replied, 'Brother, I have asked, and I will ask, that you should be concerned for your own salvation as you are bound to be, because God loves you; God has shown you to me, while I prayed for you, adorned in a white vestment, wherefore it seems to me that God loves you and that you persevere in bodily purity.'

One night when she was praying with her eyes closed a demon approached her, showing her images of dead people, of priests and of the Cross of Christ, saying, 'You know how acceptable to God it is to attend the funerals of the dead; so open your eyes and just see the dead bodies placed before you.' When she refused to do so, the devil, rejected, disappeared. On the night after the prior of Santi Apostoli in Florence was killed,[31] the devil appeared in her cell, presenting her the likeness of the prior's dead body, all caked with blood, and said, 'Look at this pitiful sight, this awful cruelty, so great a man, the prior of Santi Apostoli, so atrociously murdered and lying dead before you; you must mourn for him.' She heard but took no notice, and was not at all distracted from her prayer. Seeing her patience and resolution, the diabolical deceiver fled confounded with his phantasms.

On another occasion, before the Guelfs withdrew from Florence,[32] there was a battle in several places because of some clash of factions, and there were fires in some parts of the city, and machines were set up to propel stones at towers. The devil came to her saying, 'Get up, Umiliana, and see what's going on; look, the whole city is destroyed and consumed by fire, and the fire is getting close to your house.' It seemed to her that her body wanted to obey and was somewhat inclined to go and look, and she said, 'Brother body, if you want to look at such things, go and see; but, wanton one, you will not take my soul with you.' At this the devil instantly fled in confusion.

Often he pressed so strongly on her throat that she feared she would suffocate; and, as I believe, he often would have suffocated her if it had been permitted on high. Because he could not fulfil his desires in this particular, he constricted her arms and legs, as if she was wearing a garment of lead, and she could neither rise from the spot nor be moved. If however she had just enough strength to sign herself she expelled him with the sign of the Cross; otherwise it was necessary for the divine power itself to command him. One morning when she rose in order to pray she was so severely struck by the devil on her kidneys and shoulder-blades that it seemed to her she had been cut into four, but when she made the sign of the Cross the pain immediately vanished.

---

31 In August 1244: Papi, 'Una santa vedova', in 'In castro poenitentiae', p. 85.

32 Giovanni Villani dates this withdrawal to early 1248: Nuova cronica, 7:33; ed. G. Porta (3 vols, Parma, 1990), 1, p. 315.

How the devil appeared to her in his own true form as a serpent

Leviathan, the beguiling enemy of the human race, perceiving that she was not going to yield to impostures of this kind and desist from prayer, had recourse to his own form, that of a serpent, which women usually greatly abominate, and having assumed this huge bodily form he appeared to her, looking upon her with terrible eyes, in order at least to dent her constancy a little and obstruct the grace of her devotion. Seeing him she was struck with such terror that she could not find security in her cell, in prayer or not; but after some days, unable to bear the loss of prayer, she addressed the serpent next to her and said, 'I adjure you, horrible serpent, in the name of my Lord Jesus Christ, that if you are bodily real you depart at once, never to return; if you are my incorporeal enemy, disappear from my presence so that I may freely devote myself to my God and do not bother me any more.' At this the serpent was gradually reduced to smoke, but emitted such a stench that she could not stay in her cell. Denouncing him, she said, 'Evil and envious serpent, since you fell from heaven, you contrive on earth to attack the faithful; this is your merchandise, all stench and uncleanness, which proceed from you, full of filth. From my Lord, be he blessed above all things, proceed all good fragrance and all cleanness.' At this the Foul One retreated and such a sweet fragrance flowed in that it seemed to her that she was in the precincts of paradise.

How the devil showed her a real serpent

After some days, Satan brought with him a huge serpent, not spiritual in nature like himself, nor contrived or imaginary, but corporeal, genuinely frightful and horrible, which greatly terrified her. Still she persisted in her prayers. When she rested it kept its tail on her feet and its head at her jaw, which so terrified her that she could neither pray nor sleep with confidence. When she went to rest, she wrapped her feet in cloths and tied them round with a girdle, lest the serpent should get in and touch any part of her naked body. And although she trusted in God, she would not expose herself to such danger as to tempt God, but defended herself from it as best she could. She did not try to lay hands on it and did not want to reveal its presence to anyone else; knowing that it had been given to her for her instruction, she was unwilling to expose to anyone the devil's temptations which she daily endured. When she had patiently put up with this for several days, unable to tolerate the loss of prayer, she was stirred up against the serpent and

said to it, as it lay near her, 'I order you, serpent, in the name of my
beloved Jesus, to roll yourself up at once, here next to my hands.' At
this the serpent lowered its head and at once rolled its tail and body
round its head, as it had been commanded. The blessed Umiliana put
both hands under its body, raised it from the ground, and praising and
blessing God said, 'Blessed be that almighty love which created you'.
Carrying it to a window of the tower she commanded it, saying, ' Go
your ways and stay with me no more, for you are useless and unprofitable to me.' At this the serpent swiftly departed.

It is not to be wondered at, O revered Umiliana, if you expelled demons
with a word and the most evil beasts became pliant to your command,
for with the sweetness of your discourse you often swayed the Lord of
all, and sinners as well, and while you lived conferred many gifts on
many people.

Of certain people liberated from temptations and tribulations, and how the Lord made his divine sweetness known to many through the merits of the blessed Umiliana

On one occasion Gisla of Mugello, an exceedingly honourable and
religious woman, was greatly vexed by intolerable noises and disturbances created by people dwelling not far from her home, to the extent
that she was unable to devote herself to prayer and tranquillity. She
intended to leave her house unless she could soon be liberated from
these annoyances. It happened that the blessed Umiliana came on a visit
to her house, as she often did, and Gisla made her pious complaints to
her. Umiliana felt compassion for her in her pious heart and, wondrous
to relate, God at once had regard for her compassion and from that
hour the disturbances ceased. On another occasion, the same Gisla was
gravely tempted by the devil to desire to live entirely alone in solitude.
As solitude is dangerous for women, she commended herself to the
blessed Umiliana, who had pity on her distress; when she petitioned the
Lord on her behalf, she was completely liberated. Again, a certain friar
was oppressed by a serious temptation and commended himself to her
prayers: she prayed for him earnestly on the same night that she was
gravely afflicted by a devil, but that very same day the friar's trouble
was much alleviated, and after a short while he got over it altogether.

Sister Sobilia, a recluse in Sasso,[33] broke her arm badly and was ill-

---

33 A hermitage in the Casentino, about thirty miles south-east of Florence and five from
   the great hermitage of Camaldoli.

attended by some ignorant person. So it came about that her hand went totally dead and her nails turned black and the arm began visibly to wither. As a result she couldn't raise her hand to her mouth or do anything with it. After Easter the saint visited her and, seeing her worn out with the pain in her arm and hand, felt great compassion for her. Coming close to her she signed her arm and hand, despite the sister's protestations, for she was glad to suffer for the love of God. Umiliana said, 'I am asking God to lessen the weakness and pain in your hand and arm.' As she spoke the hand and arm began to regain their strength, so that in the evening Sobilia could raise her food to her own mouth without assistance.

Brother Buonaccorso of Todi of the order of Friars Minor, who was a great friend of hers, desiring to taste something of God, often commended himself to her, asking that through her he might obtain from God some gift of devotion. One day she said to him, as if she had been heard, 'My dearest brother, I believe that my God will soon give you some comfort from himself, for which you have often asked me.' A few days later, as she said, when the friar was alone in church he was in a wonderful manner infused with such grace that he became intoxicated and beside himself; he could not contain the fullness of grace in his confined breast and seemed in large part to have lost his bodily senses. This also happened to him while she was praying in his presence in a certain place near the city. Similarly, when Brother Michele was praying one day in her presence and feeling no devotion, he said to her, as if stirred within, 'My daughter, pray for me, for I am totally dried up.' Obeying him as an obedient daughter, she raised her eyes to heaven and prayed to the Lord, and he was at once infused with such grace that he could not contain its fullness; and then the saint herself was similarly enraptured. Monna Bene, who shared in the divine consolations, was praying once in the presence of the blessed Umiliana, before the saint's painting;[34] when she prayed that she might receive some consolation through the merits of his servant she tasted such a sweetness of grace as she could never remember before. While she lived, she obtained this grace for many others, whom it would take a long time to enumerate.

---

34 The Latin (*coram tabula ipsius Sanctae*) is ambiguous, but as the passage seems to concern spiritual benefits achieved by Umiliana during her lifetime I have taken it that the image of the Virgin and Child (see above, p. 102 n. 20) is meant.

Of the blessed Umiliana's humility

She also humbly converted many people to this grace by her words.
For she would say to someone: 'I want you to climb three steps: first
that you should weep for your sins and the time you have wasted;
secondly that you should lament your ingratitude that you have not
acknowledged the grace of God, and lament the Passion of Christ our
Lord; thirdly that you should reflect on the divinity and rejoice, to the
extent that God may allow you.' Some she exhorted to peace, others to
patience; to some she recommended the lives of the saints, urging them
to keep them uninterruptedly before their eyes, others she encouraged
to the solitary life, saying, 'Think of your house as the desert grove,
and your household as wild beasts, and live among them as in a grove,
preserving silence and devoting yourself to continuous prayer.' The
humble Umiliana held up the example of humility, so that anyone who
wanted to scale the heights should plant their foundation in humility.
She was repeatedly asked by Brother Michele why God had brought
her to such grace; overborne by his prayers she replied, 'I am sure that
it is not by my own merits, but by his mercy alone, and the grace of
humility, which according to the limits of my fragility and what he has
thought fit to grant me, that the merciful God has endowed me with so
much good.' To another lady she said that [it was] because her zeal in
almsgiving earned much for her. Truly she spoke as an imitator of the
mirror of all humility, that is, the glorious Virgin, for she sought with
all her might to follow her in the path of humility.

She was unbelievably humble in all her doings and bore a humble aspect
in every lineament of her body, for she never raised her eyes to look
about her. She went along the road like a pauper woman, lowly and
despised, and so far as she was able, banishing herself, she wished to
be despised by all. Her steps were humble and devout steps, and she
approached every one most humbly. In her speech she was so rooted in
humility that the passage of the Canticles of the Bridegroom seemed
to be entirely fulfilled in her: 'Your lips distil nectar, honey and milk
are under your tongue.'[35] It is a wonderful truth that after she began to
know God no speech passed her lips that was not of great humility. And
although she burned inwardly with the divine love, she did not dare to
speak about God, unless, involuntarily, she humbly uttered two or at
most three words of divine fire. In all her works she failed to satisfy
herself, but called herself ever wretched; and although she was full of

35 Song of Solomon 4:11.

God and so continuously concerned for her own salvation, and endowed with many gifts, never did she ascribe anything to herself, but said she was worthy of all the pains of hell. She was truly meek and humble of heart. She had wonderful patience and forbearance, for although she suffered many grave offences she was never perturbed or showed any sign of perturbation; the daughter of peace, lest she should offend the father of peace, bore all inconveniences in total peacefulness. It would take a long time to extol her virtues, for she was full of all virtues. Let us turn to other things.

How abstinent, devout and contemplative she was

Happy Umiliana, the devoted imitator of all perfection, with what compassionate zeal you followed Jesus your beloved, wanting to feel what he felt in his immaculate body for our salvation. Our God fasted for forty days on end so that he might restore us guiltless from the eating of the forbidden tree, and moderate in us the vice of gluttony; you, dearest, weaken your body with frequent fasts, not for sins you have committed, but for the love of justice (for it is just that the creature should piously and faithfully feel for her Creator), and in order to become a worthier vessel, like Daniel, of the Holy Spirit. For you reverently kept several Lenten fasts in excess of the church's usual custom, as of the Apostles before the coming of the Holy Spirit, and another before the assumption of the Blessed Virgin, and several others, and on the most solemn feast-days, which it would be lengthy to enumerate. Who could describe with what reverence you celebrated the feast-days for which you had prepared with such long fasts? spending sleepless nights, devoted to prayer and lofty contemplation, recalling what grace the Lord accorded to his saints, and the delight he took in them, in whom the companion and friend of the saints too rejoiced and gave thanks. The beloved soul loved her fellow-citizens in the heavenly Jerusalem, with whom she was to reign for ever and whom she summoned to her assistance, so that through them she might be filled with a more abundant grace. She fasted on free days outside Lent for four days in the week, that is the second, fourth and sixth days and on Saturday, unless she was prevented by bodily infirmity; and often at fast-times and on numerous other occasions she had no broth, or anything else, with her bread. She would have had it, as I believe, if she had complained, but the daughter of peace bore all offences patiently.[36]

36 This seems to imply that Umiliana's rations were sometimes cut; not all her abstinence was of her own making.

She began to fast a great deal on bread and water and to embrace great abstinence; but Fra Michele, her confessor, did not allow her to persist in this path. At mealtimes she was so intent on continuous prayer and contemplation that she couldn't eat. But a devoted maidservant called Piecilia was alerted to this and used to put food in front of her so that when she came to herself she could restore nature. When she came to herself and saw the food in front of her, she used to exclaim, 'O God, my longed-for love, when will you free me from the body of this death and from these material foodstuffs, so that I may feast at your table, as I wish, on the food of the saints?' When she began to taste the food, which was now cold after a long wait, she left it after two or three spoonfuls, overcome by an abundance of devotion; again she began to eat, and again stopped, as before, and she took her food in this state of conflict. When she was thus caught up in God (always, therefore, until the evening) she didn't eat. And sometimes she couldn't eat that day, and she passed many days not eating in this way, and sometimes she remained for three days without bodily food, nourished with the food of divine consolation. And because all flesh is tasteless when one has tasted the spirit, as Gregory says, she reached such a state of repugnance for material foodstuffs, that in a whole week she did not take more than four average loaves.[37]

One Thursday morning, seasonably and zealously reflecting on the works of creation and the stubbornness of the first man and the judgements and mercies of God and the incarnation and death of the Son of God and his Resurrection and Ascension and how he sat at the right hand of the Father, she was swept up in the sweetness of God and did not return to her ordinary senses until sunset after vespers on the Saturday. She did not eat or drink for those three days and nights on end, nor did she know anything; and, as she said when she came to herself, she believed it was Thursday, since she said she hadn't known whether she was in the body or out of it. In the evening, when she had had a little nourishment, she rested. When she had slept for a little while, the time came when she usually rose to pray, and there beside her was a boy clad in white, all radiant and holding a light in his hands, saying, 'Arise, Umiliana; you know why.' He woke her so that she might spend the night in prayer, and it is believed that it was her angel. And when she arose at the voice and touch of the boy and looked at him, wonderful as he was, he and the light vanished.

---

37 One must suppose that these *usuales panes* were not very large, perhaps rolls rather than loaves. Cf. Papi, 'Una santa vedova', in *'In castro poenitentiae'*, p. 66 n. 28.

How an angel brought her bread

Intent thus on prayer until terce[38] of the following Sunday, she experienced the great sweetness of Christ; and at terce, while she persisted in prayer, a boy (that is, the same angel, as it is believed) appeared carrying half a loaf; he said, 'Arise, and eat when you think fit.' And when she got up, she found the half-loaf (which, it cannot be doubted, had been made by the hands of angels) wonderfully white and fragrant. Looking at it she wondered whether it had been brought by the maid. But when she saw that the door of the cell was firmly locked, she believed it to be what it was, and taking the bread and giving thanks she ate. She lived on that half-loaf for almost a whole week, and gave some of it to others; and during that week the many bodily infirmities which she suffered as a result of her austerities were cured. During that week, she experienced the sweetness of God much more than usual, and all the other food which she was brought she gave to the poor. Monna Rigale her sister, Monna Luciana her aunt, and Fra Vigor of Cortona of the Friars Minor all had some of this bread. When she gave it to them she said, 'Receive this angels' bread, which our God has sent to a certain servant of his.'

How she observed silence

She preserved continual silence for all of Lent (both St Martin's Lent and the principal one)[39] and on the other new occasions which she herself had adopted in honour of the major feast-days; and for three days in the week, so that she spoke to no one unless for some unavoidable cause. She suffered severe stomach pain, and brought up abundant fresh blood, and every day she spat this out ... and by comparison with him it seemed to her that she suffered little as yet.[40] O doughty athlete, who fought so strongly against the pleasures of the body! With what diligence you followed the Creator, who was beaten for a whole day, and his punishment in the morning; for whose love you so cruelly mortified your delicate body with assiduous beating. Umiliana had a scourge

---

38 The 'third' liturgical hour, which fell in the morning, after matins and prime and before sext and nones.

39 'St Martin's Lent' ran from the saint's feast-day (11 November) to Christmas; it was observed in the Rule of the Poor Clares. See Thompson, *Cities of God*, p. 85 on its observance by lay penitents. According to one of his Lives, Homobonus kept this Lent (Piazzi, *Omobono*, p. 50).

40 There is a lacuna in the text here; some reference to the sufferings of Christ is presumably intended.

made of ropes and cords with which she frequently and vigorously beat her naked body; in addition she often beat herself with sharp twigs, and often she[41] could easily have walked a mile before she ceased to beat herself. And although she was wasted with fasting and worn down by beating, she did not have recourse to soft bed-coverings so as to be kind to herself for a moment, but afflicted her tender flesh with a harsh hair-shirt of cords interwoven with goat- and horse-hair, which she would have worn for a long time, but at Fra Michele's direction she gave it up. With this somehow resting a little on a bag of straw, which she used as a bed, she restored her body with what little sleep she could, so that she could the more easily keep vigil all night, never returning to her bed.

One night Monna Compiuta saw her, with her eyes and mouth closed and her hands extended cross-wise, standing and crying so hard that her weeping resembled rainfall rather than tears.

How she lamented the passion of her beloved Christ

Before this supreme grace of ecstasy, which she perfectly possessed, was fully over, in the silence of the night while her maid and the household slept, she bewailed the passion of her beloved Jesus with loud cries and harsh lamentations, her hair unbound. Sometimes the maidservant was awakened and saw her lying on the floor, but she didn't dare to touch her, for she knew her mistress's wish to conceal as far as possible the grace which was granted to her. She pressed her heart to the wound in the side of Christ, which she too bore in her heart. Surely she had made for herself as it were a bundle of myrrh of all the injuries of Christ, which she fixed gently in her heart, so that she might truthfully say, 'A bundle of myrrh is my beloved to me, and he will dwell between my breasts,'[42] and thus she was literally so filled that it seemed her heart could not be contained in her body. The gospel 'A good measure, pressed down, shaken together, running over, will be put into your lap' also was fulfilled in her,[43] because she was so filled bodily by abundance of spirit that it was a wonder that her bowels did not often burst bodily. For, as Fra Bernardo of Piacenza attested, one day he saw, with Fra Michele, how she was so affected by the divine love that with a slight action of her hands she snapped her own girdle, which was a strong one and could hardly have been broken at all except by a miracle.

41 One suspects that this should be 'you', but the verb, as printed, is third-person.

42 Song of Solomon 1:12.

43 Luke 6:38.

How she prepared herself to receive the Eucharist

She kept vigil the whole of Saturday night in honour of the supreme Empress Mary and to devote herself the more diligently to her Son, sweetly recalling the delightful infancy of our Redeemer and the tender care of his mother, and during the night she tasted mentally that bread of life for which those who taste it thirst. On Saturday morning she would taste that most holy bread truly and sacramentally (for every Saturday morning she received the sacrament of the Body of Christ), and she rose very early on that day, silently, like a bee fully laden.[44] Lest those of the household should notice, for she didn't want to be a bother to anyone, she changed her name and asked her companions that they should call her not by her own name but by the one she had assumed. She used this name whenever she was called early by her companions, wanting to summon her to indulgences or to visit the poor but also to hear matins. As she went on her way to receive the sacrament of the Body of Christ she asked her companion not to talk to her at all, saying, 'God is everywhere, and can be had everywhere, and gives himself freely to all as long as he finds a vessel ready; so if you want to please me, don't impede me with words. Often, when I am going along the road, and I'm among people, and when I hear sermons or the divine office, I find my Lord as fully as when I am in my cell concentrating on my prayers and devotions. And we must keep silence out of reverence for the Creator who is to be received; for if anyone were to come to receive such a sacrament dragging his own body naked over the earth he could not show it the due reverence.'

From the foregoing it is clear that she was continually in a state of devotion; for whether she was eating, or walking along the road, resting with her friends, or hearing the divine office and sermons, she experienced the immense sweetness of God, so that she was often wondrously caught up in him. She did not dare to sit up, but used to sit on the ground, leaning her head on the bench on which she was supposed to sit, or bowing it on her breast, so that she seemed rather to sleep. So, when she visited the church to receive the sacrament of the Body of Christ, she hurried as fast as she could and returned home swiftly, admitting no excuse; here she was most engaged in the grace granted to her and the contemplation of the Humanity seated on the right hand of God the Father; not negligently, but in surpassing contemplation of the supreme divinity (so far as it is given to mortals), concentrating all

---

44 Umiliana's vigil occupied the night of Friday–Saturday, ending when she rose to go to mass in the morning.

her affections on the unity of the Trinity and the Trinity of unity, in joyous celebration from which she gently drew unspeakable gifts.

Besides what has been said above about her ecstasies, there was scarcely ever a day on which she did not experience a rapture of this kind; and sometimes for two days, sometimes for a whole day and a night, sometimes for the greater part of the day, sometimes the greater part of the night, she remained in ecstasy in this way, as God appointed. Monna Dialta heard from her that she remained in ecstasy for two days and one night on end, and her brothers after the flesh opened her teeth with a knife, because they thought it was the result of some illness; she often laughed at them for doing this.[45] Monna Jacoba and Monna Gisla and Monna Compiuta said that they saw her remain in ecstasy from the middle of terce[46] until after nones; Monna Scotta said that on St Margaret's day she remained enraptured from the lunch hour until evening. The blessed Umiliana was enraptured and insensible in that state of grace for the greater part of the day in the presence of Fra Michele and Monna Altabene; and when Fra Michele exclaimed at this grace and expressed great wonder, as was his habit, she heard nothing at all. During the severe pain of the stomach illness which she suffered for a year before she died, she was enraptured when she meditated on God; and those who were present saw her at once resting peacefully, and sometimes they heard her singing, as if at some celebration, so softly that she could not be heard unless you put your ear to her mouth. They heard a sound of rejoicing, but could not distinguish what she was singing. When she came back to her senses, she was tortured with excessive pain, as if [by] a serpent, and the bystanders watching could scarcely bear her agonies. Sometimes when she was going along the road she began to be affected by the memory of the Passion of Christ, and little by little as the feelings of devotion grew she burst out into the bitterest lamentations; there could not have been so iron a heart that it would not have been softened and burst into tears and wailing.

Having seen the veiled face of Christ, you veiled the eyes of your heart and body with the bonds of love, so that you might see no one except Christ, in the manner of the blessed Apostles, of whom it is written in Matthew 17: 'Lifting their eyes they saw no one except Jesus alone.' The words of St Agnes were fulfilled in her: 'He has set his seal on my face, so that I can admit none but him as a lover.'[47]

45 This seems to be one of a number of hints that Umiliana may have suffered epileptic fits.

46 The 'hours' were in fact notional periods of three hours' duration.

47 See Jacobus de Voragine, *The Golden Legend: readings on the saints*, translated by W. G. Ryan (2 vols, Princeton, 1993), 1, p. 102.

How she never raised her eyes to gaze at anything

If it happened that on any occasion or for any reason she saw a mortal man she was greatly grieved and, wanting to be made blind, asked the Lord to deprive her of the light of her eyes. At home her eyes were half-closed, and along the road she kept them fixed on the ground, not looking to left or right. One day she was passing along the road when a madly rearing horse, caused her to raise her eyes lest she should be trampled by the horse, and momentarily she saw the rider. Wounded by an inner pain she exclaimed vehemently, 'Oh, if only I were blind, Lord, that I need see such things no more.' Again, one day, she was going along and heard someone ask 'Why haven't you taken a nice husband, with whom you could enjoy the good things of this world and be happy?' She replied, 'Would that I were blind and deaf, that I need not hear such things any more.' She took it very ill that she should hear such scurrilities and foul worldly talk. If she happened to be in company, she used to say, 'Let no one speak here unless it be of God, or I shall leave at once.' If someone took no notice, she would complain bitterly, saying, 'Alas! What are you doing? Why are you driving out the Lord so crudely and indecently and with such unprofitable words? Truly, he was in the midst of us', and at once she left. Because the sense of hearing has no natural obstacle, it often happens that we hear something displeasing, and we can avoid it only by flight. Lest she should hear the noises and vanities of the world, she stopped her ears firmly with wax.

How she faithfully loved the lovers of God

The lovable lover of the Bridegroom faithfully loved all his true lovers and especially him whom she knew burned with the greatest love. Wherefore she greatly loved a holy man named Simeon, of the order of Camaldoli, whom she had never seen, because she had learned that he was aflame with the divine love. Out of reverence for him she wanted to have some testimony of his sanctity and began to pray with insistent affection that God in his generosity should show her something of it. God heard her prayers and showed her the man, with a truly radiant face, accompanied by two shining and beautiful angels to left and right of him. This auspicious vision filled her with joy and she was enraptured by the fullness of the divine grace and tasted the sweetness of her beloved Jesus abundantly, so that for three whole days, absorbed in this delight, she took no corporeal food. You, dearest one, gazing steadfastly on the author of our faith, our redeemer Jesus, whom you loved with all your heart, summoned your companions with much reverence to the supper of the Lord, that they might faithfully follow him.

How she longed to be martyred for Christ

She longed to suffer martyrdom for Christ, saying, 'Oh, if only there were a *podestà* at Florence who would inflict severe torments on me for Christ's sake, and then beat me around the whole town and put me to death!' She also said, 'If only for Christ's sake some tyrant would burn me in a great fire!' Often, when she was forbidden to long for death with such enthusiasm, she answered, 'On this subject I cannot hear you; and if all the saints who are on heaven and earth should say this to me, I couldn't listen to them.' But as she could not find torturers to kill her for Christ's sake, she longed at least to be gravely ill so that she might suffer for the love of God and feel the pains of Christ in the pain of her own body.

She also wanted to be enclosed in her tower, saying, 'Would that my father would shut me up in this tower, with no door or window in it, for Christ's sake.' She said this, so that her father and no other should enclose her, because he sometimes threatened to wall up the door of the tower because she would not live in matrimony as he wished, and he strove to get her out of it, wanting her to live in a palace near Sant' Ambrogio, then newly built, but now destroyed.

How a kinsman of hers was struck down by God for the harm he did her

Her cousin Galgano wanted to live with his wife in the tower, in the blessed Umiliana's cell, and for this reason he strove mightily, together with her father, to get her to leave. The blessed one did not want to leave, because of the grace the Holy Spirit had bestowed on her there. Because of this persecution, both were severely smitten by God, Galgano by the death of his body, although perhaps not that of his soul, because thanks to Umiliana's prayers he was able to receive the sacrament of penance. Her father would have been more seriously stricken if the saint had not intervened with her prayers to God. She wanted to be in high mountains and in deserts and solitudes, in accessible places where she would only have herbs for her food and could meditate freely on God as she

wished and burst forth in pious praises and exclamations for the love
of her beloved Jesus Christ. She said she was imprisoned, because she
could not pour out what she had within her; and she often called her
cell a hell, although for the love of Christ she willingly remained in it,
because of the many and various diabolical temptations and harsh tribulations and cruel and frequent chastisements which the devil inflicted
on her in it.

How the Lord filled her with the spirit of prophecy

God filled her with the spirit of prophecy, so that she accurately related
many things that were to come; we will note a few. Being fervent in the
things of God, she wished to adorn daintily the panel of the Blessed
Virgin which she had in her cell. Not having the materials, she said to
a certain lady who was joined to her in friendship, 'If only the Blessed
Virgin would give me something with which I could reverently adorn
her picture.' Shortly afterwards, someone came bearing some crystal
and amber ornaments and gave them to the friend aforementioned so
that she could give them to Umiliana as from herself. When she took
them and showed them to her Umiliana was delighted and said, ' I know
where you got these, and who gave them to you, and why he gave them.'
And she added rejoicing, ' From now on, go on doing anything you can,
for if I want it, I shall not tell you.'[48]

One day, she went to visit a certain venerable religious woman who was
very dear to her, and among their other conversation she said to her,
'My dear, you may rest assured that the hair which has been brought
to you, and the other things, are truly those of the Blessed Virgin.' The
nun was amazed and said, 'Who told you about what you say I have?
For no one, except God, knows who gave them to me.' Umiliana said
nothing, not wanting to betray that she had not been told by any mortal
being, since it had clearly been revealed to her by the spirit of prophecy.
The nun had at first had her doubts that the hair and other relics were
those of the Blessed Virgin, as the secret purveyor of them had told her
they were.

She foretold the death of Monna Rubea when she was ill. One day she
visited her, and after a suitable time, when she came to leave, she said

---

48 The vernacular version omits this and other instances of Umiliana's supernatural
   insights, although Maginnis ('Images, devotion', p. 16) says that it includes 'all the
   stories about her images'.

to her, 'Dearest sister, when you are before God, will you pray for me? For now I am leaving you, and I shall not see you again in the body.' A certain sister who was present said, 'Alas, my lady, what are you saying? Of course you will see her again.' She replied, 'I am certain that what I say is true, that I shall never see her more in this mortal body.' And thus it happened as she had foretold, because after a short time [Rubea] died and she did not see her again. She also foresaw the death of the husband of her kinswoman Monna Ravenna. One day before he died she sent her maid Piecilia to Monna Ravenna, saying, 'Fortify yourself with great patience, for soon you will suffer misfortunes which will greatly afflict you.' After a few days, her husband died. She also foresaw, by the revelation of God, that her father would be gravely stricken, because in offending his daughter he had gravely offended God. The blessed one, foreseeing this tribulation, tempered it with her prayers, so that he suffered only a distortion of the mouth[49] and was spared another intolerable affliction. God was unwilling to remit all his suffering through her prayers, for he wanted him to know that he who touches his servants touches the pupil of his eye. She foresaw the death of her cousin Galgano, as we have mentioned above.

She received foreknowledge about a certain lady whom Fra Michele greatly loved and wanted to remove from the vanity of the world, desiring that she should dedicate her virginity to the Almighty and serve him in bodily purity. He often commended her to Umiliana, that she might inflame her with the divine love and strengthen her in her good intentions. The saint diligently prayed for her, because she loved her, and sent a reply to Fra Michele through Monna Gisla, saying, 'Tell Fra Michele, don't praise the flower before the fruit, for I too, praying for her, have not seen that she wants to serve God in purity of body.' This was true, because shortly afterwards she was married. One day she realised that Monna Tabernaria was worried about her son Ubertino, who had left the order of Friars Minor. She asked whether he would be received back, and Umiliana said, 'He will return to the order, and he will be received, but he will leave again afterwards, not having stayed for very long.' This was what happened: when he had completed the probationary year he freely left the order, not having made his profession; after some months he was received again, making his profession to the order as required; and after a short interval, now bound to the order, he left of his own free will. She said also that there would be a time in which the word of God would not be preached out of fear.

49 Or face: *tortuositatem passus est oris*. Umiliana's father probably had a stroke.

A certain religious person of perfect life spent seven days on end in devotion and did not take corporeal food. In the morning, at dawn, an angel of the Lord appeared to her holding half a loaf. Showing it to her, he said, 'Take this bread and restore your body with it', and she took it with devotion. This was not concealed from Umiliana. For after a suitable interval she came to the servant of God, saying, 'Dearest, give me some of that bread which was secretly given to you and which you still have.' She replied in wonderment, 'Who has thus revealed my doings to you, my dear?' And seeing that she could not deny her this bread she gave her a morsel. She took it and gave thanks and took it away with her and put it reverently in a very clean place. Not many days afterwards she was concentrating on prayer and did not eat for four days on end. At the hour of vespers she was suffering from great thirst, and having no other food ate that morsel and nothing else. When she ate it, all at once a radiant and beautiful boy stood before her, carrying a phial full of water, which he gave to her. She took it with thanks and drank and found that this water was wine with the finest and most delectable aroma, delightful to drink. She was so restored by this supper, that for four days afterwards she remained fasting, without food.

How she was several times raised from the ground into the air

God adorned her body with two special gifts which portended its glorification, that is, lightness and fragrance. Several times when she was praying she was raised into the air. On the feast of St Felicitas, the first of August, she visited Sister Sobilia in Sasso and withdrew into a part of her cell to pray. While she was praying Sobilia saw her raised into the air. One day when Fra Michele was visiting her, the saint said, 'Fra Michele, when I am praying I am raised into the air and held there, and afterwards I am released and return to the ground.' Paying no attention, Fra Michele did not understand this. When he realised that she had spoken and he didn't know what she had said, he said, 'Tell me what you just said.' At this, she remained silent and gave him no explanation.[50] Her body emitted an odour full of inexhaustible sweetness. One day when Monna Bene visited her, she came close to her and noticed a smell of great sweetness coming from her body. Monna Cecilia, a kinswoman of the blessed Umiliana, one day smelled such a sweet odour in her room in the lower part of the house that she never in her life remembered having smelled the like, and this came from Umiliana's chamber.

---

50 Both Latin and Italian are ambiguous; it is not entirely clear who is remaining silent, Michele or Umiliana.

How her little daughter was delivered from death by virtue of her prayers

One day, shortly after terce, one of her little daughters, called Rigale, came to see her and knocked at the door for her mother to open it for her. Her mother rose at her knock, and going to the door opened it, let her daughter in and closed the door again. Suddenly, the child was struck dumb, fell down as if dead and very soon turned white. Seeing this, her mother was terrified by her daughter's sudden danger, and began to nurse her sorrowfully, as is the way of mothers, waiting until nones for the troubled spirit to return and the girl to revive somehow. And when she didn't revive and didn't get any better she touched her to see if she could detect any sign of life in her, and when she examined her more carefully she found that she was cold all over. Then she went to the throat, where a pulse is usually found in a half-dead body, and when she found no pulse she thought she was dead. She was dumbstruck by the sudden death of her daughter and the trouble she feared from her kin. Rushing to the image of Our Lady, she prostrated herself before it and begged in tears, 'Kindest love, have pity on me, and free me from this scandal and tribulation which my kin will inflict on me, and restore my daughter to me.' When she had finished her prayer she arose and signed her daughter. When she had done so, a wondrously beautiful boy emerged from the panel, went to the place where the little girl lay and signed her. As soon as he made the sign of the Cross she arose fit and well, and the boy vanished at once.

How our Lord Jesus Christ appeared to her in the shape of a four-year-old boy

She thirsted with the utmost affection of her heart to see with her bodily eyes the child Jesus as he was in his childhood, at the age of three or four, when he used to be so carefully guided by the glorious Queen of Virgins. She often asked this, but timidly, for she thought herself unworthy of such a gift. But as Bernard says, love knows no rank; such was her ardour to see God that it overcame fear and impropriety, and so she did not fear to ask constantly for what she desired. But the beneficent God, who shapes the wills of those that fear him and hears their requests, hearkened to her one day in a marvellous and glorious manner, concerning both illness and her vision. One day she went on a compassionate visit to a boy who was seriously ill. When she saw him tormented by the pain of his infirmity, she said to him: 'My dearest son, surely you remember your Creator and reflect what suffering he bore for you?' He replied, 'Peace on you, good lady, I am more mindful of the pain and illness I am suffering than I am of God.' She rejoined, 'Would you like to give me your illness?' The boy said, 'I would like to be free of it, and you could have it all.' She said, 'May God do this for me: if you have this illness for the sake of your eternal salvation, may he leave you with it, so that you may achieve coronation through it; otherwise, let him give it all to me.' The boy replied, 'I don't want you to have it all, but part of it: take upon yourself the pain I am suffering in my side and groin, and take it with you now, so that I feel it no more.' Umiliana answered him, 'So be it as you have said to me'; and after a little while she went home.

What a marvel! At once the pain in his side left the boy as if it had been taken away by hand; and the saint began to be sorely afflicted with that same pain, so that for the severity of it she could find no rest, even for a moment. Unable to bear it, she had a wood fire laid so that she might mitigate the pain somewhat with the heat. When it was lit she wanted to warm herself, but worn out by excessive pain she could not support herself, but fell full-length into the fire and could not get up until it had burned right out. Her patience and humility were marvellous, for she did not want to impose any burden on any member of the household because of this sudden pain or to relieve the pain at all. But the wondrous God preserved her unscathed in the fire, so that she did not feel its heat at all. She lamented this afterwards, saying, 'I fear that my God has abandoned me, because he did not let me feel the heat of the fire.' When morning came and the pain had abated, she returned swiftly to the boy and said to him, 'Do you want to give me the other affliction you are suffering?' The boy replied, 'I do, take this sickness away from me, as you took the pain in my side, for I don't feel that any more, as if when you left me I had never felt any pain in my side or groin.' She said kindly, 'So be it, according to your word.' When she left, the boy was at once cured of every infirmity and his sickness was so imprinted on the blessed one that no one who saw her could have doubted that she had the boy's illness. This affliction is commonly called *papici*, and is otherwise known as *ignis volatilis* or *gutta salsa*.[51]

Stricken with this sickness and pain in her side she lay on her bed,

---

51 Citing this very passage, Salvatore Battaglia, *Grande dizionario della lingua italiana* (21 vols and supplement, Turin, 1961–2004) explains *papici* as 'a cutaneous eruption, mostly confined to the face'; hence the obviousness of Umiliana's affliction to the beholder. *Gotta salsa* is given as an alternative term.

not very well able to get up. It was her custom never to lie in bed if she could help it, so concerned was she with her salvation. While she was lying on her bed in her cell in the tower, which was firmly closed (she always locked the door of the cell securely from the inside, so that nothing might happen to disturb her at her prayers), a boy of four years old or less was with her, most beautiful in appearance and lovely to behold, playing energetically in front of her in the cell. When she saw him she rejoiced greatly, believing him truly to be a messenger of the supreme King, and addressing him she said, 'O sweetest love! Dear child! Don't you know how to do anything except play?' The boy, with a pleasant expression, replied, 'What else would you like me to do?' Umiliana humbly said, 'I would like you to say something good about God.' The boy said, 'Do you think it's good or befitting for someone to talk about himself?' And at this the boy Jesus disappeared, leaving her cured; the illness aforementioned disappeared altogether. Blessed the eyes that saw him whom you saw, fortunate Umiliana! To other saints and elect of God, an angel is sent to strengthen them in the Lord; to you is sent Jesus, the blessed fruit of the Virgin Mary, the only-begotten of the supreme Father, whom you had so long yearned to see with all your being. We have heard from many people that the child Jesus, our Lord, often appeared to her, in her cell and in the church of St Martin; but we have found no one whom she told that she had seen him, except Sister Sobilia of Sasso, to whom she related all that we have just said in full because, after Fra Michele, she was the confidante of her secrets. Therefore there are several things about the child Jesus which we will not put down in writing lest we should relate uncertainties rather than certainties. And let no one stumble over this, saying that perhaps he appeared to her when she was asleep. He who thinks this does so in vain, for when he appeared to her she was not sleeping but fully awake and, as stated, suffering cruel pain; and she saw him with her bodily eyes just as we see one another. We have heard and found this to be true, because she herself told several people that 'a certain lady' much wanted to see the Son of God as a child and that she saw him according to her wish. She did not say that it was herself, but 'a certain lady'; for she was a walled garden, and many great things which she knew she did not reveal, unless the grace of the Holy Spirit compelled her to do so. We have also heard it said that she kissed his feet; and we believe it, because she received many more things from Jesus than can be related and she concealed more than she declared.

How the most Holy Trinity appeared to her in the form of three spheres

One day she found a girl lying on a certain road: she was very small but monstrously scarred with leprosy, and she sat begging alms. When she saw her, the lover of the Trinity was much affected, and exclaimed, 'O mighty one, you have not deprived me of my hands and feet, like her, so that I might bear such torments for the love of your name'; but, assenting to the divine will, she at once added, 'May you be blessed for ever, Jesus, my sweet love, who according to your pleasure have endowed me with so many things and, as it has pleased you, have given me healthy limbs for the praise of your name.' And she began to proclaim with the most ardent emotion the supreme and individual Trinity, extolling it with many praises. Whence it came about a little later that one night the light went out while she was praying and three spheres appeared in her cell, brighter than the sun, which illuminated the cell far more than the material sun which we see with our bodily eyes. When she saw them, she exclaimed with great emotion, 'O Jesus, sweetest love, from night to day you reward me wonderfully.' Jumping up from the place where she was praying she ran after the spheres, grasping at them as best she could, for they were incorporeal, and said, 'O sweetest, most longed-for love, may all creatures bless you.' And all at once they were turned into one sphere, which with great care she clasped to her breast, and in her grasp she saw it disappear; she praised and blessed God, lamenting that she was carnal and physical and unable to keep hold of spiritual things.

How one day the saint, drinking water brought to her by her servant, marvellously found that it was wine

One day during Lent, when she used to abstain from wine, she was thirsty and asked her maidservant Piecilia to bring her some fresh water. She went at once and brought her a flask of water to drink as she had been ordered. When she tasted the water, which had been turned into wine, she was rather upset, and said, 'It would have been easier for you to bring water than wine, my dear, for water is cheaper than wine and there is more of it. Why then did you bring me wine instead of water?' She was somewhat upset, because she could not bear anything which was against her conscientious resolve and it seemed to her that she had greatly offended because she had tasted wine. The maid was much moved by these words, for she usually heard only humble and peaceable talk from her and she was not at fault, for she had faithfully fulfilled her mistress's command; so she said, 'My lady, God knows that I brought you pure water, as you ordered.' The saint replied, 'Say it was water you brought me, there was wine in the pitcher or it was stained with wine, at any rate it was wine which I tasted.' The maid took a bronze bucket and said, 'This vessel doesn't smell of wine, and there's certainly no wine in it. Now let's see if I bring you pure water', and running to the well, she drew some water. The saint did not trust her and ran to the window so that she could see if the maid truly went to draw water from the well, and she saw her do so, and waited until she was approaching the door to see whether she was really bringing water to her. Then she withdrew from the door and waited for her in the cell. She took the bucket, which was brimming with the clearest water, and when she put it to her lips, believing she was tasting water, she found she had tasted the finest wine, instantly made from the water. She was dumbfounded by the miracle, because she thought herself unworthy of such a gift, because God had done this for her twice and because the servant both then and previously had really brought her pure water. Still, she gave warm thanks to God, who had deigned to show her this marvel. Taking a pitcher she poured all the wine from the bucket into it, and wrapping the pitcher in a clean linen cloth hid it away, saying, 'Let no one touch that pitcher or taste that water.' We believe that she drank part of that wine and gave part to the sick of the city.

How she was miraculously cured of a wound inflicted on her forehead by one of her servants

One day when she asked another maidservant for water to drink the girl brought her a pitcher full of water and raising her hand struck her hard on the forehead, inflicting a bad wound from which quite a lot of blood flowed. She took this patiently, although she was badly hurt, and told no one about the wound, except a certain religious woman who was her confidante and who was notable for the sanctity and probity of her life; she feared that if it came to the ears of her kinsfolk, the blow would make trouble for the maidservant. It had created a putrid bloody wound which was not healing well and was becoming more and more painful. One day she was on her way to church to hear the divine office and imprinted the sign of the Cross on the wound. Then she felt a hand which made the sign of the Cross in like fashion, and at this touch the wound suddenly opened and expelled the bloody pus which was inside. The hand anointed the wound as if with some smooth and sweet-smelling ointment; it was at once healed, leaving no scar, and she felt no more pain from it.

How when she was tormented by thirst during a serious illness God miraculously came to her aid with water

On another occasion she was eaten up by fever in the stillness of the night and, sweltering with the heat of the fever, she became extremely dry and thirsty, panting heavily. She called the maid to bring her a drop of water to drink, but she didn't answer, for she was deeply asleep. Umiliana often called out and knocked to rouse her, but she was sleeping deeply and she couldn't wake her. Unable to get up because of her illness and overcome by thirst, she said, 'My Lord, my dearest love, who can do everything, you know my weakness and my infirmity, and the distress I'm in at this moment; you can certainly help me if it so pleases your goodness.' At these words, behold, a most beautiful girl appeared in her cell, with a shining face, accompanied by white-clad boys, and she carried a phial of water; approaching the sufferer, she sat by her head and inclining the phial little by little gave her something to drink; then she poured some water on to her hand and anointed her eyes and face with it. When she had done this many times her thirst was assuaged and all her sickness disappeared: restored to health and strength, she wanted to speak to the girl and to know who she was who had shown her such kindness and done her such good. The girl, however, put her finger to her lips, enjoining silence. The saint obediently kept quiet and did not dare to ask her questions, in case she should be deprived of the grace of this visitation, but the girl, after a short interval, disappeared with her companions. Much cheered by such benefits, she did not exalt herself, but in all things humbled herself much more than usual, and often said, when the grace she desired was absent, 'I am in the presence of my God like a widow, like an orphan and dependant.'

How one night she saw in her cell an unusual radiance and a great flame of fire which signified the Holy Spirit

One night when she rose from sleep to pray, she opened her eyes and saw the whole cell lit with an unaccustomed radiance. Looking towards the panel with the image of Our Lady, she saw a sort of flame of fire rising from the cloth which covered the panel up to the ceiling of the cell; she was much amazed and, fearing that the panel was burning, ran to it. She seized the cloth and, crumpling it up, rubbed it between her hands so that it should not harm the panel, taking it for granted that this was our material fire. When she realised that the cloth was undamaged and that she couldn't feel the fire with her hands, for it neither burned nor warmed, she knew what it was and was ashamed of her ignorance and pious misunderstanding of the sign; after a little while the fire disappeared. She returned to her bed so that the servant should not know what had happened, praising and blessing God, who often visited her with such joyous signs. It is to be believed that this fire manifested to her the fire of the Holy Spirit, with which Christ, through the merits of his glorious Mother, to whom she was much devoted, greatly inflamed her. This is a fire which does not burn but gives light and does not consume but illuminates, filling the hearts of his disciples very like the red fire which Moses once saw. Her maid Gisla often saw her cell shining at night as if by the light of the sun. One night Gisla was awakened by her sweet sighs and affectionate utterances, saying, 'Jesus, my sweetest love', and saw her cell bathed in such brilliant light that it seemed to be midday. Umiliana saw many things which we have not written down, and she received still more and greater things from God which she revealed to Fra Michele and which we have not been able to discover, for Fra Michele cloaked them in silence.

How she greatly longed to die on a Saturday

Umiliana humbly asked the Lord that she might die on Saturday, in reverence for Our Lady, and that no member of her father's house should be present at her death. This she obtained, for she passed to the Lord on that day and none of the aforementioned was present. On Easter Sunday she was suffering greatly from the severe illness from which she died, and began that morning to think about God. All at once she was caught up in ecstasy and remained at rest from that morning until vespers on the same day; I believe that she would have rested for much longer, had her brothers after the flesh not disturbed her and bothered her, making a great fuss and shouting, believing she was in her death-throes and unable to rouse her; which was clear, for when she came to herself, she complained about this annoyance, saying, 'O God, why am I not in the desert, so that I could freely devote myself to you, and not be bothered by mortals who so soon force me away from your sweet embraces?' On the following Monday she was bent double all day with stomach pain, and when she was asked why she was suffering more than the day before she replied, 'Yesterday God nourished me with milk, today the body is receiving its just deserts.' From this it is apparent that she had been resting in the height of ecstasy and didn't feel her stomach pain or the shouts and the shaking of her body and the way she was frequently shifted from place to place.

How before she died she predicted certain things to come

When she was close to death, Fra Michele and Fra Buonamico visited her and asked her how she was, and whether she thought she would recover from her illness. She replied, 'I firmly believe that I will never recover from this illness.' And when Fra Michele asked her and repeatedly begged her to return to him after death, she said, 'Why do you bother me with all these supplications? You will live for only a short time after me, and I see that in that time you will suffer many tribulations.' Fra Buonamico spoke to her and said, 'What have you to say to me? Will you return to me, if you die now, or not?' She did not answer him on this, although she did come to him after her death, but spoke of other things, saying, ' You will not be coming soon, but you will remain in this life: and during this time take care of yourself, brother.' The saint foretold that Fra Michele of Florence, a venerable and devout man, loved by God and men, would soon leave Santa Croce and die elsewhere, which was what happened.

Blessed Umiliana asked the women who were looking after her in her passing to buy her a tunic in which her feet were carefully wrapped, so that they would not be left bare to be touched by human beings. The lover of decency could not abide a trace of indecency even when she was dead. She foresaw the faith and devotion that the people would show her, tearing her grave clothes out of devotion. Asked about her hopes, she said she was so certain of her salvation that a consensus of men and angels saying the contrary would not prove it. O mirror of sanctity, model of all humility, exemplar of chastity, way of honour, path of devotion, rule of obedience, solace of the poor, shield of patience! What virtue, what grace, was not fully present in you? What virtuous practice was lacking to your sanctity? If we have commended you, dearest, let no one wonder, for the bishop of Florence, Ardingo of happy memory, an exemplar of holy life, also much commended you in his public preaching.[52]

52 Bishop of Florence 1230–49.

Of her illness and great suffering

Now that the end of her life had come, let us say something about her death. She began to be seriously ill in the January of the last year of her life, but out of forbearance and patience she hid it as best she could. In March, in the season of Lent, her illness worsened to the point that she lay down all the time, for she could not rise, all the strength being gone from her body. From this time she deteriorated day by day, almost totally losing the use of one side, on which she had no power to do anything for herself. She started to cough at the beginning of her illness, and then the pain in her stomach and kidneys, not to say in her whole body, got worse and caused her great suffering. Her body was much wasted and stripped of flesh, and her stomach became like a drum. Blood came from her nose and she expelled a great deal from her mouth. Somehow she took food until the second day after Easter[53] and then she ate no more, because she could not digest it. From the Monday after Easter for forty days she didn't eat, except that for eighteen days they gave her chicken broth to drink; on the remaining days they gave her only pure water. She was much tormented by the severity of the pain, so that those watching were tormented too out of compassion and sorrow. In all her sufferings she did not utter a word of lamentation or complaint, but gave thanks to God and girded herself in his embraces, crossing her arms on her breast and saying, 'Blessed be thou, my love.' I believe that she was embracing the image of Christ, which was imprinted on her memory, and which she mourned over at the same time; for she said when the she felt the pains and convulsions coming over her most severely, 'Here is my God come to visit me, I must embrace him most tenderly.' In these agonies she often seemed to be expiring and, although she was tormented by such pain, nonetheless, as was said before, she meditated on God and in her meditations was enraptured and rested in him. When she was disturbed by her kinsfolk, who slapped for a long time to revive her because they didn't know whether she was living or dying, she came to herself and said, 'For the love of God, don't inflict this nuisance on me, you are depriving me of much consolation, and tearing me away from the embraces of our Creator.'

53 Easter Sunday in 1246 fell on 8 April.

Of her passing and how she drove a demon away from her

When the hour of her death approached the devil appeared visibly to her to await the imminent departure of her soul from the body. When she saw him standing by her she began to upbraid him and denounce him mightily, saying, 'What are you doing here, you savage beast, wicked enemy? What are you waiting for, bloody beast? Leave me, enemy, get you hence, for you have no part in me.' And she threatened him not only in words but with her hands, pushing him away and saying, 'Go at once, you wretch, because my Lady is with me, who will instantly crush and smash your cunning schemes.' Not for all this did the devil retreat, but incessantly plagued her, saying that the Lord would not have mercy on her. She took this ill and said indignantly, 'You wretch, if all the angels said that along with you, they would not be believed, still less you.' Summoning the companion who was looking after her,[54] she said, 'I have wept so much and so long. The devil has dared inflict these temptations on me; I firmly believe that my God will have mercy on me.'

The companion ran swiftly to the image of Our Lady, where there was a hair of the same most worthy Mother of God, and she got blessed candles which she lit, holding them cross-wise, and placed the panel, on which there was the image of Our Lady and of the Crucified One,[55] on her breast. With the candles she illuminated it and offered incense and sprinkled holy water on her head. While this was going on, Umiliana turned to the demon and commanded it, saying, 'Leave me at once, wicked one, and do not dare to bother me henceforth.' At this the devil, defeated, vanished in confusion and she rested in total tranquillity. Opening her eyes and seeing the panel placed on her breast, she put it more honourably in a silken cloth from her cloak and rearranged it better on her breast. She rested all that night and the cold spead over her whole body. On Saturday morning, without a sob or a resistance, she yielded her spirit to heaven, at the hour when she usually received the Body of Christ, that is, at dawn, eight days before Pentecost, on 19 May, the day of St Potenziana, in the year of our Lord 1246.

Blessed Umiliana lived for twenty-seven years. Her body was taken with much joy and honour to the church of Santa Croce, the place of the Friars Minor in Florence, and she lies buried in that church, to the

---

54 Monna Gisla (not the servant of the same name), as appears from the prologue.

55 In the light of previous references to Umiliana's *tabula* it seems likely that it was a Byzantine-style icon of Mother and Child rather than a Crucifixion with Mary at the foot of the Cross; if so, *crucifixus* here is simply a synonym for 'Christ'.

praise and glory of our Lord Jesus Christ, who with the Father and the
Holy Spirit lives and reigns for ever, world without end, Amen. We
believe that once separated from the flesh she went at once to the Lord,
without other purgation, as the present writings manifest.[56]

Of her appearances and miracles after her death

After her death, on the vigil of St Mary Magdalen, as I will call it,[57] a
certain lady of upright life was praying and saw the blessed Magdalen
and Umiliana together, with their faces shining. Meditating on God in
this vision she was infused with much grace and experienced the inef-
fable sweetness of God, which she said she had through the merits of
the blessed Umiliana. Another religious woman of holy conversation,
following the path of contemplation, was disturbed because her mind
was obscured by dark clouds and she could not direct her mind to God
as she was accustomed. While she was worrying about this, and was
sleeping, she saw with half-closed eyes the blessed Umiliana, who was
already dead, who came to her and said, 'Rest in the Trinity alone,
dearest'; and so saying, she disappeared, and the religious with much
joy of spirit arose liberated, with her mental perturbation dispelled.

She restored many others from anxieties of this kind to their previous
greater state of grace, which would take a long time to describe: wherefore I leave these and the miracles which God deigned to work thanks
to her prayers to one side; except for column 28 and what follows.[58]

A certain lady was talking with some friends about the deeds of blessed
Umiliana on the Sunday after her death and all at once began to think
about Christ. The heaven was opened to her and she saw the Son of
God and the Blessed Virgin on his right, clad in white, and the blessed
Umiliana at their feet, kneeling in prayer before them and also dressed
in white. This vision was so firmly impressed on her imaginative faculty
that it did not fade from her memory before the feast of blessed Francis
[4 October].

She visited Sister Sobilia after her death, appearing in her cell, beside her
bed; holding her hands cross-wise on her breast, in her usual manner,

---

56 This forceful comment is substantiated by the following account of visions in the
period immediately after Umiliana's death.

57 That is, on 21 July; Papebroch explains the parenthesis by saying that the Magdalen's
feast, 22 July, is celebrated without a vigil.

58 Papebroch explains this as a cross-reference in the manuscript to the story of Gisla
of Mugello (above, p. 113)

and on bended knee, she called to her, saying, 'Lady Sobilia.' Sobilia asked her many things, for example whether she had suffered punishment after her death, and about Fra Michele. She told her a great deal, which Sister Sobilia did not relate to us; what she did tell us that she heard from her is here, that is, that she had not had anything to do in purgatory and that so unspeakable were the delights of the consolation which she constantly had that they could not be imagined by mortals. Fra Michele was soon to leave this world for the glory of God, but not at Florence. When she had said these and other things she disappeared in splendour, for she was of wonderful splendour and beauty.

A certain religious person, of holy life and honourable conversation, an intimate and follower of the saint and a confidante of her secrets, wanted to know about her glorious state, and by dint of much prayer obtained the concession that the Almighty would reveal it to her. While she prayed, all at once the blessed Umiliana appeared to her, clad in white and crowned with a double diadem. Her raiment was white, with purple about her hands and arms, and her shoulders and neck were fringed with varied and wonderful work, for there were tassels of reddish purple wonderfully interwoven with gold and she had a golden fringe, fuller than the others, around her breasts. The diadems differed from each other: one was of three colours, red, white and green,[59] shining seven times more brightly than the sun, clasped by three fine sapphires on the top, which glowed and sparkled indescribably, and otherwise adorned with shining green gems. The other diadem was white, shining all over and made of the most beautiful gems. Her hair was long and yellow and seemed not to be hair so much as the finest spun gold. Her face was angelic and beautiful, radiating rays of more than sunlight. She had shining eyes, whose brilliance surpassed that of the stars. From her mouth there proceeded a fragrance which filled the whole place with sweetness. She had pipes in her mouth, which looked like honeycomb, and on these she played the sweetest melodies; from her mouth two sayings were heard, that is, 'There is nothing besides Christ's love' and 'We run to the fragrance of your ointments',[60] the sweetness of which cannot well be expressed.

Her virgin crown had its own various voices, saying different things. One said, 'Come O bride of Christ, receive the crown which the Lord

---

59 Emblematic respectively of Love, Faith and Hope, the three spiritual virtues; Beatrice appears to Dante arrayed in them (Dante, *Purgatorio*, 30, lines 31–3).

60 This allusion is to the Song of Solomon 1:3, 'Trahe me, post te curremus in odorem unguentorum tuorum'; it occurs also in the Life of Zita (below, p. 165).

has prepared for you'; another, 'Come my chosen one, come my dove, come my precious, come to your coronation.' The other crown, as the reward of chastity, had its different voices, which all in unison said, 'Blessing and praise be to my God and Lord.' Seeing all this, the religious was amazed to no small degree by the pomps with which she saw the saint adorned, and said, 'Umiliana, what is this that I see? You are crowned as if with the crown of virginity.' She replied and said, 'My Lord has done this for me, because of the sorrow which I have always borne in my heart for the virginity which I lost through matrimony.' And when she was asked about the other crown which she wore, she replied, 'This has been given me because of the faithful chastity which I preserved inviolate for my Lord.' Asked what the beauty of her face and the brilliance of her eyes signified, she said, 'That is the purity of conscience which I possess.' She was asked about her garment and the fringes adorned with purple and gold, and said, 'The whiteness of the dress is humility, and good works performed in charity; the purple of the fringe, which is ruddy, designates the martyrdom which I bore in my mind, and the warmth of the desire I felt to see the Blessed Virgin in her beauty'; and shortly afterwards she disappeared.

On one occasion the blessed Umiliana appeared to Gisla of Mugello, a thoroughly religious woman, while she slept, with great joy and brilliance in her face, saying, 'Do not neglect to do penance; for because I had fully done penance, I foreknew my death twelve days before, and passed through purgatory as innocent children do.' A certain woman of Florence called Cecilia, on the day after the Saturday when the blessed Umiliana died, was standing in prayer, not asleep but fully awake, and saw the heavens open and the blessed Umiliana accompanied by an angel in the air, and through the opening she saw our Saviour raised on the image of the cross, descending with a certain most beautiful creature. The four joined together in the air, and entered the court of heaven with rejoicing, in the year of our Lord 1246.

Perhaps eight days after the death of Umiliana, a certain Friar Minor asked the Lord that he would show him something of the glory of the aforementioned saint. He was not asleep, but awake, and before the altar he saw many beautiful thrones, and some there were more beautiful than others, and among these thrones were the souls of the saints, and in the midst sat the blessed Umiliana on one of them; and many of them were empty.

We have written these things about the life and death of the blessed Umiliana, faithfully and truthfully though simply, in the year of our

Lord 1246,[61] as we have seen them with our own eyes and heard them with our own ears, and as the witnesses above-mentioned saw and heard them from her. I leave it to the wiser and more prudent to correct and faithfully emend them for us. Let the corrector, however, be careful what he adds or takes away, and above all that he does not alter what the witnesses said, or substitute things doubtful for things certain by changing the sense.

61 See comments above on the date of the Life.

IV: ANDREA GALLERANI OF SIENA (d. 1251)

The rather brief anonymous Life of the Sienese Andrea Gallerani (which is all we have) was to all appearances composed with a local and immediate audience in view. Much of it could very well have been delivered as a sermon; the reader may choose to test this proposition by reading the translation aloud with appropriate gestures. It certainly begins with a bang. A preacher whose audience was expecting to hear about a saint did not often have the opportunity to begin with his subject's exile for homicide.[1] The fanciful tale which immediately follows has Andrea (and his horse) swept up into the sky on a cloud and should have served to maintain interest. The anonymous Dominican who was the presumable author gave his audience a little bit of everything: exemplary stories which might inspire imitation and outright wonders which could scarcely do so; familiar scriptural quotations ('He who humbles himself shall be exalted [Matthew 25:12]'); and even a touch of elementary Aristotelian philosophy ('Any particular thing is perfect when it has attained its final end'). The miracles display similar variety, combining accounts of cures of mundane ailments which any audience would have recognised with pure Hollywood hokum, such as the story of the sailors who were rescued not only from shipwreck but from eight galley-loads of Saracen pirates, all of whom they killed.

The Life is organised in sections around the six virtues which the saint exemplified, each explicitly and formulaically linked to the next as if to keep the unfolding design clear in the minds of the audience, and each including illustrative wonders performed by the saint or on his behalf. The final section, on Andrea's humility, leads into an exposition of his miracles, which were the reward of that humility. The *Acta sanctorum* text adopts a division into three chapters which cuts across this structure, but it was acknowledged by the Bollandist editor that this was not the arrangement of the 'ancient manuscript', and he prints the twenty-four original rubrics at the end of his introductory commentary. These have been reintroduced into the present translation at the points where they seem most obviously to belong; eighteen of them are devoted to the miracles.

The Life is in no sense a full or sequential record of Andrea's life and is largely devoid of factual content. It seems to presuppose the existence of a fuller source of information, available to the author but no longer extant. The reader would look here in vain for any account of the saint's foundation of the Misericordia, the charitable society for which he was above all remembered by his fellow-

---

1 Thompson suggests that Andrea's victim was a blasphemer (*Cities of God*, p. 196), but this is not apparent from the Life.

citizens and in which Pier Pettinaio was enrolled a little later in the century.[2] It is only incidentally that we learn that he developed a medical specialism, which is treated as an expression of his charity. Apart from the bald statement that he was noble, nothing is said about his family background, which was doubt-less familiar to those who were likely to hear or read about him. In common with many other Italian urban notables, the Gallerani had extensive commer-cial interests and lent money to the commune. They were probably associ-ated with Corsignano in the *contado*; perhaps it was from properties there that Andrea obtained the grain which he had made into bread for the poor. That he should have been involved in feuds with members of other similar families is in itself scarcely surprising, that he proved to have leanings towards mendicant piety scarcely more so. The Dominicans of Siena, above all at the instigation of Ambrogio Sansedoni, were particularly active in recruiting the laity into various forms of pious activity.[3]

Because the saint's miracles were incorporated into the Life, they are translated here. They were explicitly abbreviated from a 'little book' in which they had originally been recorded at greater length. The author explained that he had done this so as to avoid tedium not only for hearers (as if these had priority in his intentions) but for readers. The miracles have illustrative value as covering the conventional range. They include cures of various afflictions including demonic possession, deliverance from prison and shipwreck, and punishments of incredulity. Of the fifty-four miracles recorded the majority took place after the making of a vow (*emisso voto*), but only fourteen of them occurred actually at the shrine.

In this respect, Andrea was participating in a thirteenth-century trend. In the earlier medieval period it had been normal for the majority of cures to occur at or near the shrine; after 1200 it was increasingly common for the shrine to be visited only after the cure or other deliverance was obtained. Usually the cure was triggered by a vow to make the pilgrimage and an offering in case of success.[4] One of Andrea's miracles took place even though no vow had been made. Yet his clients did not have far to come to his tomb. Although there is usually no indication of their places of origin, which may well have been among the information that was omitted by the author from his source-book, it is permissible to infer that with few exceptions they were local people, perhaps even limited to the Camporeggio neighbourhood in which the Dominican church stood or to the *terzo di Camollia*, the Sienese district of which it formed a part. That might be inferred from the fact that one exception is specifically described as living in the *terzo di San Martino*, another of the urban divisions. Others included a handful delivered from captivity or shipwreck, a nun of

2 Waley, *Siena and the Sienese*, p. 146.

3 A 'Gallerani widow who died a Franciscan tertiary' also left five pounds to the Dominicans: Waley, *Siena and the Sienese*, p. 147. Waley's other references to the Gallerani mostly come from the period after Andrea's lifetime. For Ambrogio Sanse-doni, see above, p. 29.

4 For a brief discussion see D. Webb, *Medieval European pilgrimage* (Basingstoke, 2002), pp. 58–64.

Grosseto (one of the principal cities in Siena's dependent territory) and a deaf man at Bagni di Vitriolo in the *contado* (it was he who made no vow).

We may plausibly conclude that, whether it consisted of 'hearers' or 'readers', the audience for the Life was familiar with the basic facts of the saint's life and background, including his links with the Dominicans. A woman who had left her son 'broken' in bed at home heard 'Brother Ambrogio' preaching about Andrea's miracles and obtained a cure for her son by making a vow to the saint; the writer does not think it necessary to explain who Brother Ambrogio (undoubtedly Sansedoni) was. Andrea sometimes intervened to protect members of the Dominican order. On two occasions the custodians of his tomb suffered severe injuries – one while arranging the wax offerings above the tomb – and were cured by his intercession. A lay brother *(converso)* was tempted by the devil to leave the order but was delivered when he contemplated some dust from the tomb.

In March 1274 Bishop Bernardo of Siena (himself perhaps a Gallerani) granted the indulgence for visitors to the tomb on the Monday after Palm Sunday, the first landmark in Andrea's cult.[5] With the death of Ambrogio Sansedoni fifteen years later in 1289, the Sienese Dominicans acquired a saint who was a full member of the order and in addition had played a prominent role in Sienese public life. Ambrogio was a serious candidate for canonisation, which was possibly frustrated only by the death of Pope Honorius IV, who showed interest in his cause. While Ambrogio remained essentially a Sienese saint, he benefited from his professional religious standing to become more widely known across the networks of the order of Preachers. Andrea was a much smaller fish, but his memory was maintained locally by the brethren. A confraternity in the name of the Crucified Christ, the Virgin and the Blessed Andrea, which met in the oratory below the Preachers' dormitory, was founded in 1344 and continued to flourish.

In the longer term, Gallerani was best remembered by the confraternity he had founded. On 8 June 1347 the rector and brothers of 'the religious house of St Mary of Mercy of the poor of Siena' petitioned the *Consiglio Generale* on behalf of their saint. His good works and posthumous miracles were, they said, matters of common knowledge which it was not necessary to expound at length. It would be greatly to the honour of the city if his festivity were to be publicly celebrated; he had been both a citizen and 'of such noble birth'. They therefore asked that his traditional feast-day, that is the Monday following Palm Sunday, should be publicly observed so as to secure his intercession for the city. Siena was rich in native saints, and the rector and brethren were doubtless well aware that the supporters of other holy men, Ambrogio Sansedoni and Pier Pettinaio among them, had not been backward in securing public patronage of their cults.[6]

Andrea had the distinction of being commemorated in an early example of Sienese panel painting, a small altarpiece of about 1280 from San Domenico,

5 *AS*, March, 3, p. 49.

6 Siena, Archivio di Stato, Consiglio Generale 140, fol. 42; D. Webb, *Patrons and defenders: the saints in the Italian city states* (London, 1996), pp. 277–87.

now in the Sienese Pinacoteca.[7] One panel shows him distributing alms with an assistant, another praying before a crucifix with a rosary (an aid to devotion popularised by the Dominicans) in his hand. Henk van Os has suggested, in illustration of the pious extravagances to which lay adherents of the mendicants were prone, that Andrea is depicted with a rope looped around his neck and attached to a beam in the ceiling, so that if he nodded off during his prayers he would hang himself.[8] Apart from the fact that he is in fact shown kneeling down, which would diminish the risk somewhat, this interpretation does not square with the more prosaic account which is given in the Life. Here it is stated that he fixed the rope to his *hair*; the discomfort he would experience if he fell asleep would be sharp but hardly fatal. For all his ecstasies, Andrea was a practical man.

The Life of Andrea Gallerani

There was in the city of Siena a noble man called Andrea, distinguished for conduct and honour, who originated from the noble family of the Gallerani. Not only do those who lived with him bear trustworthy witness to his laudable life, but the miracles which occurred both before his death and more frequently afterwards, and which still continue, attest the merits of his extraordinary sanctity. He was sent into exile by the *podestà* of Siena for a homicide which he had committed. Returning to the city by night from the Maremma[9] with his brother, he saw a cloud which, suddenly emerging from under a mill, snatched him, with the horse he was riding, from the sight of his brother and carried him through the air for about the space of three miles, his brother following and lamenting his loss with mournful and fearful groans. The man of God however fortified himself by calling upon the Virgin and did not cease to call upon her devoutly until at length, by her merits, he was safely restored to earth. And since to those who love God everything works for the good, the holy man understood this as the beginning of his vocation, that is, that he must avert his mind from earthly things and give himself over to heavenly contemplation, devoutly serving him who had called him from the shadows of this world into his wondrous light. This he fulfilled with foreseeing and pure eagerness; thenceforth he renounced the world and its pomps, dedicated himself totally to Christ and became distinguished for virtues by means of which,

7 Illustrated in Vauchez, *Sainthood*, pl. 21.

8 *The art of devotion in the late middle ages in Europe, 1300–1500* (London, 1994), p. 61.

9 *Maritima*: as its name suggests, a region of the Sienese territory south and west of the city and bordering on the sea.

ruling himself and dedicated to the benefit of Christians, he conformed himself happily to God; fleeing from death, thirsting for life, he was not afraid to enter on the path of life. He was full of compassion, forward in benevolence, assiduous in prayer, prompt in love, perfect in holiness, lowly in humility.

Of his compassion

This holy man was full of fellow-feeling, displaying bowels of compassion for the afflicted; the suffering of the wretched tormented him more than it did the wretched themselves. Once he encountered a poor person who had a swollen leg which was almost entirely rotten; because of his poverty he could not find a surgeon. When the man of God realised this, in his simplicity he applied a poultice, and at once the man was entirely healed. Here God clearly shows that, although he permits the suffering of pain, he was unwilling to permit the affliction of his beloved, who was so great a refuge for the afflicted. He diligently sought out the infirm and the suffering, visiting and consoling them, exhorting them to patience. One day when he was returning from the *contado* he came upon a lone woman in labour, and moved by pity he served her as a midwife, doing everything perfectly.

It happened once that his brother in a fit of temper threw a key into a window-seat where there were the phials in which the holy man kept potions of various kinds which he took to the sick; as a result the phials were completely shattered. When the holy man realised this, he remained unperturbed and going to the window found the phials unharmed. Here God clearly shows how acceptable his works of mercy were to him. When the blessed man was humbly and devoutly intent on his works of mercy, it often happened that, absorbed in the service of the poor, he was unable to return to his own house before the bells had ceased to ring.[10] Everyone in his household was enraged by this, and they were unwilling to open the door to him when he did come back. He put up with this patiently, devoutly and humbly. As his maid-servant relates, he prostrated himself in prayer before the closed doors and shortly afterwards, like the Saviour, found them open. And because that is true compassion that manifests itself in works for the relief of suffering, so the second virtue follows fitly upon the first: that is the benevolence of the helper.

10 That is, at nightfall to signal that people should no longer be out in the streets. Pier Pettinaio was once discovered by the Sienese watch out after hours; see below, p. 224.

Of the benevolence of the helper in action

Second was the benevolence of the helper; for it was his continual
concern to bring help to the wretched and to relieve want. One evening
he brought a bushel of flour to the house for the poor.[11] Having heated
the water, he called his maidservant, so that he should not miss matins.
She rose and made the bread, and the man of God knocked it back
and divided it. The dough did not give out, although at another time
so many loaves could not have been made from three bushels. The
woman was wearied by this; when she enquired and learned from him
that it was one bushel of flour, she realised that this had come about
through the merits of the man of God. Once when he wanted to take
wine which he made specially for the sick the maid found that it had all
gone; hearing this, the blessed Andrea went to the barrel and when he
made the sign of the cross, it flowed abundantly, filling the barrel by
divine power, and he sustained the poor from it for a long time. This
also happened several times with the bread: when the store was empty
and the maid had nothing to give the needy, on his approach it was
divinely replenished.

One day when it was time for the midday meal and the weather was
wet and snowy, the man of God said to his servants, 'Get ready – I'm
going to Santa Petronilla, to take them alms.' They marvelled at this
and tried to dissuade him, but he went and returned before they had
completed the preparations. Looking at and touching his clothes, which
were not in the least damp, they realised that an angel had taken him
there and back, unharmed by the rain. The same thing happened several
times when by divine inspiration he went for the same reason to Monte
Cellesio and other places; God wanted thus to make it known to all how
much he welcomed his works of mercy.[12] And because one comes to the
contemplative by way of the active, the third virtue follows befittingly,
that is his promptness in prayer, by means of which his mind flew to the
summit of contemplation from the field of action.

Of his promptness in prayer

There follows the third virtue, that is his promptness in prayer. He
devoted such passionate mental attention to prayer that, dismissing

11 'Bushel' here translates *sextarium*; see above, p. 99.
12 Santa Petronilla and Monte Cellesio were both communities of nuns: *AS*, March, 3,
    p. 54.

all other concerns, he concentrated on this alone, bodily intent on the contemplation of his Creator's countenance. He poured forth pious and miserable groans on account not only of any offences he had committed against God but of the lost condition of the human race, and also out of love for his homeland, which he felt keenly. The rivers of his eyes flowed as an acceptable sacrifice to God, to the extent that when he rose from prayer, the ground where he had been was found to be damp, as if water had flowed there in abundance. What he thus sowed in tears, he afterwards reaped in exultation. Always, if he could, between day and night, he devoutly recited fifty Paternosters and as many Ave Marias; if his work with the poor permitted, he added three times the number with great fervour. And so that he might pray more devoutly and with greater attention, he attached a cord to his hair, lest sleep intruded any interruption into the fervour of his prayer.

He devoted himself to the service of the glorious Virgin with special reverence, and out of love always hailed her as Lady. The Virgin responded to his merits not only at home but even on the road when she appeared to him. Often when the women who lived opposite the holy man rose for matins, they saw the place where he prayed radiating an immense splendour. Marvelling at this, they told the blessed Andrea's maidservant and asked her why there was such a light in the night. The maid said she knew nothing about it, but she took careful note of what had been said and on the following night rose at the hour they had mentioned and saw in the light of dawn a most beautiful lady, talking sweetly with the holy man. When she asked him the following day whether it had been the glorious Virgin, he said 'Yes', but warned her that before his death she should not tell anyone. And because the understanding is illuminated in prayer and the affections are inflamed to grasp it, the fourth follows very suitably, that is the love of charity.

Of the love of God and neighbour

Here follows the fourth, that is, the love of charity, whereby he loved God and his neighbour with sincere affection. With what affection did he love his neighbour, who totally devoted himself to the service of his neighbours? He impressed on all the counsels of holiness, in all things showing himself the mirror of honour. With what purity he loved God! Nothing except the thought of God delighted him. And since it is befitting that the beloved should visit his lover, Christ once came to him in the shape of a pilgrim, urgently asking to be given shelter. When his brother repulsed him and displayed great irritation, he brought him into his own room and securely locked the door. In the morning he went to bring him forth, but opening the room he found no one inside and understood that it had been he who said, 'If anyone loves me he will keep my counsel, and I will come to him and make my dwelling with him.'

One day when he was on his way to matins, certain people tried to ambush and kill him. As he passed through the midst of them and the chief instigator of the crime urged them to attack, their courage totally failed them. The blessed Andrea perceived this and flung himself humbly at the feet of the instigator, saying that he should freely do whatever he wished. At these words the other not only drew back from his intended wickedness but humbly begged pardon for what he had done. Whence it clearly appears that God would not suffer the holy man, who expended such a wealth of piety and charity on his neighbours, to be injured by them.

One day when he was still an exile, he entered the city secretly and hid himself in a certain tower-house. This did not escape the *podestà*, who at once sent his officers to arrest him. They were looking for the key to the tower, when the door opened without any key and the man of God emerged unseen and escaped unharmed in the presence of the bystanders. God had foreknown him as the minister of his election and very soon his most worthy confessor. And because the holy of holies alone is loved by the holy, wherefore he himself said, 'Be ye therefore holy as I am holy', the fifth well follows, that is, his eminence in holiness.

Of the excellence of his sanctity

There follows the fifth, that is his eminence in holiness; he was a saint because he was totally dedicated to the divine service; a saint, because he was firmly founded in the law of God; a saint, because he was totally cleansed of all uncleanness. He conformed himself to God with such rectitude that, conforming in all things to the divine will, he completed all his works according to his rule. He was strengthened by such constancy that no temptation could impede him in any good work, no adversity, contumely or injury move him to impatience. So perfect was his cleanness and simplicity that he shrank not merely from committing any uncleanness or dishonesty, but from even thinking of it. And because sanctity is free of all uncleanness and perfect in its immaculate cleanness, and because everything is perfect when it achieves its ultimate purpose, so the Blessed Virgin summoned this man, perfected in sanctity, to be joined to her Son, in the church of San Cristoforo. One day he was devoutly praying in San Cristoforo before the altar of San Biagio and with the doors closed. The priests and clerks who were in the sacristy heard him engaged in a delightful conversation. Emerging in order to spy out the speaker, they saw Our Lady, radiant with splendour, who at once disappeared. The man of God went home and was soon seized by a fever. Summoning his maidservant to cover him up, he said that he would die at vespers on the Lord's Day, as the blessed Virgin had foretold to him and as the event proved. It was fitting that he should give us so clear an indication of his sanctity, whereby the fame of his virtues was increased and we, inflamed by devotion as a result, should by his merits obtain from the Lord forgiveness and grace in the present and glory in the future. And because the higher the grade of perfection, the more dangerous the fall, as pride very frequently arises from it (which, as it is called the root of all vices, so it is the destruction of virtue), there fitly follows the sixth [virtue], that is the lowliness of humility.

Of the humility of his life and his exalted death

There follows the sixth virtue, that is the lowliness of humility. He was most resplendent for this virtue, by which the others are conserved.[13] He entirely despised the world and worldly vanities, but spurned nobody except himself, caring not at all if he was spurned by others. Therefore he was passionately devoted to those works which were open to contempt and insult, desiring to serve and not to be served, being founded thus in humility and following the footsteps of his Saviour, who humbled himself, and also of the glorious Virgin, whose humility, as St Bernard says, was more pleasing to the Creator than her virginity. His body he humbled as much as he could by fasting, and he wore poor and common garments.

And as it is spoken by the mouth of truth that he who humbles himself shall be exalted, it is appropriate that he who so humbled himself in life should be exalted in death by fit and novel marvels. It is related with no little wonder that in the very hour when as he foretold he rendered up his spirit, his face was seen to shine like snow, covered with fragrant flowers. Here God clearly shows how he loved him in

13 For humility as the guardian of all the virtues see pp. 178, 220 below.

the odour of sanctity, for he had displayed the odour of praiseworthy fame while he lived. A certain knight, whose eyes had for a long time been oozing humours, saw his body from a window of his palace, as it was carried to the church of the Friars Preachers in Camporeggio, where out of devotion he had chosen to be buried, and was by his merits completely cured. There were other miracles, by which the Lord made his saint marvellous and exalted him, and still does not cease to do so. The tongue cannot relate them, the hand is insufficient to convey them with the pen of memory. But let us see, in order, a few of the many. Although when an event is to be reported it is more fully and carefully examined in detail, because the prolixity of speech burdens and wearies the minds not only of hearers but of readers I shall report them in brief, leaving their full exposition to the little book in which they were first entered at length.

The faithful should note with the utmost devotion how many and how great are the miracles which have been manifested through the merits of this saint. To many, burdened by various illnesses, he has completely restored their health; he has given sight to the blind, hearing to the deaf, speech to the dumb, mobility to the lame, the power of action to the crippled, the offices of reason to the insane, the security of liberation to the possessed, a way out to the imprisoned, safe refuge to the storm-tossed, even, on several occasions, the gift of life to the dead. To these examples which have been witnessed others which have been reliably reported have been rightly added.[14]

How he liberated many from various diferent afflictions

Someone called Jacopo was at his last gasp [*in extremis*] thanks to a continual fever and a severe constriction of his chest, and it was firmly believed that he would die that evening. Monna Maria, his grandmother, made a vow to the blessed Andrea, and he was soon completely relieved by his merits.

Someone called Bartolomeo was suffering a continual fever with an abscess; his mother made a vow to the blessed Andrea, and he was completely cured of the fever.

A boy called Albrizino was *in extremis* with a continual fever and was believed to be as good as dead. When his mother made a vow to blessed

---

14 'Witnessed' here designates miracles which had been officially recorded with the names of witnesses.

Andrea he was entirely restored to health.

Someone called Benvenuta was suffering a tertian fever. Once, when she felt her temperature rising, she made a vow to blessed Andrea, and the fever at once receded, leaving her completely cured.

Someone called Bilia suffered a quartan fever for seven months; making a vow to blessed Andrea, she was completely cured.

Someone called Olliente had for a long time suffered from an ulcer in her breast which at length turned into a fistula. She had no medical help, but she made a vow to blessed Andrea, and was cured; the swollen part which had remained there because of the medications promptly shrank.

Someone called Boccabella suffered from a swelling of her stomach for six months and as a result lost all bodily strength; she made a vow to blessed Andrea and was entirely cured.

Someone called Gilia suffered quotidian and tertian fevers for twelve weeks; having made a vow, she was restored to her previous state of health before the holy man's tomb.

Someone called Bellino suffered intolerable pain for six months and was completely restored to health when he made a vow to blessed Andrea.

Someone called Sobilia was afflicted for three months with pain in her head and other ailments all over her body, which the doctors judged to be paralytic; in desperation she humbly made a vow to the man of God, Andrea, and by his merits was soon restored to health in all respects.

Somebody called Bartoluccio suffered a flow of blood from his mouth for seven days on end; he made a vow to blessed Andrea and was at once completely cured.

A certain boy had a bladder which was so inflamed that the doctors called it ruptured. His mother made a vow to St Andrea and he received a complete cure.

Someone called Lombarda had suffered the falling sickness [epilepsy] for a year; making a vow to the holy man, she was completely cured.

Fra Oliverio, a lay brother of the order of Preachers before he entered the order, was guarding the tomb of the man of God and by chance stumbled on a nail, which pierced his foot in a sinewy place, from the lower part upwards; because of this he humbled himself in prayer to God's saint and the same evening was completely cured.

Someone called Clarissima involuntarily and compulsively shook her head; when she made a vow to the saint of God, she knew that she was freed by his merits.

Someone by the name of Gemma had eaten poisoned food and as a result felt herself close to death; making a vow to blessed Andrea she was at once cured.

Someone called Francesco was afflicted with an intolerable colic; when his grandmother made a vow to blessed Andrea he obtained full health.

A little boy, childlike, put a fragment of a pottery vessel into his mouth, which stuck in his throat, and, without any remedy because of the pain, he was thought already to have given up the ghost. His mother, Parrosina, saw this and fell to the ground unconscious, but women of the neighbourhood vowed him to blessed Andrea, and he immediately ejected the fragment and was restored to his previous state of health.

Someone called Bullietto was bothered for twelve days with a pain in his throat, so that he could neither speak nor take nourishment without great difficulty. He was carried to St Andrea's tomb and fully restored to health.

A certain nun at Grosseto was paralysed, but her abbess had a piece of St Andrea's garments as a relic; by rubbing herself with this, the nun was restored to health.

A certain girl, on the second day of Holy Week, fell twenty *brachia* to the ground from an upper chamber, as her mother had dreamed the previous night; a neighbour, seeing this, commended her to blessed Andrea and through his merits she suffered no harm.[15]

Someone who was fixing a stake in a vineyard dashed his face against another stake and saw his eye ripped out and fallen to the ground; he made a vow to blessed Andrea, and it was soon relocated in his head as before.

A certain woman, hearing Brother Ambrogio preach about the miracles of the man of God, vowed her son, whom she had left collapsed in bed, to blessed Andrea, and when she returned found him completely recovered.

---

15 If a *brachium* (literally, an arm's length) was anything like a metre or a yard in length, the girl fell a long way. This story is retold in more detail below, p. 156.

Of the restoration of sight

Someone called Ghiberto, who was mocking the sanctity of the man of God, was suddenly deprived of his sight. Repenting of his malice he returned, pierced to the heart, and humbling himself to blessed Andrea sought pardon; by whose merits he fully received the gift of sight.[16]

Someone called Bonamente, who for a long time had suffered from an eye complaint and for three months had entirely lost his sight, made a vow and visited blessed Andrea's tomb and was completely cured.

Someone called Paolo could see nothing with one eye and a little with the other; when he made a vow he obtained the gift of sight in full.

Of the restoration of hearing

Someone called Grissolina, who had suffered from deafness for a long time, made a vow to blessed Andrea and completely received her hearing.

At Bagni di Vitriolo, someone called Panerio Rustici, who had been deaf from birth, had a vision in the night (he had not made a vow) that the man of God Andrea came to him and, taking saliva, put it in his ears. In the morning he found himself completely restored.

Of the cure of speech

Someone called Matteo had lost his speech for eight months. He spent the night before the tomb of the man of God and soon received the accustomed use of speech.

Someone called Cambio could not speak for three days; his brother made a vow to blessed Andrea, and he was able to speak as before.

Of the gaining of movement

Someone called Romana was suffering in her knees, legs and feet and could not walk. She made a vow to blessed Andrea and was entirely restored to health.

16 There is at least one scoffer in almost every miracle collection.

Someone called Jacopo had withered legs and could not walk; when he was borne to the tomb of the man of God he promptly improved and at length was completely cured.

Someone called Scialunga had been crippled for five years, so that she could not walk, or only a little around the house, crawling on her hands; she made a vow to blessed Andrea and was cured to the extent that she visited his tomb without a stick or any assistance.

Of the relief of crippling conditions

Someone called Matteo had such severe pains and gout, and also a hand so badly crippled, that he could not work; but when he made a vow to blessed Andrea he obtained his health in all respects.

Someone who was deformedly bent visited the holy man's tomb and stayed there devoutly for a cure and was completely relieved of this deformity.

Someone called Adalascia had twisted arms; she made a vow to blessed Andrea and received her health completely.

The nephew of someone called Marchigiares was crippled in his arms, legs and feet, but when his aunt made a vow to blessed Andrea he was entirely restored to health.

Concerning liberation from demons

Someone called Berta was insane. Coming to the tomb of the man of God, she soon began to get better and at length was fully cured.

Someone called Guido had become entirely mad, but one evening he made a vow to blessed Andrea. He began to improve in the morning and afterwards received his health in full.

Someone called Cittadina was cruelly vexed by a demon; liberated before the tomb of the man of God, she was sent home.

Someone who was troubled by a demon devoutly stayed by the tomb of the man of God. The demon left him unwillingly, saying only that the bells would not ring on his departure to hail the miracle, for as he left he would break the tongue of the bell completely, and so the event proved, for giving up and leaving him free, he broke the tongue in his rage.

Concerning liberation from prison

Someone called Pietro Baroni was captured in the battle at Montalcino and made a vow for his liberation to God's saint.[17] That evening he saw someone approaching the man who had captured him and asking him whether he was taking him to prison. He replied, 'Yes', and the other told him that in no way would he do that, and thus he let his captive go, knowing and believing that his liberator was indeed the holy man.

Someone called Uguccione of Ischia, when he was in prison, made a vow to the man of God and shortly afterwards found a nail with which he made a way out of the prison; but as it was the hour of rest, so as not to be heard he asked for rough weather and a storm blew up, so that everyone got out of the prison and none of the guards heard.

Concerning the stilling of the waves

Someone was in mortal peril from a stormy sea when he remembered the miracles and merits of the man of God and most devoutly commended himself to him. In response to his vow the storm was completely quenched by act of God.

Some people at sea were in imminent peril from a storm. One side of the ship was already broken and they were beginning to sink, with the inrush of water and the buffeting of the winds, when they heard a voice exhorting them to commend themselves devoutly to blessed Andrea. Hearing this, everyone tearfully invoked his help and soon saw the man of God sitting at the masthead, holding a lighted candle. At his appearance the tempest ceased, and with a favourable wind they sailed forty miles that night and came to the port they had most wished for. But when they were on their way back, the ship was becalmed and boarded by eight pirate galleys. All those on board were in shackles down below, with the Saracens on deck; but the captives remembered benefits received and again vowed themselves to the man of God. Once the vow was made their shackles were released; going on deck they

17 Montalcino was a little town subject to the Sienese but frequently threatened by Florentine aggression: an attack on Montalcino preceded the battle of Montaperti, on 4 September 1260, in which the Sienese Ghibellines, aided by troops of Manfred of Sicily, achieved an unexpected and overwhelming victory over the Guelfs of Tuscany, headed by the Florentines: Waley, *Siena and the Sienese*, pp. 115–17, 164. One of the first Sienese actions in the aftermath of the victory was to exact the submission of Montalcino, and it seems likely that this was the context for this miracle.

discovered the Saracens enveloped in a deep sleep and killed them all, taking possession of their galleys and their goods.

Of the resuscitation of the dead

Someone called Baroncello had died but, when his wife Landa and his daughter Ganna made a vow to the blessed Andrea for the revival and cure of the dead man, he was restored to life and health through the merits of the holy man.

Someone called Cecco, out of sorrow for his brother, whom he saw dead, gave up the ghost and was judged to be dead both by the doctors and by others; his mother however most devoutly recommending him to blessed Andrea, soon had him back alive.

A little boy had already lost sense and motion and seemed to be quite dead; but his mother, called Imelda, made a vow to blessed Andrea and at once he opened his eyes and vomited forth a long red worm with two heads; then he began to get up and was completely cured.

A certain young man was horribly trampled by a horse which ran wild and was believed to be dead or certainly about to die very shortly; but someone who witnessed the trampling made a vow to blessed Andrea and he was entirely restored to life and health.

Of a noble girl miraculously saved from death

There was a certain noble lady in the city of Siena who received a great benefit from the prayers of blessed Andrea. She said that on the night of Palm Sunday she had the following dream: that her little girl fell headlong from the window of a house. She awoke terrified from the dream and most devoutly commended her daughter to blessed Andrea. The [next] day, when the faithful begin to celebrate the feast of blessed Andrea, this lady's daughter was in a very tall house, and it happened that she fell through a window and plunged to the ground, making the dream reality. Seeing her fall, a certain woman tearfully and loudly invoked the saint's aid thus, 'Holy Andrea, holy Andrea, help her.' What a marvel! When the girl reached the ground, she landed so lightly and gently that no damage to her body could be detected by the doctor or anybody else. This came about by divine dispensation in testimony of blessed Andrea's sanctity; he who imitated his Master in his worthy life was also his imitator by right of miracle, to the glory and honour of him who miraculously raised the High Priest's daughter from the dead.

Of a certain novice lay brother delivered from the temptation to leave the order

A novice, a lay brother in the convent of the Friars Preacher of Siena, was oppressed by such powerful temptations by the enemy of the human race that he was firmly resolved to leave the order. He had in his possession some dust in a carefully bound booklet, collected at some time from the tomb on which the casket with the body of the holy man had stood. As he devoutly contemplated it, the enemy's threat and the temptation to leave the order promptly disappeared. Protected by the prayers of the glorious confessor Andrea and confirmed in the order, he was found worthy, during his novitiate, to be delivered from the burden of bodily weakness; to the praise of him who does not allow his faithful to be tempted beyond their power, but strengthens them and enables them to win manfully the battles of temptation.

Of testimony to the sanctity of blessed Andrea

A certain smith in the city of Siena, in the *terziere* of San Martino, entirely disbelieved in the sanctity of blessed Andrea. Wanting proof of his supreme sanctity, he threw a scrap of his garment into the fire; if it happened not to be burnt up by the flames, he would have no more doubts about the holiness of the saint. Wonderful! Three times he did this and the scrap remained as unharmed as if it had never touched the coals. The sceptic firmly believed in his sanctity, and related this miracle to several people, in honour of him who by his power preserved the three boys unharmed in the fiery furnace.

The same

Then there was what happened to a certain knight called Guelfo, the brother of the man blessed Andrea killed. He was highly indignant that the body of blessed Andrea had been reverently buried in the church of the Friars Preachers, given that he had manifestly committed homicide. Labouring intensely under this indignation, he was seized by divine fear; he came to the brothers' church and with his girdle around his neck, with unshod feet and his bare knees on the earth, he went from the brothers' choir to the saint's tomb, showing such humility and reverence to him that it aroused wondering devotion in the hearts of the bystanders, to the glory and honour of him who converts the enemies of his faithful to peace.

Of a crippled woman delivered in her sleep

A certain woman wonderfully experienced a great benefit in her own person by the merits of blessed Andrea. Her hands and feet were violently contracted, and she was urged by another woman to seek the protection of the blessed confessor Andrea: on her advice, she vowed herself devoutly to him. While sleeping, she saw in a dream blessed Andrea, dressed in a green cloak, emerging from his tomb and going away. Dreaming thus, she saw him return and although she was asleep she began to cry out, saying, 'He's coming back, he's coming back'. As she cried out she awoke and found herself entirely cured.

Of the custodian of his tomb

Senese, the custodian of the saint's tomb, was putting the wax images above the tomb into decent order; these proclaim Andrea's sanctity as displayed in his miracles. His foot slipped and his hand from the lower part upwards was pierced by a nail. He made a vow and fell asleep clinging to the tomb. Blessed Andrea appeared to him while he slept and, exhorting him to take good care of the poor, imprinted the sign of the holy Cross on his hand. Awaking shortly afterwards, he found he was completely cured and there was no scar remaining on his hand; to the honour and glory of him who by the touch of his own immaculate hand miraculously healed the hand of the leper.

Of someone wishing to offer at his feast

A certain man came to the church of the Friars Preacher on the feast of blessed Andrea to offer some gifts out of his devotion. On the day, as a great multitude devoutly flocked to the tomb, this man was afraid of being crushed by the people and stuck his hand out against the crowd which was approaching the tomb. He wanted to defend himself from the crush, but it happened that in the powerful onward rush of the throng his wrist was broken. In unbearable pain and half dead with suffering, he aroused great compassion in the hearts of the bystanders. Coming to himself, he made a vow, begging for a cure; as soon as he had uttered the vow his hand was restored to its former good condition.

Many other marvels are known to have been performed, both in the lifetime of this glorious saint and after his revered death, which have not been registered by the pen; these have been briefly noted to promote his sanctity and to edify the faithful, to the praise and glory of him who alone does great wonders; who, three and one God, lives and reigns for all ages. Amen.

He migrated to God in the year of our Lord 1251 on Sunday after Vespers.

V: ZITA OF LUCCA (d 1278)

The anonymous Life of Zita of Lucca was first published in *Acta sanctorum* in 1673.[1] Daniel Papebroch prepared the text from a manuscript from the ancient Tuscan monastery of Camaldoli, which he admitted to be 'much in need of correction'. He implied that he had collated it with another in the possession of the Fatinelli family of Lucca, whose ancestors (then often called 'Faitinelli') the saint had served as a housekeeper three centuries before. Papebroch called this the 'original' but, while it may well be the oldest manuscript extant, it was copied around 1380, probably some ninety years after the Life was written.[2] In fact he made little use of its text of the Life; its principal value to him was that it contained the only medieval copy of Zita's miracles, which were included in his edition. As a consequence, the numerous deficiencies and lacunae of the Camaldolese manuscript were fixed in print, except where Papebroch amended them (not always correctly) on his own initiative.

One especially creative amendment was that of Zita's date of death, wrongly given in the Camaldolese copy as Wednesday 27 April 1279 (mcclxxviiii). As Papebroch correctly noted, 27 April was not a Wednesday in 1279. The Fatinelli manuscript would have told him that the right year was 1278 (mcclxxviii), when day and date did match, but he convinced himself, by a complicated chain of reasoning, that it was 1272 and thus misled at least parts of posterity.[3] He thus postulated a six-year interval between Zita's death and the inauguration of her cult, as her recorded miracles unquestionably began in April 1278; the Life does not lend much support to this hypothesis.

In 1688 Monsignor Fatinello Fatinelli independently published the Life from his family's manuscript.[4] This edition has been much less widely used than the version in *Acta sanctorum*, but (although it oddly omits the prologue) it provides a considerably better text overall. The present translation is based on a revised text, corrected against the manuscripts, which broadly resembles this edition more closely than it does Papebroch's.[5] The prologue alone gives some measure of the more trivial corrections that the latter requires. On the best manuscript

---

1 *AS*, April, 3, pp. 499–506. The miracles are on pp. 510–27.

2 Now Lucca, Biblioteca Statale, MS 3459, fols 1–19v. The Camaldolese copy is in Florence, Biblioteca Nazionale Centrale, Conventi Soppressi G. 5, 1212, fols 193–200v.

3 *AS*, April, 3, p. 498. The *Oxford dictionary of saints* is one of several works to quote 1272 as Zita's date of death.

4 *Vita beatae Zitae Lucensis ex vetustissimo codice Ms fideliter transumpta* (Ferrara, 1688). The British Library, London, possesses two copies.

5 The present writer hopes to produce a new edition of the Life.

evidence, the author here likens scripture to 'a common fount of health', but Papebroch followed his admittedly rather unclear Camaldolese text in reading the word *sanitatis* as *sanctitatis*, which would require the translation 'common fount of sanctity'. On no apparent authority he emends the 'chaste lives' (*celibes vitae*) of the saints to 'celebrated [*celebres*] lives'. The writer's humble 'lead pipe' (*plumbi fistula*) becomes 'plebeian' (*plebeja*); the words *plumbi fistula* are in fact St Gregory's.

There are few clues to the authorship of the work, but it may well have been written by a canon of San Frediano, the church of regular canons where Zita worshipped and was buried and venerated. It was certainly written by someone with access to the works of St Gregory, principally the *Moralia in Job* and the *Regula pastoralis*, which are quoted freely and without acknowledgement. Many (but by no means all) of these allusions have been identified here, in order to give the reader some sense of the author's way of working.[6] They are mingled with narrative passages which describe Zita's miracles, virtues and good works, her death and the subsequent development of her cult. She is shown somehow managing to uphold traditional contemplative ideals in the midst of her household duties, while her dedication to good works makes a peg on which the author hangs some forceful expressions of the obligations of the wealthy to their poor neighbours, the most forceful being one of his many borrowings from Gregory.

In addition to attracting attention as a specimen of the 'servant saint', Zita has been reckoned among female saints who, although not formally affiliated to any order, 'display links with the mendicants'.[7] The Life gives no indication that she was involved with the friars during her lifetime, but records that the prior of San Frediano consulted with the Dominicans and Franciscans before translating her remains to a stone tomb. It is stranger, in view of the author's concern for the observation of canonical propriety in the veneration of saints, that he fails to mention the bishop of Lucca. A possible reason may be suggested, which may also give a clue to the date of composition of the Life.

Early in the year 1286, eight years after Zita's death, a dispute erupted between the canons of San Frediano and the Lucchese Franciscans, which rumbled on until the canons reluctantly accepted defeat in 1291.[8] Bonagiunta Tignosini, a parishioner of San Frediano, had elected in his will to be buried with the Franciscans, and the canons disputed his right to do so. Their chagrin must have been aggravated if this deserter was the same person as the 'Bonagusta' Tignosini

---

6 For ease of reference I cite Gregory's works simply by book and chapter. There are modern editions in the series *Corpus Christianorum Latinorum* and an old one in *PL*, 75–9.

7 Papi, '*In castro poenitentiae*', p. 120. On the servant-saint see M. Goodich, '*Ancilla Dei*: the servant as saint in the late middle ages', in J. Kirshner and S. F. Wemple (eds), *Women of the medieval world* (Oxford, 1985), pp. 128–30; Papi, 'La serva-patrona', in '*In castro poenitentiae*', pp. 263–303.

8 Documented in V. Tirelli and M. Tirelli Carli (eds), *Le pergamene del convento di S. Francesco in Lucca (secc. XIII–XIX)* (Rome, 1993), pp. 181–278.

who eight years previously had been a witness to one of Zita's miracles.[9] Now he apparently believed that the Franciscan convent was a holier place to be buried. It so happened that the bishop of Lucca at the time, Paganello Paganelli, was the official conservator of the privileges of the Franciscan order in Tuscany, and he sided wholeheartedly with the friars. In March 1286 Pope Honorius IV appointed judges delegate to hear the case between the Franciscans and the canons; one of the issues they had to consider was the bishop's refusal to admit any limits to his authority as conservator.

On 27 April 1286, Zita's feast-day, a miracle was recorded by a notary at San Frediano. The record seems to survive only in the two extant English manuscripts of the Life; none of the Italian copies includes it.[10] During the preceding summer, a small boy in Lucca's dependent countryside had been drowned but revived when his mother invoked Zita and vowed to offer wine and bread equal to his weight at the saint's tomb. Such miracles were the finest of all earthly demonstrations of the divine power, and some importance was evidently attributed to this one, if copies of the Life containing the story circulated as far as England. It is possible that there is a reference to the same incident towards the end of the Life, where the author recalls how, at some indefinite period after Zita's death, he had personally conversed with the father of a boy who had been resuscitated and presented at San Frediano.[11] He does not say that the boy was drowned nor does he mention his mother; at first sight the two stories might not seem to be the same. A third account however suggests that they were.

One of the English manuscripts contains a much abbreviated version of the Life in rhyming Latin couplets, following the same narrative order and devoting one couplet to each incident or episode. At the appropriate place there is a couplet which may be translated: 'A dead only son she restored alive to his father, wine measured to the son by the mother's vow he handed over.' [12] Here the account given in the Life (a child is restored to the father) is fused with that given in the notarial record (the mother vows to bring wine 'measured' to her son). It looks as if the author knew both of the other accounts and thought that they referred to the same event.

9 *Ibid.*, p. 513 (no. 24).

10 The earlier of the two English copies is among addenda made after c.1377 to the *Historia aurea* of Bury St Edmunds (Oxford, Bodleian Library, Bodley MS 240, pp. 699–708); the later in a fifteenth-century manuscript now in Lucca, Biblioteca Statale, MS 3540, fols 148–63. The Italian manuscripts all instead contain an appendix of two other miracles (one dated 1310, one undated) which were printed by Papebroch (*AS*, April, 3, pp. 509–10). This may indicate that the English copies belong to an older manuscript tradition. They certainly testify to the cult which Zita enjoyed in England from at least the mid-fourteenth century: see Caroline Barron, 'The travelling saint: Zita of Lucca and England', forthcoming in P. Hordern (ed.), *Freedom of movement in the middle ages: people, ideas and goods.* I am most grateful to Professor Barron for making a copy of her paper available to me in advance of publication.

11 Below, pp. 188–9.

12 Lucca, Biblioteca Statale, MS 3540, fol. 163v: 'Defunctum unigenitum patri vivum reddit /Vinum mensum filium ad votum matris tradidit.' It is not clear grammatically whether the father or mother 'handed over' the wine.

Perhaps, then, the Life was written after this story was reported at San Frediano in April 1286. The author indicates only that he is writing some years after the saint's death; the cult, he says, has flourished without official support and despite active detractors. Are the miracle and the dispute with the Franciscans clues to the context, perhaps even to the motivation, for the composition of the Life? In 1286 it could be publicly declared that Zita had displayed her powers impressively, at a moment when the San Frediano community was confronting a threat to its prestige and parochial rights and getting no help from the bishop – whom the author so oddly fails to mention. A date of composition shortly after 1286 cannot be certainly established, but it would harmonise with such evidence as we have. Perhaps this Life of a non-mendicant saint was produced at a particularly tense moment in the mendicant colonisation of one central Italian city.

The Life of Zita of Lucca

Prologue

All divinely inspired scripture is useful for instruction and was bestowed by the Holy Spirit for that reason, so that we might all derive from it remedies for our own afflictions, as if from some common fount of health. Wherefore it is written, 'Whatever things are written, are written for our instruction'; so that through patience and the consolation of the scriptures we should have hope. Hence too, it has been the edifying custom of the most learned men to enquire into the chaste lives of the saints and by means of the pen to give a careful and rational account of them to the memory of posterity, so that by studying their teaching all could imitate them in this world and at some time enjoy their company in the glory of eternal life. Indeed, those who do great things are praised only to the extent that the outstanding talents of writers have been able to extol them in words.

Infused with the light of wisdom, many have written in splendid language of the fragrant acts of the saints. When I compare my stunted wit with theirs – for I am watered by the streams of modest learning and moistened by scarcely a paltry drop of falling rain – I might feel obliged to break off my gasping narrative, lest my uncultured language should lay me open to the justified censure that I have impudently appropriated subject-matter which should rightly have been reserved for eloquent writers. Yet although their golden life is far beyond me, I think it no injury if my lead pipe should furnish a trickle for the uses of men. I fear only that with the passage of time the deeds and distinguished way of life of that admirable woman, the eminent virgin Zita,[13] should perish from memory.

It is apparent that in this work I have not dealt in detail with the almost innumerable wonders and prodigies she wrought after death but rather with those things which she did while alive in the body and particularly around the time of her death; for it is charity towards men and humility, not miracles, that must be venerated. That is to say that the proof of sanctity is not to perform wonders but to love everyone as oneself, to believe the truth about God and to think better of one's neighbour than of one's own self.[14] Hence it is that the Truth says, 'By this may all know that you are my disciples, if you love one another.' I have written down here only a few things out of the possible total, for if I reported everything that I have either heard from good and trustworthy people or that I have learned on my own account about this perfect, tried and tested woman, I believe the day would end before my discourse did. As I set out to write of her life and deeds, I call upon the Holy Spirit, who dwelled within her – the maker of all things and giver of all gifts, multiple and single, subtle, eloquent and agile, sure and sweet, possessing all virtues in himself, perceiving all things and allotting to all as he wishes – so that, as he bestowed virtues on her, so he from whom is every good and perfect gift may give me the words in which to narrate them.

Here begins the Life of the blessed virgin Zita

As the world turns towards its end and this corruptible life slips into old age, the splendour of the divine light has in very recent days shone forth in the venerable handmaid of God, Zita, who came from the diocese of the city of Lucca in the province of Tuscany, from a country place called Monsagrati. God, who told the light to shine out of darkness and who has chosen the weak things of the world, the foolish and the contemptible, to confound the strong, illuminated her with such rays of grace that although she was of lowly birth she was adorned with supreme virtues and filled with an abundance of merits. She was so remarkable for almost innumerable marvellous signs and wonders that her fame went out into the whole Christian world, and from the ends of the earth many came running to the fragrance of her

13 I have adopted the familiar form of the saint's name, but the Italian manuscripts have Çita, Sita and Cita, the two English manuscripts Citha and Sitha.

14 Gregory, *Moralia in Job*, 20:7:17. Gregory goes on to cite John 13:35, as the author does here.

perfume.[15] In faith she clung firmly to the primal truth, believing in God rather than in herself; in hope to the supreme benevolence, trusting in God rather in herself; in love to the supreme good, loving God above all things and more than herself. Her father was called Giovanni Lombardo, her mother Bonissima. Her uncle Graziano was a lay brother, and her sister a nun called Margarita, in a certain convent of the Cistercian order; both of whom, that is her uncle and her sister, were of such notable life that were it not for the prohibition of the law they would long have been regarded as saints by all.

Of the works of her hands

This virgin came from her country place, at about the age of twelve, to live in the city of Lucca. So that, as the Apostle says, she should provide the necessities of life for herself with her own hands, and lest she should eat the bread of sorrow or deprive the sick and needy of assistance, she entered the service of a certain noble family, the Faitinelli, citizens of Lucca, who lived not far from the revered church of San Frediano, where her venerable body now reposes. The venerable Zita spent the whole of her life in the household of these nobles, that is, until she was about sixty, serving her masters and mistresses irreproachably and without complaint, attending conscientiously to the governance of the house and of the members of the household of both sexes and all ages. If at any time she was not engaged on some household duty, she turned at once to manual labour, above all avoiding, like the bite of fiery serpents, all idleness and preoccupation with this fleeting time, that is, the weapons with which the ancient enemy captures wretched souls. She fulfilled dutifully what is written in the Book of Wisdom: whatever your hand can do, do it at once.[16] She also avoided the fearful superstitions of old women and devoted herself to the desire to earn merit. She thought that it was glorious to serve God, inglorious to serve the world.

Of her almsgiving and works of mercy

By divine gift, a certain generous pity for the poor was deeply engrained in God's handmaid; it grew from her infancy, and such kindliness filled her heart that, if it was at all possible, she never denied alms to anyone

---

15 An allusion to the Song of Songs, which appears also in the Life of Umiliana; see above, p. 138.

16 In fact Ecclesiastes 9:10.

who sought them for the love of God. So that she might have the where-withal more readily available, she not only prepared good things, or whatever lay to hand, for that purpose overnight, but carefully collected tiny scraps, even the meanest, from broths and side-dishes, much concerned that no poor person should leave her empty. She continued in this practice as best she could until her death and attained a fuller increase of grace with God. One day a pilgrim, suffering badly from both thirst and heat, sought alms from her, and she had nothing with which to succour the poor man. In great anxiety she thought what she could do.

Of the changing of water into wine

At last, by heavenly inspiration, she urged the poor pilgrim to wait until she could bring him some fresh water from the well. Taking a bronze vessel, according to the local custom, she brought freshly drawn water from the well to the pilgrim, making the sign of the Cross over it. When he tasted the water it had been divinely turned into wine, and he could really smell the aroma of the finest wine. He drank gladly and copiously, swearing afterwards that he had never in all the days of his life tasted such sweet wine.

Of her generosity and kindness to the poor

The sweetness of pity flowed in such abundance from the fountain of mercy into the lord's serving-woman that she seemed to relieve the sufferings of the wretched with maternal compassion. Her mind melted for the sick and the poor, and she extended her hands eagerly to them, loving them all with a heartfelt, fraternal affection. And so that she could thereby offer a more welcome sacrifice to God, she withheld all delicate and even essential foodstuffs from her little body and took the opportunity to bear them herself to those who were most oppressed by illness or want. She often personally visited them and took the utmost care to minister to the sick. Abstinence is more pleasing to God when the food which one abstains from is given to the needy.[17] If she could not give practical help, she at least showed them affection, with exhorta-tions to patience and consoling words. For doctrine does not penetrate the heart of the poor if it does not come recommended by the hand of

17 Gregory, *Regula pastoralis*, 3:19.

mercy; and a voice does not penetrate the heart of the hearer when it does not reinforce what it says with deeds.[18] If she saw that anyone was suffering penury or any form of want, she referred it in the sweetness of her pious heart to Christ; and as she discerned the image of Christ in all poor people, she not only generously gave any necessities she might have collected, whether clothes, fabrics, shoes or anything else, to the needy whom she encountered, but also sought them out and thought that she was returning to them what was properly theirs. For when we give necessities to those who are in want, we are returning what is theirs, not giving what is ours; we are paying a debt of justice rather than performing a work of charity.[19] She was so intent on works of mercy of this kind that on innumerable occasions she persuaded her mistress and many other people to give more generous alms to the wretched by her hands. The annual wages she received from her master she either gave to the needy or generously bestowed on the almost numberless [infants] to whom she stood godmother.[20]

Miracle

Once when the poor were lamenting that victuals were dearer than usual because of a worsening famine and their sufferings were markedly worsened by penury, they flocked eagerly to Zita as if to a mother and helpmeet in their necessities. She gave out everything she had and what she could obtain from others in this work of piety, and there was nothing left for her to give; but when a poor woman came to her, with a crowd of little children around her and clinging to her, lamenting that she and they were suffering from almost unbelievable poverty and could not survive any longer, the kindly handmaid of God was pierced by the sword of compassion. Not having the means to extend a helping hand to her, she was divinely directed, for in times of need everything is to be shared and the heavenly rather than the earthly Lord must be obeyed. She went at once to one of her master's stores, which contained an abundance of beans, that is, a certain number of bushels, and gave some to the poor woman and children so that they could avoid the danger of starvation. For those who claim private rights in the common

18 A conflation of *Regula pastoralis*, 2:7 and *Moralia in Job*, 19:7:13.

19 *Regula pastoralis*, 2:21.

20 The text as printed by Papebroch (*AS*, April, 3, p. 500) differs radically here, not mentioning Zita's mistress and making her wages 'slender' (*tenuis*) rather than 'annual'.

gift of God are wrong to consider themselves blameless. Almost every day they are killing as many poor dying people as those whose means of support they keep to themselves; as long as they fail to give out what they have received, they are effecting the deaths of their neighbours.[21] So, on the following days, she gave from the aforementioned store to as many poor people as came begging for alms. Although she greatly feared the scolding and abuse of her master, without whose knowledge or consent she was distributing the beans to the poor, she said to herself: 'So be it, I will put up with whatever he inflicts on me, I will take it on myself', ready and willing for the blows and the punishments. When Zita's almsgiving, unknown to anyone, had almost emptied the store of beans as far down as her hands and arms could reach, the master of the household, unaware of this, decided that the beans which he had stored in that bin were to be sold, and (having first made an estimate of the value) he ordered them to be measured out. In faith and fear Zita called upon the Lord God to make her master lenient towards her, so that he should not treat her roughly on account of the loss of the beans. But behold! By divine agency the bin was found to be full of beans, and their measure was not at all diminished. Thus God, in whom she trusted, wondrously and in a manner incomprehensible to humans protected his servant from all threat of trouble. Zita, noting that her master was not annoyed with her, expressed her gratitude to his wife, that is, her mistress, thanking God and praising him exceedingly for his manifold goodness. But since one must beware lest, while one is living well, the mind, despising others, may be puffed up by self-importance,[22] she humbly concealed what had happened and did not try to attribute it to a miracle, although several people who knew about it lauded the divine power and her merits in so great a miracle.

Another miracle

The handmaid of God Zita was an imitator of the apostolic bishop St Martin, who, as we read, was deemed worthy to clothe Christ (or one of his angels) in his own person.[23] On the most holy night of the Nativity of the Lord Saviour, she wanted to attend the matin vigils

---

21 These radical sentiments are Gregory's, in *Regula pastoralis*, 2:21.

22 Gregory again: *Moralia in Job*, 6:31:49.

23 This much used *topos* was probably particularly agreeable to a Lucchese audience, for St Martin was titular saint of the cathedral, and a sculpted group of his act of charity stood above the main portal.

which Holy Church especially solemnises then. It was more intensely cold than normal, and the master of the house said to her, 'O Zita, how can you rush off to church like this on a night which is so cold that we can scarcely put up with the icy conditions indoors and fully clothed? especially as you are eaten up with fasting, and wearing poor thin clothes, and you're going to sit on a damp and cold marble floor. Either spare yourself and perform your religious exercises here, or put my fur-trimmed cloak on your shoulders against the cold.' Although Zita refused not to go to church on such a holy night, she accepted the fur cloak and hurried off to church. Her master said to her, prophetically as the event showed: 'Look here, Zita, take care that you don't give the cloak to someone or put it down somewhere; for if it's lost, I shall be much put out by my loss and you will suffer for it from me.' She replied, ' Your cloak will be kept safe and sound for you, master.'

When she entered the church, her gaze immediately fell on a poor man who was half-naked and moaning, his teeth chattering in the extreme cold. At once Zita's heart melted in pity for the state of the trembling pauper. Going up to him, she said, 'Well now, brother, what's the matter and why are you moaning so?' He turned a pleasant gaze upon her, put out his hand and touched the cloak. Zita took it from her shoulders and wrapped the poor man in it, saying to him, 'Keep these furs on you until the divine office is over, brother, but then give them back to me; and don't go away, because I will take you home and protect you from the cold by the fire.' So saying, she withdrew to the part of the church where it was her custom to stand in prayer and holy meditation, listening to the office. When it was over and all the men and women who had attended had gone, she too had to go home. Looking everywhere for the pauper, inside the church and out, and finding him nowhere, she said to herself, 'Where do you think he's gone? Surely someone hasn't taken the cloak away from him, and for shame he doesn't dare show himself to me? And yet he looked a decent person, and I can't believe that he's run away so as to steal the cloak.'

In this and like manner she piously made excuses to herself for the pauper, unwilling in any way to accuse him of theft or robbery. When she had spent long enough wandering around looking for him and could not find him, she returned home in shame, still putting her hope firmly in God that he would either placate her master or inspire the fugitive pauper to return the cloak to her. When she came home without the cloak, her master attacked her with bitter reproaches, piling on his complaints. He got no sign or word of impatience from her, but listened to her explanation of what had happened and her exhortation not to give up hope and did not stop grumbling until lunchtime came. But oh the immense clemency of the divine goodness! At the hour of terce, the pauper appeared in the middle of the stairs, presenting the most beautiful aspect to the beholders and carrying the cloak in his arms; he gave it back to Zita, with her master looking on and listening, and thanked her for the great kindness she had done him. And suddenly, when both Zita and her master started to speak to him, he disappeared from them, like a lightning-flash, leaving in their hearts a new and unfamiliar sensation of heavenly joy, at which they wondered and rejoiced, marvelling at it for a long time with delight.

Of her harsh penitence and austerity of life

The blessed Zita mortified her flesh and its vices with such stern discipline, and restrained the sensual stirrings which she felt (although rarely) with such a strict rule of modesty, that she scarcely consumed what was necessary for the support of nature. She rarely tasted any portion of the cooked food which was reserved for her by her employers, but kept it to give to some poor or sick person, herself content to eat the smallest and meanest things. She rationed her drinking, especially of wine, to such a degree that on many days in the course of a year she tasted no wine at all. And because continence leads to perfect purity when the flesh is subdued by abstinence she inflicted such frequent fasts on herself that, although she looked plump, there was scarcely anything on her bones. Her face was pale with fasting, and her mind was inflamed with heavenly longings, so that often she resembled a phantasm or spirit no less than a human body. Nor, as many people do, did she afterwards more readily prepare a more lavish or richer supper for herself, lest she should pay attention to the longings of the flesh; on the contrary, she strove in fact to forbid those who tried to prepare [food] for her to do so, lest she should become a burden to anyone in this respect.

She did not care about the preciousness or meanness of the clothes which covered her little body, their colour or any quality or quantity in them. She paid not the least attention to all this, above all seeking to avoid ensnaring her spirit, which she wanted always to be free, and wisely stating that Christian perfection consisted not in quality of dress, but in breadth of charity. The more highly the human mind elevates itself and contemplates things eternal, the more it fears disturbance by temporal concerns. She went barefoot at all times and would never wear shoes even in the harsh winter weather. She was girded around her loins with a cord or rope next to the bare skin, with which she bound herself so tightly that (as was revealed after her death) the flesh grew over the rope, and in many places the torn skin really cut into her. Furthermore, although she had a perfectly comfortable bed, she rarely slept in it; rather she introduced paupers and pilgrims and rested them on her bed. Often she invited prostitutes or other light women, enslaved to the lures and uncleanness of the flesh, and put them in her bed, reasoning in her simplicity that she could at least preserve them from one night's defilement, burning as she was with the most ardent zeal for the salvation of all souls. The bare earth or, very often, a wooden board furnished a bed for her weary little body; it was so worn out with innumerable labours and genuflexions and all her comings and goings and pious rounds that if you had seen her you would have thought the spirit had gone out of her. Yet, as will become immediately apparent in what follows, she offered, to him whom she served with the most fragrant love, powers of endurance of hunger and thirst, cold and nakedness.

Miracle

One day the most devout Zita most devoutly set out, fasting, on a pilgrimage to the church of San Jacopo in Podio, near Pisa, in the company of a certain friend of hers. When she had reached the church and humbly offered her prayer she set out, according to plan, to continue her journey to the church of San Pietro a Grado, which is about five miles from Pisa towards the sea. The aforementioned companion left her when she entered the city of Pisa and returned home. And since whoever intends a greater good thereby makes a lesser good impermissible, which before was permissible,[24] Zita did not give up her fixed intention, and went on to the church of the Prince of the Apostles, combining humble prayer with devout fasting. At about the hour of vespers, when she was returning through the city of Pisa, she was offered hospitality but refused it, and reached the baths of Monte Pisano as the sun was setting. She was asked to stay by someone who was well known to her, but she would not agree to remain there. In fervour of spirit she boldly crossed that difficult mountain tract which is called San Giuliano, where a certain hermit urgently besought her that she should rest, for fear that she should fall prey to robbers or wild

24 Gregory, *Regula pastoralis*, 2:27.

beasts; but she turned a deaf ear and passed on, her spirit controlling her flesh. She also passed the *castello* of Massa, where some watchmen invited her [to stop] and marvelled at the endurance of this feeble woman. Her physical condition began to deteriorate, and, suffering from hunger because of her fasting and travel-weariness, she sat down by a spring around the time of the first cockcrow. Although her flesh was almost worn out and irresistibly giving way her spirit, undefeated by her flagging limbs, was exultant.

When the handmaid of God had drunk a little water a woman appeared to her, the Mother of the Son of God as it is piously believed, and greeted her, standing in the most friendly fashion at her side and saying 'Do you want to come on, to get back?' At her most gracious voice Zita was not only unafraid, but drew such strength, confidence and courage from her sweet and kindly speech that all her weakness and tiredness, hunger and thirst, vanished and she promptly replied, 'Gladly. I want to get on; let's go together.' They went on together and came to Pontetetto about the middle of the night. Here the gate to the bridge, which had been closed and barred in the usual way, stood open for them and closed and locked itself again after them. Then they came to the gate of the city and found this too carefully secured with iron bars; but again, at the sight of them, in the blinking of an eye it let them freely through. At last they came to the door of Zita's dwelling; at her call the serving-maid, with much mumbling and grumbling, opened the door, and the woman who had been accompanying Zita vanished. Wanting to invite her companion in, Zita put out her hand and turned towards her; when she found no one there, she was amazed and deeply disturbed, inwardly wondering where she had gone and who she was who had escorted her thus; she had so enjoyed her sweet conversation along the way that the road had not wearied her, and she seemed to be feeding on celestial nourishment.

Another miracle

Let us relate another wonderful story. For as long as she lived, God's servant Zita had the custom of going to the church of Sant' Angelo al Monte once a week, especially on a Saturday. This church is on a hill by a river, about six miles from Lucca. Nothing deterred her from this journey, neither torrential rain nor menacing thunderstorms. One day, because she had been much tied up in domestic matters, it was late in the day, and evening was already coming on when she set out on her accustomed journey. A man on a fast horse came up and followed close behind her; he was going towards the same church on private business. When he saw her walking slowly and feebly ahead of him, he addressed her thus: 'Where are you going, stupid woman, at this late hour? The shades of night will soon surround you and lead you into danger.' She replied humbly, as if she thought nothing of it, 'Go your way, Christ will guide me safely.' The horseman at once passed Zita at high speed, and, in a hurry to arrive at his destination on time, he galloped part of the way. When he was passing by the church, he saw Zita, not in imagination but in reality, praying in front of the church door; she had arrived before him, guided by God, in whom she trusted with total purity and simplicity. When the horseman asked in great wonderment how she had got ahead of him and arrived so quickly, she said in the words of St Job, 'As it pleased God, so it was done.'

Of her concentration on prayer and sweetness of contemplation

Zita, the handmaid of Jesus Christ, felt that in the body she was distant from the Lord, and lest she should at any time be without the consolation of her beloved Bridegroom, she prayed ceaselessly and strove by praying to present her spirit before God. And, so that her soul's understanding might be made the purer by the illumination of the divine light, she prayed so continually that even when she was engaged on manual work she thoughtfully uttered words of petition, in her heart and with her lips, lest by entirely abandoning tranquillity she should quench the fire of heavenly love within her. As a result it sometimes happened that her handiwork became clumsy, because her heart was more in her prayers than in her work. Walking and sitting, working and at leisure, indoors and out, her mind was so intent on prayer that she seemed to have dedicated not only her heart and body but her time and her work to God.

She was often caught up in holy ecstasy, in such an excess of devotion, fixed on the peak of perception of the sights of heaven, that, caught up above herself, and sensing something beyond human sense, she had no idea of what was going on around her; but, after many tears and after fixing her eyes on heaven, it often seemed to her that she had been present in the ranks of the angels and was leaving the confines of the flesh in heavenly contemplation, drinking in the sweetest fragrances of a splendour that was more than light and a love that was more than fire. So that she could more peacefully receive these infusions of spiritual consolation, drunk with the overabundance of the divine love, she sought out a secluded place within the confines of the house, and frequently spent the night there. Here the members of the household often saw a radiance at night, as if the sun, the fountain of light, had risen there; those of better judgement reckoned that she was being consoled by the presence of the author of light, or by angelic visitation.

Throughout her life she rose for the matin vigils and most often went to the church of San Frediano, which was nearby, and remained there, intent on the matin office, standing alone in the lower part of the church, which is quite spacious, reciting her prayers and beating her breast with her hand or with a stone, and in different ways sharing all the secrets of her hidden thoughts with God. She was especially accustomed to pray before a certain crucifix which was almost worn out with age and had therefore been placed in a by-way of the cemetery. There her soul melted, while she was sweetly and gently restored by the flesh of the Lamb who was roasted in the oven of the Cross. The thought of the Passion of Christ was so intimately impressed on her innermost heart that it both burned her mind within with a fire of love and infused it with the wormwood of compassion. In the fount of his love she burned the more fiercely the more violently she lamented his Passion; and when she saw the marks of the wounds on the crucifix and saw them also internally with the eyes of her mind, she could scarcely restrain tearful groans; feeling, in her virginal bowels, with endless sighs, how the bloody fluids burst forth from Christ's heavenly limbs and how he, the supremely blessed, exhaled his spirit with them; and she did not cease to beat her breast until, at God's invisible chiding, tranquillity returned. And, just as a man talks to his friend, so she talked, groaning, with the Lord, as if he were there present in the flesh. Going over the whole delectable sequence of the Lord's Passion, she was seized with such a sweetness of pleasure and perception of heavenly things, tasting in advance the draughts of heaven, that the custodian of the church, often wanting to shut her out when the divine office or the mass was over, could scarcely extricate her from the immense sweetness of contemplation even by scolding.

It was her habit to leave the church last and to enter it ahead of others; nonetheless, when she was shut out she often prayed in front of the closed church door. The size and prominence of the callouses which at her death she was found to have on the backs of her hands and on her knees affirmed the foregoing; what her spirit had always done in life, her flesh in death attested. Usually she did not stand among the other women in church, because they are known very often to spend their time in idle chatter, but she used to choose a place near the men in which to pray. She conducted herself in church with such modesty and silence that not only did she try never to look anyone in the face, but nothing was on her mind or on her lips except her prayers; for often, while the tongue is not at all restrained from idle talk, it is let loose in presumptuous and foolish chatter.

Miracle

It happened on one occasion that Zita remained longer than usual in prayer after matins. When she brought her prayer to an end and realised that dawn had broken, she was seized with fear, because she remembered that there was no bread in her master's house and it was her responsibility that morning to make the bread. She knew that the time for doing this had passed and returned at high speed to the house to attend to the job as fast as possible. When she came to the cupboard, she found loaves properly prepared, which she put in the oven, and quickly came back to thank her mistress, in fear and shame, because she thought she had prepared the loaves. It had however been done by heavenly agency, as was clearly revealed afterwards; for on diligent investigation no mortal person was discovered to have made them. In fact, as we have already said, although she eagerly prayed at night, in church or in a secluded place in the house, still by day she personally visited pious and holy places, poor hospitals, churches and monasteries, and wherever she knew that a saint's feast was being celebrated, or the first mass of some new priest was being sung, she promptly attended, out of faithful devotion and to obtain the remission and usual indulgences, the more readily seeking the aid of God and the saints, as she was able to devote herself the more freely to supplication where she was quite unknown.

Another miracle

On one occasion, when the devout feast of the blessed Mary Magdalen was approaching, Zita, according to her previous custom, set out to go to her church, about ten miles away from Lucca, in the remote place which is called Crebaria. No one dared go to that church because of the hazards of the wars which were afflicting the Lucchese and the

Pisans; there was a lot of brigandage in those parts, and people going there were sometimes killed. But the handmaid of God, fixed in the fervour of her spirit, would not for that reason miss going there with the utmost devotion, bearing in her hands a taper to burn in honour of the blessed Magdalen. Travelling alone and resolutely crossing the deserted region, she arrived around the end of the day and the beginning of night and found the church carefully shut and barred and no one about since, thanks to the wars which we have mentioned, the place was uninhabited. She prostrated herself in prayer on the threshold and, bowed down thus in the open air, persisted in prayer until out of bodily weariness and the outpouring of supplication she was overcome by sleep. That night there was a torrential downpour of rain and a furious outbreak of wind and tempest. As dawn approached, the venerable Zita, unafraid and unharmed, arose from prayer and sleep and found that her taper, which she had brought with her unlighted, had been ignited in her hand by divine fire, and neither wind nor rain had been able to extinguish it; while the doors of the church before her, standing open by divine will, offered her free entry. Later, the people who arrived after sunrise with the priest found her in there praying, and they were dumbfounded with surprise.

Of her chastity and virginity

Furthermore, I do not believe that Zita received her name by chance, but by divine prevision and the disposition of supernatural grace, to whom things future are as if present; for Zita, in the Romance tongue, signifies 'Virgin'.[25] She was indeed the purest of virgins, and therefore guarded herself with the strictest vigilance, taking the utmost care of that inestimable treasure, that is, chastity and virginity, in their earthen vessel. And since nothing is so easy as wrongdoing even if no one is teaching you or forcing you, so, when she was young and as she got older, she insisted with the utmost severity not on indulgence but on austerity, constantly mortifying her flesh; for experience had reliably taught her that that evil enemies are put to flight by what is hard and rough, but greatly strengthened in their power to tempt by what is soft and delicate. The mind is concentrated on seeking heavenly things to the extent that the body is restrained from what is forbidden. By exercises of this kind she began to shine in her senses with the beauty

25 *Lingua romana* signifies the Italian vernacular. Papebroch noted that, while the word *zita* had already fallen out of use in the seventeenth century, its diminutive *zitella* was still current. It survives in modern Italian, meaning a spinster or 'old maid'.

of purity; her mind, having achieved command over the flesh, seemed to have entered into a treaty with her eyes[26] that it would not only shrink from carnal sights, but avoid even the casual inspection of any vanity. Nothing seemed to her more conducive to a holy life than to close off the bodily senses, as it were, and to become removed from the flesh and the world and turned within herself, keeping her senses and her soul apart from human concerns, devoted to herself alone and to God. Having therefore achieved purity of heart and body, she so subdued and totally overcame the inner enemy that she preserved the white vestment of her soul from the flames of pleasure and was seen to be the most transparent vessel of sanctification. She sternly refused even to hear immoral talk, being dedicated to preserving the purity of her conscience inviolate. Often carnal words insistently enter our ears and start a war of temptation in the heart; and although reason rejects them and the tongue reproves them, victory is won with difficulty within, when it can be authoritatively decided without. Therefore it is essential that what the vigilant mind repels from the threshold of thought does not reach our ears; because eventually we are stirred by the memory of evildoing we have committed and are struck by unlawful thoughts against our will.[27]

In her younger days, one of the household servants, with shameless audacity, once tried with scurrilous words to persuade her into lewd[28] embraces, adding improper actions to his words. He reached out his hands and attacked her as bold as brass, so that she might fall into the night of the foulest evildoing before she could cautiously recognise the enticements of pleasure. She was small of stature and physically almost powerless but, while she did not want to make the impudent boy's attempts public, she was inflamed with zeal to preserve her chastity and defended herself vigorously with all her strength. She scratched his face somewhat with her fingernails, aware that, as guilt begins to allure, the mind should realise into what danger it is being drawn; and so, with God's assistance, the shameless one in no way prevailed over the handmaid of God. With harsh words she reprimanded his lustfulness, also threatening, if he spoke to her with this forwardness again, to denounce him to their master, who would severely punish him; so too would God, if he did not lament his guilt. To the degree that the mind knows it is the more deeply soiled by consent it must be cleansed of

26 Job 31:1; there is extended exegesis of this passage in *Moralia in Job*, 32:2–3.

27 This passage juxtaposes *Moralia in Job*, 7:13:15 and 9:54:82.

28 The phrase is *in incestuosos amplexus*; *incestuosus* here probably has its less specific meaning of 'lewd' or 'immoral'.

pollution with a stricter application of penitence.[29] And although this battle could not be entirely concealed from the master of the house, who discreetly found out from the servant why and by whom his face had been damaged, Zita answered his questions skilfully and modestly, without telling the smallest lie; she did not want to avenge her injuries or expose her neighbour's attempt to accusation.

Of her perfect humility and careful preservation of it

Humility, the guardian and adornment of all the virtues,[30] so fortified Zita, the servant of God, with its strength that although a manifold selection of virtues shone in her, and many people venerated her for the sanctity of her life, in her own estimation, according to which she was a sinner, she was nothing but some sort of mean earthen vessel; when in truth she was a elected vessel of sanctification, adorned with the multiple grace of the virtues and dedicated to sanctity. It was very difficult for her, achieving great things as she did, not to have mental confidence in her own great achievements. Precisely because one struggles mightily against vice, presumptuous thoughts arise in the heart; as the mind valiantly overcomes external faults, often it becomes secretly puffed up inside and, attributing some great merit to itself, it does not think, in its self-estimation, that it has sinned. In the eyes of the severe judge, the offence is greater the more covertly, and therefore the more incorrigibly, a fault is committed; and the devouring pit yawns more widely the more generously life glories in itself.[31] Therefore she controlled herself carefully, lest the commendation of previous glory should increase the demerit of subsequent guilt. She made every effort to belittle herself, in her own eyes and others', and to expose her hidden defects, not only to the priest in sacramental confession (which she much frequented), but in public declarations, while the gifts, revelations and graces which she received she kept secret in her breast, so that they were not exposed to praise which could be the occasion of ruin. Presumption based on vain and empty reputation is for men a great impediment to virtue, because often the dust of sin is produced by a good work, and what cleans the hearts of the hearers dirties the footsteps of the speaker.[32]

29 *Ibid.*, 4:18:34.
30 Gregory calls humility the *custos virtutis* in *Homilia in Evangelia*, 1:76. Cf. the Life of Pier Pettinaio, below, p. 220.
31 *Moralia in Job*, 2:52:83.
32 *Ibid.*, 1:23:31.

In order to fulfil the whole law of perfect humility, which distinguished her more than all the other virtues, she tried to demean herself not only to her masters, superiors and equals but to her inferiors, to the extent that she never refused obedience to any order or demand, however onerous or difficult it might seem; but immediately on any suggestion, persuasion or command, she freely, cheerfully and totally dedicated herself to its fulfilment, not putting forward, by word or gesture, any excuse of time, place or difficulty, but (as she was mild in speech and full of a dovelike simplicity) replying at once that she would do what she could, treating herself as if she were dirt.

Miracle

On one occasion, she was sent by the young ladies of the household, on some frivolous pretext, to a distant place during a heavy shower of rain, as a joke, so that they could have a good laugh at her when she came back soaking wet. She hurried along and faithfully fulfilled their orders, and came back so completely untouched by the rain, thanks to her obedience and humility, that she looked as if not a single drop had fallen on her.

When she was on some pious journey, in any sort of company, she conducted herself so submissively that she would not stop, or walk, or eat, or drink, or talk with anyone, except if and when she was invited by others to do so; and whenever she was so invited, with studied moderation and in a respectful voice she replied, 'As you please' or 'However you like.' She always had her hands humbly folded and in her manners and deportment signalled her mental humility, never otherwise expressing her will; she showed herself outwardly in speech to be what she was inwardly in conscience. She tried in her speech to declare and in her life to demonstrate humility, the mistress and mother of all the virtues;[33] she wanted to be rather than to seem humble. If she ever happened to hear anyone speak in praise or commendation of her, however lightly, she showed by word and gesture that she was gravely upset and mortally wounded, calling herself unhappy, wretched, miserable. The just man is indeed wounded when he is praised. Oh what a perfect laywoman, worthy of imitation not only by other laypeople, but by ecclesiastical persons, including nuns and regulars, so adorned by the emblems of humility that she was justly regarded by all a true

33 This alternative description of humility is to be found *ibid.*, 23:13:23.

imitator of the Virgin Mother!

So greatly did Zita venerate the Mother of God that out of pious reverence for her she regarded any woman who was called Mary, of however
lowly condition, to be altogether her superior in merit, out of a pious
sentiment of reverence for the mother of the Son of God. The gentle
Zita achieved such a habit and perfection of humility that, as if dead
to the world, she never replied crossly or unpleasantly to anyone who
grumbled at her or reproached her, who cursed or offended or insulted
her, nor did she betray perturbation in her mind or her face, however
sorely she was tried; but, following the example of the Lord, who so
forgave all injuries that he did not condemn when avenging, did not
destroy when reproaching and loved no less when accusing, she used
to say, with a calm and pleasant face, in a modest and agreeable manner,
and in the softest voice, 'Pardon me', or 'May God forgive you', or 'Don't
upset yourself, it does you no good to speak or act thus, rather seek
perfect patience.' He is perfect who is not impatient with the imperfection of his neighbour.[34]

Furthermore, if it happened that the master or mistress of the household or anyone else was, human-like, upset about something that had
happened and spoke crossly or otherwise criticised her or any other
person, the gentle Zita flung herself at their feet, humbly begging pardon
for her fault and tearfully whispering, ' Oh, I am to blame for this!' Nor
was it easy to restrain her from this demonstration of humility. If she
received any offence from anyone, she tried to forestall the guilty party
in asking pardon; for this is religious duty, to give satisfaction with a
word if anyone seems to be wounded by the darts of suspicion. It is
human nature to suspect that others are doing to oneself what one does
oneself; people who are in the habit of belittling the behaviour of the
good think that they themselves are being belittled, and they suspect
that everyone is against them because they themselves are in conflict
with everyone else.[35]

O who could tell with what zeal she sought to relieve the troubles
of others, in her assiduous care for the household and especially for
the upbringing of little children? To them she showed more than a
mother's compassion, conscientiously undertaking a nurse's difficulties
and hardships. When she took on the responsibilities of housekeeping,
she considered what was due to herself and to her neighbour; she would

34 *Ibid.*, 5:16:33.

35 This combines passages from *Moralia in Job*, 14:3:3 and 14:14:16.

not neglect her own interests by overdoing any duty, nor would she disregard other people's interests out of concern for her own benefit.[36] In a marvellous manner she fulfilled all the requirements of total perfection, because she did not slacken her care for things internal by her external occupations, and she did not abandon her care for external things because of her concern for the internal.[37] She behaved with such discretion that never at any time or anywhere did she deliberately harm anyone or slight them in word or deed, of whatever condition or status they might be. Rather she offered joy to the grief-stricken, compassion to the afflicted, profitable counsels to the desolate and salutary advice to the unlearned; not with sophisticated eloquence or in the learned words of human wisdom, but by the display of spirit and life. Many think themselves more learned than others when they presume to speak inappropriately about unfamiliar things, and believe that they appear the more learned the bigger the display of loquacity they can make.[38] Although as far as worldly affairs were concerned, whatever their substance or cause, the handmaid of God was of such simplicity as to appear totally strange to such things and not of this world, nonetheless, in the fulfilment of God's commands and those things which might affect the salvation of souls, and the understanding of holy scripture, she seemed to be of such wisdom and virtue, according to her measure, that she attained the understanding of the most learned, illuminated by the rays of the eternal light, like one inhabited by the Holy Spirit, the teacher of all scripture.

These signs of profound humility were also present in the handmaid of God: love of humble people, avoidance of all conspicuousness, contempt for her own desires, an appetite for lowly duties; despising no one, seeking counsel of the best people, patiently bearing insulting words, showing herself prompt in obedience in all things and zealous in the pursuit of good. In this last commendation she was found to be great and to surpass everyone. She kept her heart under guard, knowing that God, for whom she was ceaselessly preparing a fit habitation in her mind, is the inspector of all hearts; hence it was that, according to the saying 'It is the sign of a good mind to acknowledge fault where no fault is to be found',[39] she bewailed her least and tiniest faults, not only in deed but in thought, and her slightest motions, and confessed

---

36 Largely *ibid.*, 2:48:75.

37 *Regula pastoralis*, 2:1; also 2:7.

38 This fuses passages from *Moralia in Job*, 16:5 and 26:23.

39 Gregory, *Epistulae*, 11:64.

them humbly to the priest in penitential confession. Often the mind, which overcomes many powerful obstacles, fails to overcome one, in itself perhaps the least, although it exercises the greatest vigilance. The mind of the just, although free from sinful deeds, sometimes nonetheless slips into sinful thought.[40]

Of her love and charity toward God and her neighbour

The zeal for heavenly salvation, emerging from the furnace of charity like a sharp and flaming sword, so pierced the bowels of the venerable Zita that she seemed totally inflamed by a competitive ardour and smitten with the anguish of compassion. So when she saw souls, redeemed by the precious blood of Jesus Christ, mired in some sort of filth or the contamination of sin, she was deeply stung by sorrow and mourned with tender pity like a mother who, as the Apostle says, daily gave birth to them in Christ, eagerly hoping that no such contamination should take place; for guilt is more swiftly forgiven which is incurred without deliberate malice, and guilt is easily corrected when it is blushed for. Undoubtedly, neither to do nor to love what is good is to sin deliberately.[41] If anyone ever told her that someone had done this or that evil, or had sinned by doing such and such, or had committed some offence, she at once made some fitting excuse or said firmly that it was unbelievable; even if the story was true, it was not to be repeated or made public or spread abroad in the telling, since we should maintain silence about our neighbour's evils if we cannot correct them, and even tolerate them thus, lest the poison of sorrow be concealed in the spirit.[42] She groaned deeply if the fact that a sin had been committed was established beyond doubt; since it is of little profit to constrain the flesh, if the mind cannot through compassion expand in love of its neighbour. And because there is no bodily chastity which is not recommended by sweetness of mind,[43] she persuaded everyone she could to works of piety and charity, desiring the redemption of all sinners.

She did not talk about or interfere in other people's business, like a flatterer; she was not one of those for whom nothing is more enjoyable than to talk and concern themselves about the affairs of others,

40 A combination of *Moralia in Job*, 4:23:43 and 18:5:11.

41 In succession *ibid.*, 32:22:45 and 25:11:28.

42 Close to *ibid.*, 10:6:8.

43 *Ibid.*, 6: 34: 53.

especially when it is the case that they are prejudiced by either love or hatred, by which the truth is often concealed and distorted. She closed her ears against slanders and rumours; she set a guard of silence on her mouth and imposed such a strict guard on her lips that she rarely spoke without proper consideration or useful need, bewaring of all idle talk, which happens when it lacks the justification of necessity or the purpose of pious utility.[44] However, out of a zeal for righteousness, she often reproved wrongdoers in the household; and so that she could do this in good faith, she took every precaution, as far as is possible for human nature, to preserve herself from guilt. No one can honestly reprove another for something in which he is not sure that he is irreproachable; for it is humane not to wax wrathful with others, certainly about things in which one over-indulges oneself.

Also, when she heard the sound of bells announcing the death sentence, as is the custom of the rulers of cities when some malefactor is condemned to death, she at once burst into a flood of tears and praying with sweet and benevolent emotion said, 'O Lord, succour the soul of this dying wretch. Help the soul of the sinner, O Lord.' Nor did she cease, for two or three days, or even until the seventh day, to implore God for the salvation of the soul of the condemned man. The ardour of perfect charity, by which this beloved of the Bridegroom was moved both towards God and her neighbour, can be sufficiently discerned from what has already been said but especially from this, that, pierced by a most fervent zeal for souls, she exerted every effort to thirst with the crucified Lord for the salvation of all who could be saved. She knew, as she used to say, that we must love our neighbour, because it is God's command, because he shares our nature, and because he is the image of God; and because to love him is proof, nourishment and increase of the love of God. She was greatly inflamed in her fervid love of him by the divine mercies which he shows to us, for she often considered how long he waits for the sinner and for the conversion of the depraved will, his remission and interior consolation of all iniquity, the help he gives our weakness to make satisfaction, to endure and to resist, and finally the purely gracious gift of the kingdom of heaven. By the fervour of her love and in the practice of the spiritual life she was every day made a new creature, so that she despised this present world, did not love transitory things, fixed her inmost mind in humility on God and her neighbour, maintained patience against insults and with studied

44 A virtually identical definition of *sermo otiosus* can be found in *Moralia in Job*, 8:37:58; *Regula pastoralis*, 2:14; and *Homilia in Evangelia*, 1:6:6.

patience repelled sorrow from her heart, gave what was her own to the needy, never meddled with others' affairs, loved her friends in God and her enemies because of God, and lamented the suffering of her neighbour.[45] All these things were great signs of perfection in her.

Of her fervour and progress in her old age

When the venerable Zita had achieved the summit and perfection of all the virtues and also an advanced age, the noble people whom she had served for so long wisely decided that they could no longer regard her as their servant but as the servant of the supreme God. Henceforth they allowed her freely to do whatever she liked and treated her with befitting reverence, both for her old age and for her holy reputation. Whatever they could do for her they did as if for one of their daughters. Zita, however, as she ascended to ever greater heights in fervour of spirit, did not cease to embrace voluntary poverty, which had always been dear to her; nor did she allow her old age (when others often take life more easily), the weakness of her sex or her physical frailty to soften or diminish her austere regime. She did not want to diminish her works of penance or for any reason to abandon her accustomed vigils and fasts or other bodily austerities or to leave off the condition of servitude or subjection, but with dedicated attention and extreme deliberation, polished by endless beating and rubbing, she earned the right to be swept up to the celestial dwellings and hailed by the resplendent heralds of sanctity. Ever increasing in fervour, despising transitory things, she was carried to the love of the Creator by exertion in marvellous works. For all ascent is in exertion, all descent in pleasure; by effort the step leads upwards, but by relaxation it leads downwards.[46]

In her mind all transitory things were inferior, and she soared ever higher above the whole passing round, thinking of nothing but heavenly things. Already all earthly things had become vile for her and she had accumulated treasure for herself in heaven. It is entirely fitting that anyone who is inflamed with desire for the eternal mansions should be released from all earthly loves; but he who is overcome by the love of earthly things in no wise takes delight in God.[47] Thirsting, like the stag for the waters, for the fount of the blessed life and panting for

---

45 *Homilia in Ezechiel*, 1:10. There are similar passages elsewhere in Gregory.

46 *Moralia in Job*, 7:25:30.

47 Successively *ibid.*, 4:33:67 and 18:9:16.

the celestial fatherland, she burned with melting soul and eager spirit to come to the bedchamber of the heavenly Bridegroom and to enjoy the delicious banquet of eternal sweetness. Death, which to almost everyone is a punishment, she loved as the entry to life and the reward of her labours;[48] as cold in her enthusiasm for this world as she was increasing in warmth in the love of God, desiring, as the Apostle says, to be dissolved and one with Christ. Since her mind was firmly focused on God, whatever seemed bitter in this life she regarded as sweet; all affliction she thought repose; she longed to pass over the mountain, to obtain the fullness of a better life and reach the summit of eternal felicity.[49]

Of her death and passing

Almighty God, the true and faithful (who does not defraud the labourers in the vineyard of penitence of their daily hire, as the gospel trumpet proclaims, 'Come to me all ye who labour and are heavy laden'), wanting now to give rest and refreshment to his beloved handmaid, thought fit to lead her to the heavenly nuptials of the Lamb in this manner. In about the sixtieth year of her age, the weak members of this elderly virgin were shaken by a mild fever for about five days. The sickness grew slowly worse, and she was forced to take to her bed, although it was not her habit to lie on her bed in any illness and she used to stay on the floor, her spirit having the upper hand over her age, abstinence and labours. In the year of the Nativity of the Lord 1278, on the twenty-seventh day of April, on the fourth day [Wednesday], at the third hour, attended by certain devout women, the most happy virgin Zita, by desire a martyr, fortified by the most devout reception of the sacraments of the church, showing no sign of sorrow or anxiety, her eyes fixed on heaven and her hands folded in supplication, mentally praying and rejoicing, departed for heaven; and her most blessed soul, released from the flesh to take possession of the boundless Trinity, was absorbed into the glory of the eternal light and peace; for no one can come to the perfect joys of freedom unless they pay the debt of human nature. How great and deserving she was with God, and what heavenly exaltation she had merited, who with profound humility had demeaned herself, the divine goodness revealed immediately on the passing of her spirit. For a brilliant star appeared above the city of Lucca, evident to

48 This is from the Proemium to Gregory's *Dialogi*.
49 Mostly from *Moralia in Job*, 7:16.

all, which the brightness of the sun did not conceal, as it does the other stars; whereby it was clearly revealed, as the devout proclaimed and the abundance of miracles subsequently proved, that a new rose had sprung up in the celestial rose-garden of the saints, and the city of Lucca was illuminated by the light of a new star.

On the very day of her passing, he who unlooses the tongues of infants perfected her praise out of the mouths of babes and sucklings. Immediately after the departure of that happy soul, children tirelessly shouted in the squares and public places of the city, not because anyone had announced it but by the revelation of God, 'Let's go, let's go, let's run to the church of San Frediano, for St Zita has died.' Thus by the will of God it came about that while the noble Faitinelli were preparing fit exequies for the burial of the blessed Zita, their household servant, a numberless multitude of the inhabitants, of both sexes and all ages, flocked to the church of San Frediano and filled the great cloister and the adjacent squares. Only with considerable difficulty was that most precious treasure, her body, borne into the church, preceded by the assembled community. Each and everyone competed, in an unruly battle, to touch the body of the venerable servant of God, Zita; the clergy could not get on with the funeral rites, nor, for the space of several days, could they bury the body, since day and night a throng of people remained constantly around the corpse and did all they could, out of their great devotion, to carry away some part of her garments; so that on several occasions, although repeatedly wrapped up, she was left semi-naked. So that the holy body should not be destroyed by the irrational multitude, who reject restraint, certain people who were more distinguished by faith and devotion adopted various stratagems and deceptions and moved the venerable body from place to place to safeguard it; now it was enclosed in the choir, now in the cloister, now in the chapter-house, now in the refectory, now in the guesthouse and other parts of the convent. They enclosed it in wooden caskets, which were eventually several times broken.

Of various cures

Meanwhile and thereafter, signs and marvels shone forth, wonders occurred; and between the very hands and before the very eyes of men who wept for joy frequent and manifest miracles were performed. The blind saw, the deaf heard, life returned to withered and defective limbs, the lame and the bent were straightened, and the dumb spoke. The feverish were restored to health, people in pain were cured, unclean spirits were chased from bodies, the bloody flux was suppressed, those in peril in childbirth were succoured, the sterile made fertile, the heavy lightened, the ulcerous cleansed, those bitten or seized by wild beasts delivered, the shipwrecked rescued, the imprisoned released, men tortured on the rack felt no pain, and for many fire lost its heat and water its liquidity; men hung on the gallows escaped from the very jaws of death, the feverish, despaired of by the doctors, through her recovered; in short, all kinds of danger, harm and sickness were evaded through her merits. Wherefore the people were not deterred by hunger or sleepiness, nor by heat, sweat and the tremendous crush, but continued to come, one after the other, to the venerable tomb.[50] Jacopo, the prior of the church, and his brethren accorded little or no faith to her sanctity, although they were otherwise very religious men. They took counsel with the prudent and religious brethren of both the order of Preachers and the Friars Minor, and had the venerable corpse, which emitted a tremendous fragrance, enclosed in a stone sarcophagus. By the agreed advice of the persons aforementioned, they awaited the result. If the whole business was ill-founded and of merely human origin, it would soon cease; if it were of divine origin and proceeded from divine providence, no mortal would be able to resist it, but despite all opposition it would prosper and grow mightily.

And so, from day to day, the outcome became public knowledge. After just a few days a health-giving liquid began to seep from the tomb in which the holy body lay; the limbs of the weak and sick, when anointed with it, were restored to health; and as that virginal body was free of all carnal uncleanness, so to this very day it remains free from the usual dissolution and corruption of other corpses, except inasmuch as it looks slightly withered. Several cardinals of the Holy Roman Church, and also archbishops, bishops and many other venerable men, coming from various parts of the world, have seen this and can testify to it; so too a multitude of secular princes, barons, knights and prominent *popolani* who have come at various times and have seen it with their own eyes. They have come often and still come daily to venerate her (albeit within the limits of the law), especially those who have experienced her assistance and beneficence in their necessities, and by whom she has been devoutly invoked in danger by sea and land.

---

50 This translation takes *memoria* to mean (as it often does) the 'tomb' of the saint; this also has good grammatical warrant. The manuscripts are variably punctuated. Papebroch followed his Camaldolese copy in taking *veneranda memoria* to mean the 'venerable memory' of Prior Jacopo.

What is particularly worthy of devout wonder and wonderful devotion is the fact that although no one has promoted or favoured or publicised by preaching the pre-eminent sanctity of her life and the excessive abundance of her miracles (indeed, she has had many detractors), nevertheless there is not only every year an assembly of numberless people from different regions, cities and dioceses in almost the whole of Italy, who come on the anniversary of the day of her glorification and passing and bear witness to her saintly merits, but also a daily concourse of visitors to her tomb, people from both sides of the mountains,[51] to whom she gives and has given help when they call upon her in their dangers and necessities and who proclaim her, not only in word but in deed, by manifest signs and favours, to be distinguished and in favour with God.

Among others, finally, who have written of the miracles of the handmaid of the supreme God, Ugolino of Parma, learned professor of laws, says this: 'She has cured fifty-three people of different nations and sexes who were troubled by contraction [of the limbs], of whom some were suffering all over their bodies, some in certain parts. She has cured sixteen who had lost their eyesight; some lacked the sight of both eyes, some of one. There were six mutes, of whom some were afflicted by nature, some as the result of an accident. In addition, the divine mercy has healed four deaf people, twelve demoniacs and many suffering from other infirmities and painful conditions, through the intercession of the pious virgin.' So says he. We ourselves can testify, in clear corroboration of the truth, not only that the blessed Zita has helped more than 150 people, suffering from a variety of troublesome and serious afflictions and assailed by danger (as described one by one in official documents by the trustworthy notary Faitinelli, on receipt of sworn testimony),[52] but that there is a host of people to whom, at different times and in different places, she has rendered all sorts of assistance and bodily healing, and does not cease to do so. These not only exceed 1000 in number, but would seem incredible to anyone who heard them. I myself have seen a boy brought back to life, and living, walking upright and talking; his father, a man worthy of belief as far as can be told, voluntarily swore

---

51 Presumably the Apennines, which divide Tuscany and central Italy from the Lombard plain.

52 The number of extant records in Lucca, Biblioteca Statale, MS 3459, is only ninety-nine. It seems therefore that about a third of the original number had been lost by the time the manuscript was copied, probably around 1380. The notary Faitinello di Migliore, who compiled the record, is noted between 1250 and 1275 by Andreas Meyer, *Felix et inclitus notarius: Studien zum italienischen Notariat vom 7 bis zum 15 Jahrhundert* (Tübingen, 2000), p. 548.

on the gospels on the altar, in the presence of me and several others, that his only son was truly thought to be dead but by the merits of this holy virgin was awakened from death at his urgent prayers and piteous devotions.[53]

Miracle

Within a year[54] of the death of this handmaid of God a certain young man, Pietro de' Faitinelli, who had been brought up in the Faitinelli household in Lucca, was travelling in Provence when he fell gravely ill. He was so eaten up with this affliction that three well-known doctors who were attending on him despaired of his recovery and unanimously agreed among themselves that he would die the following day. When the sick man realised this he called upon the blessed Zita with all his heart, in the gentle and familiar speech which he had used as a little boy, beseeching her, among other things, that since he was far from home and did not have the help, support and advice of father or mother or any of his own people, she should not leave him helpless but would deign to bring him friendly assistance from God. And behold, on the following night, while the woman who was looking after him was neither asleep nor fully awake, the venerable Zita appeared to him, in a silken garment which displayed marvellous workmanship in its skilful weave and wearing a lofty crown on her head adorned with large precious stones; but she had the face of her old age, as she had had in life, so that Pietro recognised her beyond any doubt. She was preceded by two splendid lights from tapers or candles. Although Pietro did not see who was carrying the lights, he saw her plainly and recognised her, and he addressed her thus: 'O my lady Zita, save me, for I'm completely abandoned and afflicted, and there is none of our people who is able to help me.' And she replied, 'Don't be afraid.' And he spoke to her again, asking 'Who is with you?' And she said, 'Quiet; don't ask any questions; be brave.' Stretching out her hand she touched the forehead of the sick youth and immediately healed him, vanishing at once from his sight. He rose up cured and said to his attendant, 'Bring me something to eat, because I'm well.' But she said, 'O my son, rest, if only you were well. Tell me, who was that you were speaking with just now? For I heard you talking and another person that you were talking with replying.'

---

53 For this miracle and the possible dating of the Life see above, p. 162.

54 Because of a lacuna in his manuscript Papebroch left a blank at this point, inviting his readers to fill in what time-indication they preferred!

The young man told her the whole story, and added that he would see the three doctors who had prophesied his death dead before he died himself; which indeed came true not long afterwards.

Behold, beloved, the God of peace, who lifts up the needy from the dust and raises the poor man from the dungheap; who endows the word of those who spread the gospel with great power and who wished the deeds of this virgin to be set down for our use and instruction. For the examples of the saints are transmitted thus in writing so that all, according to their sex and their age, may imitate their way of life and study the life of the good in the mirror of pious contemplation. What has been written above has been set forth for the glory of the illustrious virgin Zita; but while I strive to show in these words what she was and what everyone should be in life, I have been a bad painter depicting a beautiful person, and I am pointing others to the shore of perfection, while I am still tossed on the waves of wrongdoing. Therefore, O most splendid virgin, favoured of God and the angels, support me, I beg you, in the shipwreck of this life on the plank of your prayers; so that, because my own weight presses me down, the hands of your merit may raise me up,[55] while we all pray as best we can that you will think fit to remember us, so that he who has awarded you the palm of all your labours, Jesus Christ our Lord, may grant us forgiveness of sins, with prosperity and well-being; to whom be eternal praise in glory, honour, strength, beauty and power for all ages. Amen.

---

55 This echoes Gregory's prayer and apology for his work at the end of the *Regula pastoralis*.

VI: PIER PETTINAIO OF SIENA (d. 1289)

The Life of Pietro Pettinaio presents problems akin in some respects to those raised by that of Raimondo Palmario. The original Latin version by the Franciscan Pietro da Montarone was written in 1330, over forty years after the death of the saint. The manuscript was lost in a fire at San Francesco in the sixteenth century, but by 1507 it had been translated into Italian by Serafino Ferri, an Augustinian hermit of Lecceto near Siena, and in this form it was printed in 1529. In 1802 Maestro de' Angelis, a Sienese Franciscan, republished this Italian text, embellishing it with footnotes mostly of a doctrinal and devotional character.[1] Although he claimed to have corrected his original in places, a comparison with the 1529 edition indicates that in fact he did very little more than adjust some of the sixteenth-century orthography according to more modern norms: to take a very obvious and frequent example, the plural definite article 'li' is everywhere altered to 'gli'.

We are therefore once again faced with a question of judgement: what reliance can we place on the early sixteenth-century rendering of Pietro da Montarone's lost Latin? No more than his contemporary, the translator of the Life of Raimondo Palmario, did Ferri claim or admit that he had amended the fourteenth-century original to conform to changed ideals of piety or propriety, although he remarked that he had performed his task with some difficulty, as the Latin legend was 'extremely incorrect'. It is possible only to say, once again, that there is nothing in the Life as we have it that seems implausible for its supposed date.

Why was a Life produced in 1330 and not before? There is no indication that there was an earlier one; indeed Pietro's preface strongly suggests that there was not. Steps were taken to venerate Pier Pettinaio immediately on his death, and in December 1289 the ruling council of Siena voted to contribute 200 pounds to the cost of an altar and ciborium in the chapel where he was buried.[2] The civic authorities were still sending an offering to the commemoration of the saint in the 1320s, but late in 1328, ostensibly for reasons of economy, proposals were made to abolish all participation by the chief magistrates in any *festa* (except presumably that of the Assumption of the Virgin, the city's supreme patron). Early in 1329 the orders of friars mobilised to prevent this demotion

---

1 *Vita del B. Pietro Pettinajo sanese del terz' ordine di San Francesco volgarizzato da una leggenda latina del 1333 per F. Serafino Ferri Agostiniano da Lecceto l'anno 1508, corretta e riordinata con annotazioni ed aggiunte dal Padre Maestro de Angelis Minor Conventuale* (Siena, 1802).

2 F. Cristofani, 'Memorie del B. Pietro Pettinagno da Siena', *Miscellanea Francescana*, 5 (1890), pp. 34–52, publishes numerous documents relating to the cult.

of their several saints (and the loss of offerings), headed by the Dominicans in defence of Ambrogio Sansedoni, with the Franciscans scarcely a step behind. The Franciscans laid special stress on the value of multiple heavenly protectors to the city, Pier prominent among them.[3]

In his Life, Pietro da Montarone quoted Pier's deathbed prophecies of woe to Pistoia, Florence and Siena. As far as Pistoia and Florence were concerned, the prophecies had already been fulfilled. Pistoia, riven by faction in the late years of the thirteenth century, had fallen under the control of its more powerful Tuscan neighbours, while Florence had sustained grievous defeats at Montecatini (in 1315) and Altopascio (1325). Siena had as yet suffered no such outright disaster, and it was to be piously hoped that through the intercession of the Virgin and Pier Pettinaio this happy state of affairs would continue. These are unremarkable sentiments in themselves, but they fit with the arguments put forward by the Franciscans in 1329 for the continued official civic veneration of their saint. Pietro da Montarone however makes no explicit reference to any such context for his work. He says that it was instigated by his superiors and others, and his own conscience pricked him to it, as he had benefited in some unspecified manner from the saint's intercession.

Pietro had conscientiously sought out surviving witnesses to Pier's life and presents him as an exemplar of a particular kind of holy life, lived by a layman under the aegis of the Franciscan order and firmly embedded in the urban society around him. That he enjoyed contemporary fame as a spiritual counsellor was attested by the radical Franciscan Ubertino da Casale, who in the prologue to his *Arbor vitae crucifixi Iesu*, written in 1305, recalled how at his first coming into Tuscany (in 1289, at the very end of Pietro's life) he had benefited from the advice of 'Pietro of Siena' and the virgin Cecilia of Florence, both now dead.[4] These two, he said, had introduced him to 'the hidden things of Jesus' in such a manner that their spiritual perspicuity would cause wonderment if described. The best-known testimony comes from Dante, who is not lavish in his references to the holy men and women who were so numerous in the central Italy of his time. In *Purgatorio* 13 (lines 127–8) the arrogant Pia de' Tolomei, accusing herself of the sin of envy, admits that she would be less far advanced towards salvation were it not for the prayers of Pier Pettinaio. Dante was writing about 1315; for the great Florentine (and no great friend of the Sienese) the saint's memory was alive a quarter of a century after his death.

Augustine Thompson has observed that 'The adoption of Pietro into the Franciscan family was postmortem wishful thinking' and that 'Nothing in Pietro's life suggests that he understood his penance as somehow Franciscan.'[5] Pietro

---

3 A. Vauchez, 'La commune de Sienne, les ordres mendiants et le culte des saints: histoire et renseignements d'une crise (novembre 1328–avril 1329)', *Mélanges de l'Ecole Française de Rome*, 89 (1977), pp. 758–67; Webb, *Patrons and defenders*, pp. 280–5.

4 Vauchez, *Sainthood*, p. 205. The *Arbor vitae* was printed at Venice in 1485.

5 *Cities of God*, pp. 82–3. Thompson states that the Franciscans claimed that the habit Pier adopted was their grey, not the black of the Dominicans. The Life says only that he abandoned the coloured garments of his youth in favour of the habit of the

da Montarone in fact implicitly recognises that there were other elements and influences at work in Pier's long life, including a period when he lived near and frequented the Sienese Dominican church. He moved into the neighbour-hood of the Franciscans later, and it seems to have been ill health, fairly late in his life and certainly after the death of his wife, that caused him to take up residence with them. His 'penance' may well, therefore, not have been Fran-ciscan in origin, whatever it subsequently became; naturally enough Pietro da Montarone (our only source) is eager to emphasise his connection with his own order. We may reasonably thank the Franciscan hagiographer for the Life's unusual stress on the godliness of Pier's economic activities and also his marked civic patriotism.[6]

Two peculiarities of the present translation should be noted. In homage to Dante's usage, I have called the saint throughout 'Pier', and I have frequently omitted to translate the words *servo di Cristo* or *amico di Dio* ('servant of Christ', 'friend of God') which as often as not accompany it.

The Life of Pier Pettinaio by the Franciscan Pietro da Montarone

Proemium

Let us praise our glorious protector, greatly beloved of God and of men, the precious confessor of Christ, the blessed Pier Pettinaio; God has given the glory of this excellent man to be eternal in him in memory and in his blessing. For by virtue of the humility of his heart he merited the loving regard of the mighty God and by singular gifts freely given achieved purity of heart, truth of speech and a multiplicity of virtuous works. This blessed Pier appeared like the evening star in the twilight of this world, radiant in the example of his unique life and his salutary counsels, enlightening the minds of mortals who were sitting in the shadow of death and guiding them to perpetual light. Like an angelic spirit, he continuously practised the contemplative life; hence he was often filled with the spirit of prophecy and, following in the footsteps of the Apostles, spurning human arrogance, with fervent charity and with the authentic faith of the ancient patriarchs and holy martyrs of Christ, he was entirely caught up in God. Yet he did not confine himself to all this, but tirelessly practised the active life of charity towards his neighbour and with singular prudence renewed in himself the harshest penances of the confessors of Christ. Wherefore he deserved of almighty

---

Third Order of St Francis, made of 'cheap cloth' (*di vile panno*) which he subsequently patched: Ferri, p. 13. There is no reference here or elsewhere to its colour, but the patches were of *diversi colori* (*ibid.*, p. 79; see below, p. 223).

6 See the remarks in the Introduction, above, p. 36.

God to be made like his saints in glory and to be magnified in the fear of God; he was exalted by God in the sight of his people, with immense power against his enemies, making the fame of his sanctity, demonstrated by many miracles, known to all, as we shall explain below.

I know for certain that I am unworthy and insufficient to describe the life of this venerable man of Christ, which is worthy of the sincerest imitation, as being full of wonders and outstanding miracles. I would never have attempted such a thing, were it not that I have been spurred to it by some of my superiors and brothers in Christ and friends and devotees of this holy man, and that the singular reverence and devotion which I bear towards that saint constrains me; for I confess that when I have called upon his merits, I have received the greatest grace from Christ Jesus. So I do not doubt that I would be justly marked down as ungrateful if I kept silent about his praises and his merits. This has been the chief reason why, with great labour, I have undertaken to tell of the virtues of this saint. Although I cannot make a complete collection of the saint's virtues, acts and words, I thought I would describe them as best as I could, in the most truthful and sincere fashion, so that such precious, outstanding and desirable virtues should not perish; however, they are like scattered testimonies, for I have learned of his life from different people who lived with the blessed Pier. And so that I should write the truth about the life of this saint as clearly and reliably as possible (for I intend, so far as in me lies, that it should be useful to posterity), being in the place where the holy man lived and peacefully ended his days, I have talked with those who knew him, whom I have sought out with all diligence, and especially with those who knew the virtues of the saint; I thought I could place unquestioned faith in them, for their proven truth in the religious life is well known.

It is to be noted that in this legend I shall not always maintain chronological sequence, and this is in order to avert confusion. I intend rather to preserve the order of the subject-matter, writing of similar things which were observed of the blessed man at different times, but never deviating from the full and entire truth of the most holy life of this blessed Pier. From beginning to end, we shall divide the life into ten distinct chapters, for the greater ease of reference of the readers, according to the variety of the subject-matter, as follows.

His origins, manner of life and honourable conduct

The blessed confessor of Christ originated from a *villa* called Campi, situated in the Chianti, seven miles distant from our ancient and renowned city of Siena. He came to live in Siena in his early childhood, and there, when in time he grew up, he always remained. This Pier always lived happily, being of a cheerful disposition, although (so it was said by those who knew him when he was young) he was a hot-tempered youth and very boisterous. Nonetheless, with the aid of the divine protection, he was always immune from the vices in which that age-group is usually sunk. At this time he learned the trade of making combs, a craft which he practised until his old age. When he became a man, Pier took a wife, by whom he never had children, and lived with her in a Christian manner, avoiding the pleasure-seeking and idle company of other young men, which is the ruin of so many. The hand of the Lord came on Pier and suddenly he changed into another man altogether, and began devoutly to frequent the church and to listen with the greatest attention to what he heard of Holy Scripture in the divine office or in sermons. Not forgetful of the poor of Christ, already their lover and benefactor, he was displaying the holy and particular principles of his future holy life. And this he did like a good imitator of the patriarch Abraham, when he bought the field in Hebron in which he could make the double cave for himself and his successors.[7]

The trade of comb-making which he had learned he practised with such justice and purity that he seemed to be not a craftsman or merchant of the world, but the most devout and God-fearing religious. It happened that he went to Pisa to buy raw materials for his craft, and when he arrived he found, with some merchants of Pisa, good and bad stuff mixed up together. Pier asked the masters to sell him good and not poor-quality materials, but they refused and he was forced to buy both; they behaved like men who feared damage to their business more than to their conscience, which is what happens to people who are excessively attached to worldly concerns. But Pier, already full of the love of God and his neighbour, bought the good and bad together as it was, so that no one else should have reason to offend God because of this merchandise. When he had done so he went on to the bridge over the river called the Arno, which flows through Pisa, and there, like an angel of God commanded to separate the good from the guilty, he put to one

---

7 The cave (*spelunca*) was in the field which Abraham purchased and was intended as a burial-place (Genesis 23:17). Perhaps the author intends an allusion to Pier's future 'double life' as exponent both of action and contemplation.

side the good merchandise and to the other the substandard and threw the latter into the river.

On another occasion Pier went to a Sienese butcher to buy bones or horn suitable for the practice of his craft. The butcher wanted twelve *soldi* for them, but the servant of God knew they were worth twice the price and replied, 'My dear brother, you don't know the real value of these bones: they're worth twenty-four *soldi*, not twelve; so take their value, and peace be with you.' Pier always made his combs from the best material he could find and sold them justly to all, so that if a purchaser said to him, 'Tell me, Pier, is this a good comb?', the servant of God would reply (when the comb was not particularly good), 'Brother, this comb is neither particularly good nor particularly bad'; but if the purchaser said, 'Pick me one out which is good', then Pier faithfully selected one, saying, 'For myself, I would choose this one.' But when the purchaser asked, 'What are you asking?' Pier always answered with the just price, and never either increased or diminished what it was worth. If the purchaser, as is the way of the world, insisted that it was worth less, the servant of God replied, 'Brother (or sister) mine, the comb is worth so much; if you don't like it, leave it, and go with the grace of God.'

Often Pier used to take his combs into the communal piazza on a Saturday to get a quicker sale, because he depended on them for most of his income. But because his fame was already widespread, not only in the city of Siena but also in the *contado*, almost everyone who wanted to buy combs flocked to Pier (and out of devotion, too). As a result, as usually happens, the other merchants or craftsmen got extremely annoyed with Pier, because they could not dispose of their merchandise as they wished. Taking note of this, Pier, full of charity, so that his neighbour should not be scandalised by his doing, began not to go to the piazza to sell his combs until after vespers, so that the other comb-sellers could have a better chance of selling theirs. When all the purchasers saw this, especially those who did not have a long journey from the city, they waited until after vespers to buy from Pier, or went to his house to find him. The servant of God operated in this manner so that the other merchants should have no cause for complaint, being able to sell their merchandise notwithstanding.

To his wife he showed such respect that she seemed to be his mother or lady rather than his wife. At all times he tried to show consideration for her, which he thought was pleasing to God, so that if it happened that he was talking to someone when the hour for lunch or dinner arrived, he would gently say to them, 'My dearest brothers, peace be with you, because it's the hour at which my lady is waiting for me, and so as not to upset her I want to go home.' Whence it can easily be seen that in all things the servant of God tried to fulfil the divine precepts, for, according to the Apostle, the husband must love his wife as the Saviour Christ loved his church. And such agreement in good between husband and wife cannot exist without pleasing God, as is written in the book entitled Ecclesiasticus [25:1]: the divine spirit takes pleasure in three things which are approved in the sight of God and of men, that is concord among brothers, love of one's neighbour, and husband and wife when they conduct themselves well in God. All of these things the servant of God well observed, as will appear below; he showed himself favoured in the sight of God, amiable and nonetheless worthy of veneration to men.

Pier achieved such purity, as it is believed, that rather like Abraham he had knowledge of his wife solely out of the desire to have children for the service of God. Seeing that she was sterile, they decided to live together observing perfect chastity; and after the death of his wife he always lived in the utmost continence. When it pleased God to call his wife to himself and she saw that she was near to death, she called Pier to herself most lovingly and said to him, 'My dearest husband, I have always known you to be a servant of God, and through him I ask two things of you, praying that you will not deny them to me before I die. The first is that I commend my soul to you, that you will continually pray to God for me. The second is that I commend to you my friend, who you well know is tried and trusted and has always been loyal to me; and I commend to you also her little son, whom I have always loved tenderly.'

Hearing this, the servant of God, full of charity, replied kindly to his wife, saying, 'Be of good courage, my dearest sister, for everything you have asked of me I will fulfil with all my heart.' When his wife had departed this life, the man of God conducted himself as conscientiously towards the mother and child commended to him as if she had been his sister and the little boy his son. But the mother did not survive long and died, and Pier took charge of the boy like a son and put him to learn the trade of tailoring with a master who was a friend of his and also of God, so that he also should instruct him in good morals. Pier often brought food to the boy, as if from God, so that he should not have cause to become a vagabond out of reluctance or shame to ask for it, as can happen.

His contempt for himself and the world; his love of poverty

As an observer of the gospel, Pier despised himself and the world so
that he seemed to be not a secular person but a true disciple of Christ;
wherefore he was not bothered, as happens with men of the world,
about wearing clothes of various colours, but was content with one
outer garment and concentrated solely on changing himself for the
better in God. The man of God was therefore, by mental elevation in
God, clad in the spirit of poverty and singular humility, with feelings of
inner piety; and, reflecting continually that our Saviour Christ became
poor for us and lived poor and died most poor on the Cross for us, Pier
thought of nothing else but that he could, for the love of Christ, humbly
serve the poor. He continually visited the hospital of Santa Maria della
Scala of Siena,[8] where he particularly served the poor of Christ, and
with great joy and solicitude gave them whatever alms he could from
his own resources. With a gracious expression he asked them all if
he could in any way serve them, and when he knew, he did what he
could himself, by either word or deed. He devotedly washed the hands
and feet of the sick, and cleaned and bound even horrible wounds, like
another blessed Francis. He despised himself so that he could the more
easily spurn the world and dedicated himself, insofar as he was in the
world, all his effort and power, to the perpetual service of the poor;
like another Martha he was always engaged on the active life in similar
activities, not abandoning the contemplation of heavenly things with
Mary. The more lowly the activity, the more willingly he performed it
for the love of Christ, judging that the sick person represented to him
none other than the person of the needy Saviour Christ, recalling the
gospel saying, 'I was sick and you visited me'. And because the man
of God so fervently gave himself to works of mercy for the love of
Christ, God recompensed him with such sweetness of contemplation of
himself that everything seemed burdensome to him apart from the love
of Christ. He achieved such favour with God and men that (wonderful
to relate) no one ever made any complaint aganst him, everyone holding
him in the highest reverence, as we shall tell below.

He gave up the coloured garments that he used to wear in his youth
according to considerations of propriety and rank and occasion and,
like a true despiser of himself, made himself a habit of the Third Order
of St Francis, whom he had adopted as his special advocate, out of cheap
cloth. When this habit began to wear out the man of God did not discard

8 Waley, *Siena and the Sienese*, pp. 137–8.

it, although he had the means to make another, but went on patching it. An acquaintance of his, a prudent man of good reputation called Salvi di Orlando, on one occasion said to him, 'Pier, it seems to me that, talking as you do with men of standing, and as you are often bidden to attend the councils, thanks to the grace that God has given you, you shouldn't wear such a cheap patched cloak; you should rather have some respect for these people, who think that you are a person of note, tactful and modest.'[9] Pier replied to him, 'Listen to me, brother Salvi: you may know that when I want to wear a better cloak than this, I have the means, as you know; but you can rest assured, my dearest brother, that he who cares for God cannot care for the world, and we must attend to God alone and not to this passing world, and these external appearances, believe me, are the thing that destroys human life.'

The man of God, while his wife yet lived, sold what he possessed and as a despiser of money and fervent lover of poverty gave abundantly to the poor along the wayside, to prisoners and above all to the decent poor, to such an extent that a tactful and prudent religious once warned him that in his giving he must at least reserve his wife's dowry, because while she lived he must not alienate it. So the man of God just kept the house with a vineyard, with the produce of which, like another Tobit, he gave as much assistance to the poor as he could. After his wife died Pier went one day to tend his vineyard and spent more time in it than usual, with such pleasure that when he came back he found that vespers, which he usually attended with great devotion, was over. Regretting this greatly, he addressed the vineyard sorrowfully, saying, 'Vineyard mine, I have been looking after you for a long time, and with your temporal fruits and passing delights, you have deprived me of spiritual devotion, and this has happened because you are a transient creature, and every love of creature, without God, is in itself a vice, so that St Gregory well says that man distances himself the more from the love of God the more he approaches earthly love. And because you, vineyard, have separated me from my Creator, you are certainly of no use to my soul.' So Pier went and like a lover of poverty sold the vineyard; and with the money he got for it he first executed his wife's will and with the rest gave alms to the poor, spending part on other good works and keeping for himself only what he needed for a very scanty living.

9 Salvi implies that (like Ambrogio Sansedoni) Pier was sometimes asked to attend meetings of the urban ruling councils.

His companions and devotees

According to the gospel saying, the brother, sister or mother of Jesus
Christ is whoever does the will of his Father which is in heaven, and
those alone are called good and must be loved as brothers and dearest
sons, who living according to God are full of good works; as the Apostle
says to the Romans, those are sons of God who are justly guided by his
grace. Therefore the man of God Pier associated only with those who
knew how to walk according to the will of God, and these he loved
like holy angels and was joined with them in holy friendship, mindful
of the saying of Ecclesiasticus: he can be called blessed who in this life
deserves to find a friend according to his heart.[10] Pier was particularly
close to certain people with whom he lived as with the best of brothers
and was venerated by them with pious affection like a father. It seemed
to him, as is indeed the case, that men of God should love one another
much more than men of the world, just as, when people find themselves
together far from their native land, they show greater affection for one
another than they do for other people. So it was with Pier; it seemed to
him that he was an exile from his celestial fatherland, and he associated
lovingly with people whom he knew to be servants of God, as with his
special brothers.

His association was with eight men, and he was the ninth, although he
was the first in devotion. Rather like the nine choirs of angels which,
although they differ in nature or substance, nonetheless have one and
the same will in serving and praising God, so in these nine companions, who, although they were of different ranks, degrees and conditions, there was always one single intent towards God. The names of
these companions were: the man of God Pier Pettinaio; Guglielmo da
Pancole; the notary Ser Compagno; Frate Baldino; Tolomeo Barcigli;
Mino Luglioli; Bartolomeo di Vincenzo; the notary Ser Buonfigliuolo;
and Jacomo Falconi. All of these had for the love of God spurned the
world, concentrating on nothing but prayer and works of mercy. On
Sundays five of these men always met in the great hospital of Siena
and there took counsel together as to how during the next week they
could most diligently serve the sick and the needy. They split up, each
taking a companion with a bag around his neck; some, with a vessel for
carrying soup, went around the various districts of Siena seeking alms,
which they charitably disbursed to the needy. The others, among them
the man of God Pier, on these days did nothing but concentrate with

10 There are similar sentiments, but not these precise words, in Ecclesiasticus 6:14–17.

Mary Magdalen on the contemplative life; they had already won favour with God by the performance of the active life, and now browsed solely on the divine harvest.[11] And thus these nine servants of God, although diverse in status like the angels in substance, were nonetheless united in charity and the love of God.

His charity and pity

As the Apostle well says, and the expounder of the apostle St Augustine, the fullness of the Law and the Holy Scripture is nothing other than the love of God and one's neighbour. Wherefore, he lives as a Christian who loves all things in due order, as did the true servant of Christ Pier, who, entirely swept up in the divine love, fervently loved him, and his neighbour for his love. What this love was and how great it was I well know, and there is no need for me to recount it. All the same, I shall not refrain, according to my poor ability, from saying what I can in his praise and as an example to others. The man of Christ resembled a burning coal, ignited by the divine love, and thus sometimes, indeed often, it happened that if he heard talk of God he became inflamed and fell into ecstasy, so that he seemed to all a man bereft of human senses and for some time resembled a corpse. This happened only when he was overcome by supernatural sweetness. Wherefore it is written, he is much loved by God who delights much in him.

It happened once that Pier went into the church of San Francesco at Siena, as he often did, and found four men there who were associates and great friends of his, talking together. When they had greeted one another he asked what they were discussing among themselves, and one of them replied, 'Dearest Pier, we were just saying that surviving in this miserable world certainly seems burdensome to us; we have to go to great expense to support our families, we make very little from our trades, and it seems difficult to live in the world without committing offences against God.' The man of God replied to them, with great cheerfulness, 'Whoever can be afraid of poverty, or of any other trial of this world, does not have his confidence and his mind fixed wholly on God; do we not know that our God is rich and great in all those who rightly call on him?' And uttering these words with great mental force Pier was suddenly seized by ecstasy and, snatched up into heavenly contemplation, looked for an hour like a man half-dead. His four

---

11 This implies that Pier had already decided to pass from active involvement in charity to contemplation.

companions, standing by, knowing what he was like, did not bother him or permit anyone who entered the church to approach him but guarded him reverently, waiting for him to return to himself. When he did, wishing out of humility to show that this ecstasy was bodily weakness and not elevation in God, he sighed and said briefly to his companions, with a smiling face, 'Great indeed are the miseries of this our fragile body; peace be with you, my brothers', and so saying he went at once to the cell he had in San Francesco.

The man of God bore a special reverence towards Mary the glorious Virgin and Mother of God, reflecting that she gave birth, for our salvation and restoration, to the divine Majesty and Creator of the universe; and he reposed all his faith and hope in her, after Jesus Christ, and as his special advocate continually rendered honour to her, fasting on Saturdays, and day and night often and devoutly commending himself to her in holy prayers. Often, when the man of God was in some tribulation or temptation, or the diabolic conflicts which were frequent with him, he called upon her out loud, sweetly saying, 'My lady and mistress, do not abandon me, but succour your servant in this necessity and affliction.'

On one occasion Pier was asked by the priest of San Giorgio, which is a mile and a half outside Siena, if he would consent to go and dine. The priest did this out of the desire he had to hear Pier speak, because his words were of great weight. Pier totally refused, as he always fled from similar invitations and meetings, but, when the priest had asked several times, he was compelled to go to appease many friends of his, who had also been solicited by the priest. Taking with him two brothers of San Francesco and some other devout men and their servants they set out for San Giorgio about the hour of terce, and on the way met his friend Salvi, who was mentioned above; he called to him, saying, 'I beg you, come with me.' They went on together and had scarcely left the city when Pier began to say, 'Friends, you hurry on, go on ahead, for I must stay behind for a little while.' His companions, out of reverence, did not argue with him but went on. Pier was the devotee of the glorious Virgin Mary, who had been mentioned as they walked together, and such sweetness of the love of her came over him, when he was near the place called Ravacciano, that he could keep quiet no longer but began to call upon her fervently in a loud voice, saying, 'My lady Madonna and special advocate, do not abandon me', and having said this he fell into an ecstasy and was borne up on high; as he spoke he saw the glorious Virgin Mary there, and he stayed thus for a long time. Returning to himself, he followed his companions. It seemed to them that he was totally cut off from the world (as indeed he was). They reached the church together and gave alms; the priest, according to his means, had provided a sufficient variety of food but the man of God Pier ate very little, concerned only to feed himself and his companions on the sweetest words of the Virgin Mary. He uttered wonderful and weighty words, and when they had eaten they returned to the city, still talking about God.

On one occasion some friends of the man of God from Florence came to visit him in Siena. Pier was still living in his own house and received them with a joyful countenance and heartfelt charity, like a man who thought it a privilege to be able to talk with servants of Christ and for his love to show them some tokens of generosity and love. He called in some others of his Sienese spiritual friends, and when they were all together in his house began with great affection and care to prepare bodily food for them all. The man of God did not lack food of the divine words, and while he was with them at the table he was swept up into a mental ecstasy. Seeing him thus rapt, his fellows did not know what to say, except to give immense thanks to the divine mercy and mutually to exhort one another to serve God, who does such marvellous things with his servants, with greater fervour. When the man of God returned to himself, being a studious lover of humility and not wishing those present to believe that what had happened was the result of mental devotion, but rather of human infirmity, he said, 'O my dearest brothers, while we are in this wretched life, it often happens that thanks to the frailty of human flesh we feel these things, as if the flesh can't bear them. Blessed be God' (notable words) 'in whose hands we are always.'

When both types of refreshment[12] were over, the man of God invited them to visit certain holy places around Siena, constantly talking of God along the way. When they came to the piazza de' Conti, they saw a poor woman passing by, calling out, 'Who wants to buy brooms?' When he saw her, the man of God, like one who referred everything to the spirit, turned to his companions and said, 'Oh! Wouldn't it be good if just as an earthly house is swept and cleaned with these brooms, so, with the spiritual brooms of discipline,[13] of fitting penance, with amendment of sin and perseverance in good, the interior house of the conscience could be cleaned and purged, so that when the Celestial Spouse comes to live in it, finding it cleaned with these brooms, he should say, "Come, come to the bedchamber of your spouse, my sister, in whom there is no spot."'

12 That is, both the food and the spiritual improvement derived from Pier's talk and the spectacle of his ecstasy.
13 Probably in the technical sense of flagellation.

And so saying he was immediately caught up in spirit and elevated above the earth for some space of time, as it seemed to his companions. Little by little he returned to earth, but was not fully restored to his senses. He remained for a good hour in this overflow of mind, as if he had heard the voice of the Eternal Bridegroom and beloved of whom he had just spoken with his companions. When Pier came back to his senses he at once parted from his companions alone, and each of them, as they had come, returned to their own place.

Another time, during the fig season, the man of God was going towards Florence with some companions, in order to buy things necessary to his craft. When he came to Castellina he found someone selling figs along the road and bought some. Coming to a beautiful spring, he stopped with his companions and began to eat the figs. The man of God took one and, as it pleased God, found it sweet and pleasant. Turning to his companions, he said, 'My dearest brothers, if God has implanted such sweetness in his earthly fruits, how incomparably much greater must be the sweetness he has implanted in his celestial fruits, on which the blessed feed in the everlasting life'; and having said this, with inward and devout contemplation, he at once fell into ecstasy.

Pier loved his neighbour according to the Christian rule of love, for he loved as he himself wished to be loved. It happened that he was selling a house in the Poggio de' Malavolti, where he had lived for a long time, and his brother-in-law, that is his wife's brother, who was called Gezio, came to him. Gezio was building a new house in the Ovile district and could not afford to furnish it; so he asked the man of God for a loan of 200 *lire*. Pier responded graciously, 'My dearest brother, here are 200 *lire* which I don't need for the time being, so take them, as you have need of them, and do what you like with them, and keep them for as long as you have need.' His brother-in-law took the money and furnished the house he had begun. The man of God never asked for the money, although he often found himself in need, thinking that his brother-in-law needed it. When Gezio thought of returning the money to Pier, he said to him, in gratitude, 'Pier, here is the money you so kindly lent me. I've kept it longer than I should, and prevented you from making the gains you could have got from it; I don't want to be ungrateful, so take this amount, not in usury, which I know is not pleasing to you, but by way of legitimate business and the profit that you could have got from it; your conscience need not trouble you, for I am giving it to you of my own free will.' The man of God, full of charity, replied: 'My dearest brother, I ought to thank you, for you have honestly and faithfully kept my money for such a long time, and therefore you don't need to make satisfaction to me, but I to you; so I beg you to take whatever part of this 200 pounds that you like, or keep it all and use it according to your needs.' And the servant of God insisted that his brother-in-law took whatever part of it he wanted.

The reason why the man of God Pier sold this house, so they say, was a horrible vision that he had in Piazza San Domenico when he was going to matins, as we shall relate below. He reported this vision the following morning to a friend, for no other reason than to persuade him to contempt of the world, all the same begging him to keep it secret. However, as is the way of things, he told someone else, and the someone else told other people, until it came to the ears of the family of the dead person of whom the man of God had had this horrible vision. The family were indignant against the man of Christ, through whom this had come to the knowledge of many people, and they began to utter many wrong and evil words against the servant of God. When he realised this, not wanting to be a cause of disturbance but to give way before anger, he sold the house and went to live in the Ovile district.

At one time during the winter, the man of God was in almost constant contact with the Friars Minor. It happened that a certain young friar was suffering greatly as a result of the intense cold and, leaving the divine office in the choir, went in search of a fire so as not to die of cold. The man of God, seeing him go off like this, and being full of the most ardent charity, looked at him with a cheerful expression and called him to him, saying, 'My dearest brother, where are you going?' He replied reverently, as to a person whose fame and sanctity had already spread all over Tuscany, especially with the friars with whom he was much associated, 'Father, I am going to see if I can find a fire to warm myself, for I am almost dying of cold.' Pier, inflamed by heavenly charity, said to him, 'Come here to me, and open your ears to the words of my mouth'; and taking the friar by the hand he went on, 'O my son, remember the immense fire and ardent love with which Jesus Christ loved you, he who as Lord of the Universe of his own free will for you bore the greatest cold, heat, hunger, thirst and poverty, and at the last died, placed on the wood of the cross; so don't flinch, don't be terrified by a little cold or other adversity which you can bear for him. If you are mindful of what he has borne for you, you will easily, with his grace, put up with any adversity, well knowing, as the Apostle says, that God is faithful and will not suffer us to be tried beyond our strength; but with that trial he makes us fit to suffer these trials.' The man of God had no sooner uttered these words, than the young friar, already thoroughly heated, said, 'Leave me, leave me, my father, go away and don't keep me any longer, for I tell you truly that from the moment you began to speak to me, I became so warm that I can't bear any more.' Pier let him go, warmed externally as he was internally inflamed by the divine love, and remained in his own accustomed consolations.

Pier was full of such love for all the afflicted, imprisoned and other poor persons suffering any infirmity that it cannot be expressed; so that on many occasions the man of God was privileged by Christ Jesus, through the immense piety, generosity and love which he felt for the poor and afflicted, to perform healing miracles. It happened on one occasion that a friend of the man of God called Maffeo Canestri became so ill as a result of a cold in the head that no human remedy could be found to cure him. Hearing of this, Pier went to visit him and coming to him he greeted him kindly and said, 'O Brother Maffeo, have faith in God and don't be afraid. Why are you lying in bed and why do you seem frightened?' The sick man replied, 'How fortunate I am to see you today! But I tell you that I can scarcely rest for the pain in my head; so I beg you to pray for me, for I hope that will cure me.' The man of God, comforting him with gentle words and looking at him, said, 'My friend Maffeo, it seems to me that you have got so much cloth wrapped round your head that if you were cured it would be enough to make you ill again'; and so saying he reached out his hands and took all the cloths off his head, making the sign of the Cross over him and invoking the name of the Indivisible Trinity and of the glorious Mother of Jesus Christ. At once Maffeo, cured, got up by himself; he had not been able to rise before without assistance.

Similarly, the man of God heard from a certain brother of the hospital of Siena that a friar of San Francesco was gravely ill in Siena and it was thought that he must die; at once, with burning charity, he went to visit him and comforted him in the Lord, and when he had commended him to God he was at once cured. Another time in the parish of San Pietro a Ovile in Siena there was a young girl who from the girdle downwards was so completely wasted that she seemed to be without feeling. One day Pier, the friend of God, came out of his great charity to console her and to exhort the girl's mother, who was a friend of his, to patience. He had entered the house, and she, having heard of the reputation of her friend Pier for sanctity, approached him in a reverent manner and took some of his hairs, which hung from his head under his cap. When she had taken them and wrapped them in a cloth she put them with great faith and devotion on the neck of her sick daughter. She was cured at once and began to move around the house, at which her mother, seeing this with amazement, called her neighbours, who had known about her daughter's illness. When he heard about this, the servant of God went at once to his friend, begging her that while he lived she would not tell anyone about it.

On one occasion Pier went to Pistoia to visit the church of San Jacopo Maggiore and to obtain the indulgence which there is believed to be in that church.[14] He lodged in the house of a good man, a Pistoiese friend of his. Being with him in the house in the usual way, he saw that his friend had a grown-up daughter. Pier said to him, 'Tell me why you haven't taken steps to get your daughter married, or, if she wants, to put her in a convent.' The girl's father replied, 'O my dear friend, nothing should be hidden from you, I will tell you the reason', and, calling his daughter to him, he lifted the covering she wore on her head and showed him how on a certain part of her head the girl had a horrible ulcer which continually oozed pus, which is in the world's eyes repulsive not only in women but in men as well. When the man of God Pier saw this, he was moved by immense pity and prayed over her, saying, 'O most merciful God, to whom nothing is impossible and who created the universe out of nothing, mercifully deign to remove this ulcer from this girl's forehead; put it rather, Lord, on my forehead, for there it will do little harm, while to her it is a great handicap.' And as he prayed thus, inflamed with fervent charity, he put his hand on the ulcer, and no sooner had he touched it than the mercy of God was present, relieving the girl of the infirmity; it fell from her forehead into the hand of the man of God like a piece of flesh in the likeness of an egg. There remained on her head a hole of the size of the ulcer that had been removed; Pier made the sign of the Cross over it and it was completely healed, without leaving a mark. This done, the man of God turned to the father, mother and daughter and exhorted them not to be ungrateful to God for his gifts and benefits. Seeing that the bystanders were dumbstruck by this event, Pier at once secretly fled back to Siena, to safeguard his humility, before his action could become public.

Pier found himself in the city of Pistoia, where he had many devout friends of good reputation, on another occasion. One of them had a stepson who had been paralysed and bedridden for many years. This boy's stepfather had already heard of the man of God's reputation for

---

14 On the cult of St James at Pistoia see D. Webb, 'St James in Tuscany', *Journal of Ecclesiastical History*, 50 (1999), pp. 207–34. Pier was probably going to obtain an indulgence on the saint's principal feast, 25 July.

sanctity, and talking with his wife, the boy's mother, he said, 'I hear that our friend the man of God Pier is in this city; so I have thought that if he puts his holy hands on our son, he will be cured through his merits.' In this faith he left the house and went in search of the man of God and finding him said, 'I beg you to come to my house, for my wife and her son very much want to see you.' Knowing him, Pier went with him and entering the house found the sick boy. Greeting him, in a Christian fashion, he touched him and comforted him with a blessing; and when he was touched by the man of God he was at once cured. Seeing this, Pier departed, as an enemy of human praise, and would never consent to return to that house.

Pier had a wonderful compassion for the poor, whom he always regarded with the eye of merciful concern. So when he once saw Fra Baldino, also a man of Christ, whom we mentioned above and who was like a father to the poor, going around barefoot during a period of severe cold with a crowd of poor people following him for whom he was earnestly begging alms, he called to him and said, 'O my dearest Fra Baldino, don't you know the truth? You should know that God has made you the father of these poor people, and if through your fault or carelessness you sicken and die, you will not be able any longer to serve God in this holy enterprise; and these poor of Christ will have difficulty in finding themselves another such father; so I beg and advise you, dearest brother, that at least when it is as bitterly cold as this, you will go around with shoes on.' Hearing Pier's advice, Fra Baldino immediately went and put some shoes on, still fervently serving the poor of Christ.

On one occasion certain kinsfolk of one of the eight companions above mentioned, Jacomino Falconi, complained to Pier, saying, 'O Pier! How can you keep a robber as your friend and associate? You should know that Jacomino, your companion and our kinsman, is a thief and a robber, because he steals all he can from us, his kinsfolk.' The servant of Christ was aware that Jacomino, knowing the way of life and the avarice of his family, for their own good and for the support of the poor of Christ, took from them what he could to give to the poor and needy, and he replied, humbly and full of charity, 'You well know how the devil of hell has many robbers, assassins and brigands in this world, who in various ways wrongfully rob other people; so should we marvel, as we are true Christians, that God, the maker, Lord and King of the universe, too has one thief and robber, who doesn't rob others but only takes and steals what is his own, and gives it to his true sons and masters, that is, the poor of Jesus Christ, whom the divine goodness does not disdain to call brothers and sons?' Jacomino's brothers knew they were confounded by this true and Christian reply, for it seemed to them that they had been identified by the servant of Jesus Christ as thieves and robbers of the devil of hell; and bowing their heads they went away.

Prayer, contemplation, prophetic spirit, reverence for the divine office and other graces conceded to Pier by God

Pier desired in his works only to please God, and it did not seem to him that what he desired was contrary to God's will. Carefully and with great effort he gave himself to devout prayer, in which the well-disposed mind readily instructs and directs itself in the divine will and seeks its own salvation, as the Saviour said to the disciples, 'Pray, and the spirit of my father will make you capable of all things.' The man of Christ learned therefore through the practice of assiduous prayer to obey God perfectly in all things, and in order to perform his prayers more devoutly, he conscientiously arose at night, going to the church of San Domenico in Siena, and entering the church said matins to himself, devoutly standing in prayer. He was held in veneration by the brethren, and they opened the door to him as soon as they knew he was there.

One day the man of Christ was going to the church before they had rung for matins, although he thought the bell had already been rung. When he came near the church he saw two demons, in the horrifying shape of Ethiopians, on the tomb of a knight who had passed from this life a few days previously. He had lived in the same neighbourhood as Pier, and his tomb was outside the door of the church. Pier saw one of the demons with an iron hook which he put inside the tomb and turned the wretched corpse back and forth in the fire; the other demon seemed to have an iron fork in his hand with which he continually stoked the fire, pressing the corpse on to the flames. When Pier saw this he returned to his house, thinking much about this horrible vision, and there he stayed until they rang for matins, whereupon, without any fear on account of this vision, he went devoutly and calmly made his accustomed prayers, and did not see the fearful vision again. Nonetheless the man of Christ soon sold the house in which he lived near San Domenico and bought one in the Ovile neighbourhood, to be near San Francesco. However, because that church was outside Siena[15] he could not go there at night, but he did not for that reason cease to perform his holy works.

15 That is, outside the thirteenth-century walls and therefore 'out of bounds' after nightfall. This account completes the explanation of Pier's move away from San Domenico.

Living now in the Ovile neighbourhood he fell gravely ill, and the Friars Minor came to visit him as soon as they knew about it. Greeting them, Pier humbly begged that they would stay with him that night, fearing that he must die and wishing to pass from this life in the care of the aforesaid friars. They replied compassionately, 'You must know, dear Brother Pier, that we are ready to fulfil your every wish and do you every service according to our capacity; but that we should stay the night with you is not possible. You well know that our superiors, who are conscientious men of holy life and great learning, do not like the brethren to stay outside the convent at night. It would be better, so that we can be with you day and night, if we carry you to the convent, where we can serve you according to your wish.' Pier liked this idea, and when he was somewhat recovered he followed the friars' advice and himself went to live in the convent of San Francesco. He spent all his time there, and his devotion to God and the merits of his excellent life increased, so that not only did he rise at night at the hour of matins, but also long before that hour the man of God was to be found totally caught up in devotion to the Blessed Virgin Mary, making the most devout prayers every day and night.

Pier had the habit of often going at night to the cathedral of Siena to venerate his advocate the Virgin Mary.[16] When he found the doors locked they immediately, by divine virtue, opened of themselves, and when he had entered locked themselves again as before. This was known to many clergy and servants of the cathedral, in which church Pier, praying in holy silence before the image of the glorious Virgin, felt within himself marvellous consolations of heavenly things.

Among the other revelations made to Pier while he was standing and spending the night in devout contemplation in the aforesaid church, it happened that, while he raised his mind to God in prayer, he began to wonder in his heart what saint, among the others who had been acceptable to God after the holy Apostles, had most imitated the Saviour Jesus Christ, to have him as advocate and patron, and to imitate him, so far as God should concede it to him, with all his might. Praying thus and weeping bitterly, Pier lamented that the holy apostolic life was in his time so extinct in this wretched world that it revealed itself scarcely or not at all. And because Jesus Christ, true and beloved spouse of the human mind, wished to console his friend and servant, he revealed to

16 These nocturnal visits to the cathedral, which was dedicated to Mary, must date from the period before Pier moved into San Francesco, outside the city walls. On the Sienese cult and art of the Virgin, see D. Norman, *Siena and the Virgin* (New Haven, 1999).

Pier the vision described below, as clearly as he could desire.

As the man of God stood watching, behold, certain holy angels in the form of the most beautiful youths entered the cathedral. They seemed to be carrying vessels full of fine clean ash, which they sprinkled over the floor of the church from the main door to the high altar; and then it seemed to him that he saw two most ornate royal thrones placed on the high altar which is dedicated to the Blessed Virgin. Then he saw the door open, not by human hand, and through it, it seemed to him, the Saviour Jesus Christ entered barefoot and in the poorest clothing, with the Stigmata on his blessed feet. The Saviour walked over the ash, and it seemed clearly to Pier that the prints of those spotless feet remained marked in the ash, all the way to the high altar. When Christ arrived there, he was immediately clothed in royal vestments and he sat on one of the thrones, and on the other was placed the glorious Queen of Heaven, the Blessed Virgin Mary, with a vast escort of blessed angels around the Saviour and King of the universe and his mother.

Then it seemed to Pier that the twelve holy Apostles entered by the door of the church, walking directly, planting one foot after the other, in the footprints left by the Saviour, and thus they came to the place where Jesus Christ sat with his mother and were received by him with joy and honour. And then it seemed to Pier that there came a multitude of saints, male and female, of diverse ranks and conditions, and although many of them walked in the footprints, it seemed nonetheless that they did not plant their feet so exactly in the marks that they did not to some degree deviate from them or enlarge them or depart from them, some more, some less, so that it seemed to Pier that the original footprints of Jesus Christ could not be seen for the multitude who had in this way with difficulty followed them. Those who were with difficulty following those traces, which were almost totally covered over, coming at last to the throne of Jesus Christ were honoured and more or less esteemed by him according to how well they had followed the footprints of the Saviour.

Then it seemed to Pier that after this multitude had passed no one could discern what or where the footmarks had been, and standing there it seemed to him that he saw the King Jesus Christ, with the aforesaid multitude of those who had already arrived, standing and waiting to see if anyone else was coming. And behold: it seemed to Pier that a poor little barefoot Friar Minor entered by the door aforementioned, with the Stigmata on his feet, and following him there seemed to be a great company, and this poor little friar stood sadly by the door, not seeing any sign of the footprints. Grieving thus, it seemed that with great effort and no less ingenuity he went about finding the footprints, creating a draught over them with his tunic and with his lips to remove the dust with which the multitude of saints passing over had covered them. So doing, with difficulty he discovered two and placed his feet directly in them, and then with great care went on to find those following, until with the divine grace and much effort he was brought before Jesus Christ, by whom he was received with especial favour; it seemed to Pier that he was placed in the open side of Jesus, who so much loved him. And at once the vision vanished from Pier's eyes and imagination. He remained greatly comforted, giving infinite thanks to Jesus that he had deigned to grant him so beautiful and gracious a vision of the Blessed Francis, his singular imitator.

And thus the man of Christ grew in the special devotion to St Francis, whom of all the saints after the Blessed Virgin he had as his particular advocate, and he especially loved the friars his successors, and the better to associate with them he went to live in the convent of San Francesco. He was kindly received by them, and they assigned him a cell near the infirmary chapel and also a devout and circumspect religious to minister to his needs. In this cell the man of God Pier received numerous special spiritual consolations from the Saviour Jesus Christ and from his mother, the Blessed Virgin, and he was often visited by holy angels, so far as can be understood from certain devout religious and fathers of the convent of San Francesco, who for their own consolation carefully positioned themselves where they could clearly hear the sweet exchanges which the servant of Christ, shut in his cell, shared with Christ Jesus, with his mother, many times with the angels and often with certain saints, especially the blessed Francis to whom he was devoted; from which exquisite comfort Pier, as his words revealed, received the utmost consolation. These brothers, as they said, sometimes heard Pier addressing and replying to the Blessed Virgin, as two people do when they talk together, but they were only ever able to hear Pier's voice. It seemed to them also that when the Blessed Virgin Mary had to depart Pier was distressed and afflicted, like one who could not possibly find better company. Left alone, and standing in ecstasy, Pier called out 'O Blessed Virgin, O Queen of Heaven and Earth, don't be so quick to leave your servant, for without you I am enfeebled.'

Pier was many times caught up above himself in holy devotion of mind, so that he was as if cut off from his human senses, performing all his external actions as if he were outside his body, transported in his mind to heaven, his spirit constantly united with God. He was most assiduous in continuous mental prayer, often also including the most devout vocal prayer. Wherefore, as happens to true servants of Christ, Pier suffered horrible persecutions from the devil, who tried to disturb him most of all at times of prayer and contemplation. Not only in his spiritual exercises, but often also when he was at table with his confessor, the envious enemy tried to harm him. On one occasion they were together thus and Pier was not eating. His confessor said to him, 'My dear brother, why aren't you eating?' and Pier replied, smiling, 'Father, don't you see what a bad companion I've got here? He's trying to upset me by sitting on the plate so that I can't take a mouthful, and if I drive him from there with the sign of the Cross, he immediately sits himself on the cup and doesn't let me drink; and so in various ways he tries to harm me, but he will be defeated, so I hope in God, by patience; I trust in the glorious Virgin Mary that by perseverance in fervent charitable prayer he will be overcome.' His confessor, who was not accustomed to conflicts of this kind, was alarmed and replied, 'The blessed God be with us to defend us, for we certainly have bad company.' To which Pier replied, 'Don't be afraid, Father, for our salvation will soon come'; and raising his eyes to heaven, praying mentally, with a radiant face he comforted his confessor, saying, 'Now you can eat in safety, dearest father; our bad companion has fled, for the aid of the Blessed Virgin has come over us and the holy angel who watchfully looks after us has been present.'

Pier was on one occasion standing in the church of San Francesco waiting for his confessor (who was a holy man, and after his death God manifested through him several miracles). The demons did not cease to distress him greatly by coming close before his eyes; Pier, making the sign of the Cross with great faith in Christ Jesus, said to them in a loud voice, 'Depart from me, accursed and worst of enemies of Jesus and of the human race; for I believe in Jesus Christ, and in his mother the glorious Virgin, so you will not be able to impede me, their servant, in their holy service.' The man of Christ endured many horrible diabolic conflicts, the severest annoyances and physical beatings, so that he was often heard to cry out and call on the aid of Jesus and the saints, and especially on his glorious advocate the Virgin Mary, saying, 'Blessed Virgin, my lady, help me and defend your servant.'

Such was the celestial illumination which Pier received in the inward contemplation of his heart that not only in his mind but around him and in the place where he was praying there often appeared a great and corporeal light which could be seen by other people. Once, out of devotion, Pier went with two brothers of San Francesco to Mount

Alverna, to visit the place where it is said that St Francis received the holy Stigmata. They lodged there in the house of a very devout and good woman of that order, and the two brothers told her in conversation about Pier's virtues and holy life, especially how he was a man of great contemplation and mental elevation, and therefore willingly spent the night alone. Hearing this, the lady prepared the remotest chamber in the house for the repose of the man of God, so that being alone Pier could devote himself to his prayers. But the devout woman, wanting to experience something of the virtues of the man of God, placed herself where she could not see, but could hear, what he did at night. The servant of Christ, when he thought that everyone was asleep, piously rose from his bed around midnight as was his custom, and leaving the chamber went into one side of the loggia; setting himself to pray, he entered upon such a degree of contemplation that he was illuminated not only in his heart, but also without. Such a wonderful light shone in the loggia around the servant of Christ that although the night was extremely dark, there seemed to be the greatest brilliance as if a sun had specially lit up the place. When the devout woman saw this, she went down noiselessly to call the brothers, who came at once to see this wonderful thing and, coming hastily with her, saw it just as she had described it. These brothers, when they returned, spread the story among the people.

Pier rated the virtue of prayer so highly that he thought it must be placed immediately behind the virtue of charity, saying that in continual and devout prayer the soul is instructed in all things which are necessary to salvation. On one occasion Pier was asked by a certain young friar of the order of San Francesco, who was extremely devout and was called Brother Ugolino da Querceto, by what virtue he could come most quickly into the grace of God. Pier replied, as one well instructed in the things of God, 'I believe, dearest brother, that nothing is wanting to the salvation of that man who practises continual and devout prayer and contemplation; for in and through this prayer, the excellence of the Creator is made known; so too is the nature of the creature and the vileness and lowliness of man; and so I tell you, brother, that I do not think a man can learn what is needful for his salvation through any virtue better than prayer, by which we are aided in tribulation and supported in temptation, so that we do not fail; by means of it we learn how to moderate ourselves in prosperity, so that we do not enter into a foolish elevation of mind, and in adversity, so that we do not fall into despair.'

On another occasion a Friar Minor came to Pier saying: 'O Pier, I come to you as to a servant of Christ, desiring that you give me advice in a difficulty; know that I am much troubled in my conscience, because, constantly attending the canonical hours in choir, and other prayers besides, I confess to you that I never feel any spiritual consolation, so that I have thought of leaving them off, believing that my prayer is not pleasing to God.' Pier benevolently replied, as one well practised in prayer: 'My dearest brother, don't do that and let yourself be beaten by our foul adversary, who is prompting you to abandon them; but carry on and persevere with this prayer and don't leave it before you have finished it as best you can, and as far as is possible force yourself to go on with it devoutly, even if you feel no consolation from it; for such prayer cannot fail to be pleasing to God, and the more so for the double struggle which the person experiences in it, with the devil and with his indisposition. The good God reserves the fruit to give in his own time, which is not the case with that prayer from which one feels some instant spiritual consolation; just as it is right that someone who has not been paid at all for his work should receive more than he does who has already been paid in part for his labour. And I say the same thing to you, brother, about the divine office; even if you feel bored saying it in choir (as can sometimes happen by diabolical suggestion), you mustn't for that reason abandon it or leave the choir; when we persevere in well-doing, we must believe that the good Jesus will turn it not to punishment but to increase our reward.' And thus this friar, encouraged by Pier's words to follow his advice, in the future always persevered with greater fervour to the end, in holy and fervent prayer and in the divine office.

When Pier was living in the convent of San Francesco he was going from his cell into the church around midnight to pray when he met a young friar in the first cloister, running from the church. Pier said to him, 'Why are you running away, my dearest son?' The young friar replied, 'I'm running, father, because I wanted to say my prayers in the church and I heard such a loud noise, as if the roof was falling in, and I think that part of it has already come down.' Comforting him Pier said, 'Our old adversary has already got part of you; he was trying to fool you, not letting you go on with your prayer, which thwarts him mightily, and so he hates it; therefore, my son, so that you get total victory over him, and not he over you, fight bravely with the weapons of holy prayer and come back with me into the church. Don't be afraid, my son, you will see the church roof still firmly in place and not fallen in any part.' Trusting in Pier the friar returned with him into the church to make his holy prayers, and persevering in them he had the victory by this means over the adversary, like Moses over Amalech.

Pier was assiduous in prayer, devoted to the divine office, and attentive to sermons and the word of Holy Scripture, remembering the saying of Ecclesiasticus, 'Be assiduous in hearing the word of God, so that you may understand; and offer a true reply with wisdom.' He was in the habit of confessing frequently and with great devotion, even though he had no need of it to be a complete servant of Christ; nonetheless in his heart he thought himself a great sinner and so with great contrition he frequented the sacrament of holy confession and very often restored himself with the most holy Communion.

Standing one night in the church in prayer, he wanted to communicate afterwards. The brothers were saying matins, and he heard them sing the Canticle of the Children, which begins 'Bless all the works of the Lord to the Lord', in which all creatures are invited to praise their Creator. As he stood and listened, Pier saw a friar passing on his way to the sacristy and calling to him asked, 'Tell me, brother, what are the brethren saying, or singing, at the moment?' He replied, 'Father, they're saying the hymn of the three children, in which all creatures are called upon to praise their Creator.' Then Pier said, 'If irrational and insensible creatures are bound to praise the Creator, how much more are we obliged to praise him constantly, when we have received innumerable benefits from him and we have the use of reason, which commits us to do so more than the other creatures?' And so saying Pier fell into ecstasy and so remained for a good hour before he returned fully to his senses.

Pier was continually and devotedly at prayer and in extreme mental elevation; wherefore he often had great revelations from God about the future and spoke forth like a man full of the divine spirit, as we shall fully relate below.

Once when Pier was standing in San Francesco at his prayers, a man called Mino of Siena came into the church. He had received an injury from another man and at the prompting of the devil believed he had been greatly offended. He had resolved to murder his enemy and had not told anyone. Resolving one night to carry out this homicide, he went into San Francesco the following morning to see the elevation of the host and to commend himself to it, and then to go and carry out his evil intent. But the divine goodness, which never abandons those who trust in him, revealed this to Pier, who called Mino aside to him in the church and said, 'My dearest brother, although you haven't revealed the secret of your heart, all the same God has revealed to me the evil you have in mind, and you must see that you are doing it for nothing; and so I say to you, on God's behalf, that if you carry out this murder you will die a horrible death in body and in soul, and everything will go badly with you; know that this morning, as you commend yourself to Christ the Saviour, he is giving you this counsel, and know that this is the will of God.' Mino reflected that no one could have known this except by divine revelation, as he had not said a word about it to any living soul, and judging, rightly, that Pier had had it from God, to whom all is revealed, he said gently to him, 'My dearest, blessed father, pray to God for me that he will pardon me, for I have offended against his goodness in my evil desire to commit murder; and, because when I commended myself to his most holy Body, he has come so swiftly to my aid and called me back from this evil, I tell you that I am going home in much peace and tranquillity of spirit, giving endless thanks to the divine goodness; and I pray you again, dearest Pier, that you will receive me into the number of your companions.'[17]

Pier, by virtue of holy prayer, knew the hidden secrets of men, and God revealed to him not only things future but also things present. As one example, it happened on one occasion that Messer Jacomo of Chiusi, at the time when he was a judge in Siena, was moved by pity, seeing a poor needy person, and secretly gave her generous alms. He thought this was known to God alone (whom alone he wished to please) but the Holy Spirit, not a human being, revealed it to Pier as he stood in prayer. Going by chance through Siena, Pier met this judge and taking him confidentially to one side he said, 'Messer Jacomo, God has indeed seen your almsgiving and has gladly accepted the excellent intentions of your heart, and so I tell you that if you persevere in holy works of piety you will make a good and just end.' The judge marvelled at how this thing had become known to Pier and said, 'O, servant of Christ, how did you get to know this secret? To whom has it ever been revealed? Pier replied, 'Don't worry about how I know it; rather take note of what I am telling you, that is, to persevere to the end in similar holy works of piety.'

While Pier was still living with his dearest wife near San Domenico and he was at prayer in that church, his wife fell down the stairs and split her head wide open. Her neighbours came running at the noise and found her on the ground half-dead. Some of them rushed, one after the other, to find Pier, who was still standing in San Domenico, praying devoutly, and when they found him they said, 'Pier, your wife has had a fall and is close to death.' He answered, 'My dears, I know very well that my wife has had a fall; but I am trusting in the divine goodness that this fall is not going to be the death of my dear companion, but that

17 A Mino Luglioli is named above (p. 200) among Pier's associates.

the divine power will be manifested in it'; and praying fervently for her, and knowing by revelation that he had been heard, he at once left the church with the others and went home. Finding his wife as if half-dead, he began to comfort her with sweet and gentle words. With his hands he lifted up the cloths and other human remedies applied by the neighbours to her head; he signed her with the holy Cross and touched her with his hand. All at once the wounds were closed up and the bruises healed, as if she had never suffered any injury.

Pier, who had placed all the desires of his heart in God, was enabled like the prophet Elijah to revive those who had departed this life; and among the other miraculous virtues and graces which the good God granted to his servant, I will relate this, which I had from a person worthy of belief. A devout man called Ventura Marciaio, who lived in the *contrada* of San Martino and who was an acquaintance of Pier, had an only son, who when he was small by chance fell down from a high window. The neighbours ran to pick him up and judged that he was dead. Carrying him into the house they could see no sign of life in him. The father and mother were grief-stricken but they could do nothing but mourn, and the father left the house and went alone to arrange the burial. He met the servant of Christ, who, seeing him so upset, said to him, 'What's the matter, brother?' He replied, 'You may know, Pier, that my son today has had this fall. Leaving him for dead, I am going to arrange the funeral; and I beg you therefore that you will pray God to grant me patience.' Pier compassionately comforted him with gentle words and at once let him go on. Finding himself near the church of San Martino, he went in and prostrated himself devoutly and fervently in prayer, praying Christ the Saviour and his Virgin Mother the sweetest Mary for the child. Oh what a marvel! The little boy, who had been completely dead, once Pier's prayer was over, was made live and well as if he had never suffered any injury.

The sorrowing father returned from arranging the burial, entered the house in wonderment and, finding his son alive and well, almost went out of his mind; as if drunk with amazement and joy he flung himself on the child, embracing and kissing him tenderly, and asked the bystanders how such a great miracle had happened, that his son, left by him as if dead, had so soon been revived. The bystanders and the mother said, 'When you left the house, the child was close to death; little by little we saw him expire, and there he was for some while dead, with us all grieving about him, and suddenly he came back, live and well as you see him, to our great fright and joy, and we are greatly amazed by it, not knowing how it's come about.' The father, reflecting, like an intelligent man, that he had talked with Pier, said, 'Without doubt, the prayers of our friend Pier have obtained this miracle.' He had seen him go into the church of San Martino and, believing that he had not yet come out, he at once ran to the church and found the servant of Christ still in prayer. 'O, friend of God and my dearest benefactor,' he said, 'don't weary yourself further in prayer for my son, but know that by virtue of your holy prayers, he has been made live and well.' Pier replied, 'I am delighted with what you tell me, but don't attribute it to any virtue of mine, for I am not such a person or of such great merit in God's sight that I could do such a thing; so don't jump to conclusions, and don't while you live tell it to a soul.' So saying, Pier left and went on his way.

It happened on another occasion that this same Ventura was seized for five days on end with a severe pain in his side, to the extent that during this period he could not rest or take in anything by mouth. He was sure that he was going to die, and sent for his friend Pier, the servant of Christ, to come and visit him. Pier came at once and, raising his eyes to heaven and mentally praying to God in compassion for such pain, touched him with his hands and encouraged him with gentle words to trust in God alone. At once his friend, who had been so tormented, was entirely cured.

One day before Pier sold his vineyard he went there at the time of the vintage, returning to the house with a fine bunch of ripe grapes. Seeing it so fine, he embarked on many thoughts and praises of the Creator. There came into his memory a friend of his, a very God-fearing man, who at that time lived in Rome, and he said to himself, almost as if he were praying, 'O, would that it should have pleased the good God and my Saviour Jesus Christ and his sweetest mother, that my friend at Rome could have had these grapes.' And thus, fixing the grapes to a beam,[18] he thought no more about it. Not long afterwards, this friend came to Siena from Rome and came to visit Pier, for they were very fond of each other, and said to him, 'O my good friend, I owe you many thanks for the splendid present, when you sent me those grapes all the way to Rome.' Hearing this Pier looked up at the beam and not seeing the grapes hanging there, replied, 'My dear friend, don't thank me, but thank the Saviour and his sweetest mother, for they and not I sent them to you.' And so Pier's friend learned that the good God was graciously inclined to his servant Pier and by means of an angel had sent the grapes to Rome.

18 Presumably to dry them as raisins.

A God-fearing nobleman and citizen of Siena called Vanni Malepaste came to visit his friend the servant of Christ Pier, while he was still living with his wife in their old house. Vanni entered the house; Pier's wife was not at home, being as it happened out, and Pier was at that hour in a certain place upstairs at prayer. Vanni waited for Pier to come down, and while he was waiting it seemed to him that he could certainly hear the holy angels talking with Pier, encouraging him and defending him against demons, which Vanni could also hear creating an uproar to obstruct the servant of Christ in his prayer and contemplation. Vanni began to climb the stairs to see this battle, which he could hear, and when he got upstairs he saw Pier alone in ecstasy. Seeing this Vanni at once fearfully left the house.

His humility, control of his tongue and purity of mind

Pier the man of God recalled the opinion of Ecclesiasticus, who says: 'As pride is the beginning of all sin, so the beginning of our salvation is humility, the summit, beauty and guardian of all the virtues.'[19] Pier was full of humility and completely despised himself, judging himself to be a great sinner, although he was in fact to be reckoned among the true, just and holy servants of God. Out of humility he so mastered his tongue that, without great necessity, he never or rarely spoke and what he said was always useful, either to himself or to his neighbour. This gift of mastery of his tongue Pier had by special grace; he had sought it from God for many years with great effort and persistent prayer and finally obtained it. So, following the counsel of the wise Ecclesiasticus, he conducted himself prudently in speaking, that is to say, either he was silent or, if he did speak, he ventured nothing that was not salutary. It was his habit, whether he was walking or standing, almost always to hold his hand over his mouth like a man altogether careful in all his speech and fearful of saying an unprofitable word.[20]

Talking sometimes with his friends about the difficulty of restraining his tongue, Pier was asked whence and how he had so well achieved this

---

19 The words *Initium omnis peccati est superbia* occur in the Vulgate text of Ecclesiasticus 10:15; in the New Revised Standard Version the verse (numbered 10:13) is contrastingly translated 'the beginning of pride is sin'. The description of humility that follows is also used by the author of the Life of Zita (above, p. 178).

20 Ecclesiasticus 5:14 advises that if you do not know how to answer your neighbour, 'put your hand over your mouth'. Pier is depicted thus in art: see notably the panel on the reliquary cupboard doors (the 'Arliquieria') painted by Vecchietta c.1450 for the hospital of Santa Maria della Scala (now in the Sienese Pinacoteca) and also a fresco in the nave of San Francesco at Siena.

grace. He replied, 'My dear brothers, I don't believe, nor do I say, that I possess this essential and special virtue, but I do tell you that for four-teen years I have struggled to perfect it.' There is no doubt that Pier had perfectly acquired the virtue of controlling his tongue, for he spoke little and rarely and his speeches were very cautious, prudent, profit-able and well conceived. One day he was asked by a certain man how he could achieve the virtue of perfect humility and he replied, 'Brother, if you want to achieve this virtue easily, it's necessary to think yourself inferior to all and not to despise anyone; all of your sins must seem big to you, and the good that you do must always seem slight, and any offence that you do to your neighbour, however small, you must think great, and any service which you do to your neighbour you must think base, tiny and unworthy of reward.'

Pier was going along the road towards the Porta Salaria, with the eyes of his mind always fixed on heaven, although it was his custom always to walk with his eyes on the ground so as not to see anything that could disturb the purity of his heart. He met along the way certain young men who were noble according to the flesh but ignoble in their habits. They called Pier over to them, and he, like a humble servant of Christ, stood and listened. Possibly not with any evil intention, but wanting to hear some weighty saying from him, like youths stained with the immoral ways of the world, they asked Pier a foolish and indecent question, saying, 'Tell us, Pier, if by chance you found yourself alone in a locked room with a very beautiful woman and no one would know, then or ever, what would you do?' The holy and genuinely modest Pier humbly replied: 'Don't talk of such things, brothers, for it is not proper for good Christians to say or do dishonourable things, especially for servants of Christ, of whom I wish to be one. Nevertheless, so that you may under-stand our nature, I shall reply to your impudent question, although you've asked it with good intentions; and I tell you this, that no one is so just, not I who am a sinner, who while he lives in this wretched flesh can presume on himself for any good, unless he has received it as a special grace from God. So, according to your question: if, which God forbid, I were put in such a position, I well know what I should do, but I don't know what I would do. But I tell you this, that I would guard myself from sin, even if no one was going to know, just as I would if all the world were clearly seeing me, because it is not for love of men, from whom many things are concealed, that we must abstain from sin, but only for the love of God, to whom all things past, present and to come are manifest, down to the smallest motions of our hearts and thoughts. God be with you, brothers, peace to you.' At this reply the young men were dumbstruck and mentally confounded, and they thought among themselves of reforming their lives.

Pier knew that vainglory was a type of pride and closely allied to it; therefore he fled from it and viewed it with horror like a venomous snake. He never spoke or exhorted others to any well-doing or virtue before he had himself perfectly fulfilled it. Walking once through Siena the servant of God heard some people praising his sanctity; he went up to them, like a lover of holy humility, and said, 'O my dearest brothers, don't put dust and ashes, such as I am, before the wind, since every creature, if it is not made firm by God, is unstable and like a hollow reed is easily shaken by the wind.' So saying, he fled from them so that the empty smoke should not rise.

On another day he was devoutly engaged in contemplation when certain men of Siena said to him, as if for the sake of piety, 'O Pier, God has granted you such grace in this city that everything which you might ask to be given to the poor would be granted; why then do you not apply yourself to these works of mercy, relieving the want and misery of so many people, rather than concentrating in leisure on your contemplation?' The servant of Christ answered them benignly, 'Brothers, you must know that there are many paths to spiritual advancement, and I can say from experience, and know with absolute certainty, that it is no longer safe for me to be involved with the world, where I do not feel I can achieve any good except at the cost of my own perdition.' The men replied by pointing out that Ser Compagno, whom we have mentioned above as a devout man dear to God, was still involved in works of mercy. Pier replied humbly in praise of Ser Compagno, saying, 'Brothers, we cannot all run at the same pace, and I am not like Ser Compagno. He has this grace from God, that just as the sun shining on mud doesn't get dirty and shining on water doesn't get wet, so he, performing these works, does not suffer the harm that I would; so I do not feel fit for it, nor is it safe for me; peace be with you.'

We will tell of another virtue granted to Pier, so as to exhort sinners to holy confession. In order to preserve his mind devout, pure, clean, humble and submissive to the Saviour, he confessed every day, or very often, although it was not particularly necessary for him to do so, and with such contrition as if he had been the greatest of sinners, which in his own mind he thought he was. Once, in order to have a better recollection of his sins, he wrote down on a piece of paper everything from his infancy up to the present day in which he thought he had offended God. Taking this piece of paper, the better to weep over what it contained, he left Siena one day and went to a certain lonely place where the blessed Francis had spent some time, called Ravacciano, and entering the hermitage there the devout servant of Christ began with the greatest contrition to read and lament over what he had written on the paper. So bitterly did he weep that he knew from God that he had received forgiveness, and this was a sign: that when his tears were over the piece of paper that had been written on was as blank as if nothing had ever been written on it.

Chastity, abstinence, pilgrimages

The servant of Christ Pier paid constant and vigilant attention to the preservation of the special treasure of holy chastity, which, as the Apostle says, we possess in earthen vessels very prone to fracture. Pier went to great efforts to preserve it, with great mental purity and holiness and bodily decency. He devoted much time to abstinence, which in him was hidden and discreet, in that he ate all permitted things according to their seasons, but so soberly and sparingly that it scarcely sufficed for the support of nature. He always fasted from All Saints to Christmas, and throughout Lent, with other prescribed vigils, and on Friday and Saturday he never failed to fast devoutly. He slept very little and, following the apostolic precept, remained ceaselessly in prayer and contemplation; the little that he slept was on a very hard bed, to which nothing but extreme necessity could induce him. He dressed in the cheapest fabrics, which he often patched in different colours. He mortified the flesh with various tiring pilgrimages, going now to Rome for the holy indulgences, now to San Francesco at Assisi (he held this indulgence in particular faith and devotion), now to Pisa on the Feast of the Ascension, now to Pistoia in the church of San Jacopo Maggiore. The man of God with great fervour compelled his body to serve the spirit, and both to serve Almighty God.

His justice, discretion and good counsel

By means of his great prudence and discretion Pier had achieved the singular virtue of justice, compelling himself in everything to render to each according to their entitlement. First of all, to God he rendered the most passionate love, with filial fear and honour; to his neighbour the sincerest affection; to his own soul special purity and devotion; to his body endless toil and a bare subsistence, exerting himself always to do good to himself and his neighbour, and to the utmost of his ability avoiding all evil.

One night, while he was still living in his own house, he rose about midnight and left the house to go to the cathedral, as was his custom, to pray and meditate before the image of the glorious Virgin Mary. On the way he encountered the men who go around the city at night keeping watch, that is, the household servants of the Bargello.[21] They could see two lighted torches with their own eyes but could not see who was carrying them; they only saw the man of God Pier walking in the middle between them. They were amazed by this and out of reverence said nothing to him. But Pier saw them, and called them to him, saying, 'My dearest brothers, you don't want to swear to anything falsely; I know very well that you have taken an oath to your superior and promised to report anyone you find going about the city at this hour, so tomorrow morning, by all means, so that you don't perjure yourselves, tell the judge that you have seen me.' The officers replied to him, 'Go in peace, man of God, we will do our duty.'

The following day Pier went of his own accord to find the *podestà* of the city, and said to him, 'Messer, you know the statute which you have sworn to observe; it states that anyone who is found at night going around the city must pay a certain amount of money, according to the form of the proclamation which you issued when you took office. Now you must know that this last night I was found by your officers going around the city, and so, as I have contravened the proclamation, I have brought you the money which I must pay: so take it and put it into the communal treasury.' The *podestà*, observing Pier's justice and marvelling at such punctilious observation of the statutes, said, like a prudent man, 'Go, servant of Christ, I know all about your life and your sanctity; take your money, for the law wasn't made for you, but for criminals and ill-livers; I know perfectly well that you only go around at night in order to do good. And so that you can do so in future with a clear conscience, I am exempting you from this statute, giving you total licence and freedom to go wherever and however you want, at any hour of night, and I want this permission to last for my entire period of office; and I do not want you to be subject to any impost which may be imposed by this commune.' Pier thanked him for the first concession, that is, the freedom to go around at night, but on the second, about the

---

21 That is, of the *podestà*. At Florence the palace of the *podestà* is still popularly known as 'the Bargello'.

communal taxes, he replied, being a just man: 'Messer *podestà*, I do not want this second privilege, because, if I make use of the amenities of this city – land, water, air, fire, the company of others, the security of this way of life, and many other common goods – it is not good for me to be exempt from the city's imposts.' Marvelling at this reply, the *podestà* said to him, 'Go in peace, man of God, and pray for me.'

The commune of Siena had raised a large army to overcome a fortress in the *contado* which had often been a source of injury in that it was a refuge of many brigands, exiles and rebels against the city of Siena. For this reason the commune was forced to go to large extraordinary expenses, and a tax was proclaimed on all Sienese citizens, which was to be paid according to wealth. Pier did not know about this immediately, but after several days he heard some of his neighbours complaining about the tax and he asked them, 'Dear brothers, what is this that you're all complaining about?' They replied, 'Don't you know about the tax imposed by the commune on the whole land?' Pier said, 'Certainly not, I know nothing about it. But tell me, how much is it per person?' They told him the amount of the levy, and immediately Pier went into his house and carefully calculated what he should pay according to the amount of his property; having worked it out, he took the amount of money that his conscience dictated and went at once to the citizens who had been appointed to receive the aforesaid tax, saying to them, 'Sirs, it's bad news for me that for several days, being in ignorance, I've kept back this money which I owe to my commune; today I've heard about the tax and I've brought my share; so take it and forgive me my ignorance.' They marvelled at such justice and observance of the law and said to him, 'Man of God, there is no need for us to forgive you, because you have not been defrauding us, and in fact the assessors had decided not to say anything to you, because we know very well that you are not rich in the things of this world. It will be enough for us, and this is what we would ask of you, that you pray for us and for your city and ours. So take your money, take it back and go in peace.' The just man answered them, 'My dear sirs, I am always desirous of going in the peace of God, but I am not taking this money, which belongs to my commune, for it is not mine'; and leaving it, he departed at once.

Pier had a friend in Florence, a man who was not well founded in the ways of God, wanting to have one foot in heaven and keep the other on the earth. Now this man asked Pier in a letter for advice as to how he could live this life in a manner pleasing to Christ as a good Christian. Pier had several times given him advice on this subject, but he had given little heed to similar admonitions and counsels. Wanting to satisfy him, Pier replied figuratively in this manner: he blunted a table knife and made cuts in it all round, and sent it to him. By means of this knife, treated thus, he wanted him to understand that just as this knife would be of little use at table, because while with one edge it cut the food, with the other it would cut your hand; similarly he who wants truly to serve in the ways of God must leave the world, for it is impossible for the same heart and mind to devote himself at once to God and to the world; as the Supreme Truth says, 'No one can serve two masters'; especially when they are opposites, as are Almighty God and this wretched world.

His prudence and counsel

Pier possessed the greatest prudence, which enabled him to foresee, for himself and others, the good (so as to achieve it) and the evil (so as to avoid it) and to give the most excellent and Christian advice to others. In that time there was as *podestà* at Siena a nobleman of the March of Ancona who, hearing of Pier's sanctity and remarkable prudence, sent word to the guardian of San Francesco, where Pier was living permanently, asking him to come to him, bringing Pier with him, because he wanted to see and talk with him. So the guardian, not telling Pier the reason, took him with several other friars to the palace of the *podestà*. When they came before him, all the friars were silent, and Pier, being a just and God-fearing man, was also humbly silent, not presuming to say a word in the presence of such people without the permission of the guardian. Seeing that he was silent, the guardian said to him, 'Pier, know that we have come here because Messer the *podestà* wants to hear something of God from you.' Then the servant of Christ said to the *podestà*, 'Tell me, Messer *podestà*, when you came to this city, did you bring any debts with you?' The *podestà* reflected and, reckoning that he did not think he had, replied, 'Servant of Christ, I don't recall that at the moment I have any debts.' Pier answered, 'If up to now you have not got into debt, I exhort you for the future not to do so.' And so saying he left (I believe because he felt he was close to a state of ecstasy and ravishment of spirit). These words could mean only that Pier wanted by them to exhort the *podestà* to do nothing by which he could offend Almighty God. When Pier had gone, the *podestà* said to the bystanders, 'Verily I believe that this holy man has in him the spirit and wisdom of God, for in a very few words he has given a mighty piece of advice.'

A friar of San Francesco was very conscientious in hearing the confessions of different people and came once to seek the advice of the servant of Christ, saying, 'Oh Pier, I hear many confessions of different people, and sins; and I want advice from you as to how I should conduct myself in imposing penance on them, that is, should I impose large or middling or small penances, for I don't want to get this wrong.' Pier replied, 'My dearest brother, I say to you that if the heavenly King and Lord of the universe is not only generous to me, but lavish with his goods, you are not the master, but only the dispenser, you give not what is yours, but what is his; why should you be mean? But I advise you to administer penance to penitents, according as you see in them more or less contrition and a better disposition to do what is imposed on them; always make yourself incline more to mercy than to justice, for our Saviour Christ asks of the sinner only contrition for sin and a genuine intention in the future to abstain from it.'

At the time when the servant of Christ was living in San Francesco, a very learned friar was appointed in San Francesco, according to the custom of the province, to read holy theology. This friar had previously in the world been a great philosopher, and in his doctrine he followed natural philosophy rather than sacred theology. For this reason he was often implicated in some philosophical error in his teaching. One day he was lecturing on theology and dealing with the subject of divine foreknowledge, like a philosopher rather than a theologian. In his lecture he stated publicly that God's foreknowledge knew everything from the beginning and always, things past as well as present and future. He was right in saying this, but what he went on to say was false: that since God's prescience knows all things, he consequently knows whether a man is to be saved or damned; and because the divine foreknowledge is immutable, no virtuous actions can save someone who is to be damned, nor can someone be damned who is to be saved.

A young student friar, hearing this, was at the prompting of the devil thrown into such agony and perturbation of mind that he considered returning to the world, saying to himself, 'If so learned a man as my master, our lector, holds this opinion, that is, that if I am foreknown by God I cannot save myself by any good work, nor if I am predestined by God can I damn myself by any evil work; if then what is to become of me will happen whatever way of life I maintain, I would rather return to the world and enjoy myself, for God knows very well what must finally happen to me.' However, the divine clemency, which neither can nor does abandon him who truly serves him nor (as the

Apostle says) permits us to be tempted beyond our capacity, put it into the young friar's head that before he put his evil intention into operation, he should seek the advice of the servant of Christ Pier, for whose sanctity he had a very high regard. So he went to the church, where he found Pier in prayer; and out of reverence, not wanting to disturb him, he waited, silently and in much distress. Pier, inspired by God, seeing him standing there, called to him saying, 'My dearest son, did you want something of me?' The friar in reply told him everything in order, that is what his master and lector had said, and his own thoughts and his present intentions.

When he heard all this, the zealous man of God was marvellously disturbed, and, raging within himself as if he were intoxicated in spirit, he began to groan, walking up and down the church several times, saying, 'Alas! Alas! Wisdom has gone astray like folly, the light has gone dark, truth has fled, and iniquity has come and had taken the place of wisdom in the chair!' When he had gone round the church several times groaning, he returned to the friar, who was now completely dumbfounded at the sight of what Pier was doing, and said to him, 'O my son, you must know that you have got your sums wrong, and therefore I want us to redo them together. You say that you want to leave holy religion and return to the evil life of the world, saying that God knows very well whether you must be saved or damned. My son, your reasoning is false, and therefore not good, and so I, with the help of God, will guide you into another, better and truer.

'The first argument I will give you is this. If an angel from heaven brought me a book in which my total damnation was written, I would not for that reason depart from the service of God because, even if not at the end, at least in this world I want God with me, for it is written that he lives with his servants. Hearken, my son, to another argument which must recall you from your plan, and that is: given that you must be damned, since you have committed sin and have the guilt on your conscience, this guilt is nothing other than the punishment of damnation before a man is damned to hell, and I can give you a parallel: if someone in prison is condemned to death by the judge, he musn't be constantly overwhelmed by that sentence before the hour comes, but must make the best dispositions he can for the saving of his soul, and bear the sentence with patience.

'Listen, my son, to the third argument. God never created a person in order to damn him, indeed God wishes, as the holy Apostle says, that all men should be saved and come to the knowledge of the truth, and

God loves the rational soul more than the soul loves him, in the person of his son Jesus, who underwent such torments for that soul; so I say to you that no one will be damned by divine foreknowledge, which does not impose the necessity of either salvation or damnation on man, but he is damned only by his own guilt. Hearken, my son, to the fourth argument. You must know that just as in heaven there are, as the gospel says, many mansions, that is different crowns of victory, so in hell there are different punishments, according to the different nature of the guilt; and just as we must always aspire to the greater crown, the greater glory, which is acquired by doing good, so must a man choose the least possible punishment and infernal torment that is acquired by evildoing; so I say to you, assuming that a man must be damned, he must always choose to do as little evil as possible.

'The fifth argument, my dearest son, must recall you from this foolish plan. That is, you must imagine that the good God has provided the path that can lead finally to the longed-for goal of salvation, and so you must reckon that his goodness has so worked on you, taking you from this miserable world into this holy religious life, where, living according to the past example of its fathers, you can achieve perpetual happiness. I now bring forward the sixth argument, that is, that it is the duty of the good and prudent creature to wish sooner to be damned with the will of God than saved in despite of it – I say this assuming that it were possible. So, dearest son, everything must be reposed in the pure will of our Creator and Saviour, who, as I said before, wants every man to be saved and nobody damned unless by their own fault and ill will.

'The seventh and last argument is that you must know that the good God has given such power to our free will that it cannot be constrained by any creature under almighty God; much less then can our cunning adversary impede our salvation against our will, and even though he continually afflicts us with his temptations, still, when we are overcome by our fragility and fall into sin, our God is always merciful, turning us back to him to receive us in penitence. So I say to you, dearest son, that for all these reasons and many more which could go on to infinity, you must reckon that because the supreme truth is incomprehensible, the divine foreknowledge (wrongly understood by your master and doctor) does not impose the necessity of a man's salvation or damnation.'

The young friar, hearing these holy arguments and exhortations, was totally comforted and restored to himself, and with great reverence thanked Pier and departed. Constantly persevering in the religious life he progressed to ever greater good; he achieved the highest rank and was an ever more excellent shepherd and ruler of others.

On another occasion the bishop of Siena had died, and the canons and electors gathering together elected as their bishop a religious of holy life and great learning, an excellent preacher called Brother Ambrogio, of the order of Preachers.[22] When he was thus elected, he was for many reasons exhorted by his brethren to accept this dignity. He replied, 'My dearest brothers, it seems to me that this election is a matter of great importance, therefore I don't want to answer yes or no, I want to think about it and do what God inspires me to do.' Reflecting thus, he was inspired by God to seek the advice of Pier, the servant of Christ. He went secretly and, discussing the matter with him, got this reply from Pier: 'Brother Ambrogio, as you know better than I do, the seed which is sown in the earth mustn't be hollow but plump and firm, if it is to bear fruit; I think it's the same with the preacher of the word of God, that is, he bears little or no fruit when he doesn't reconcile good life with learning. You are reckoned a good servant of God, and a fine preacher; you have been preaching for a long time, and you have always exhorted the people to despise the world and its vanities. Now I don't know how effective your exhortations against worldly pomps and dignities can still be in the hearts of the faithful if they see that you yourself have sought them and got mixed up in them. All the same, you are wise and prudent; do what seems best to you, I have told you only what God has inspired me to say.' Hearing this reply Brother Ambrogio, like a good and prudent man, decided that Pier's advice was excellent and salutary, and so he refused the election.

At that time there was great conflict in Siena between the Guelfs and the Ghibellines. The Ghibelline party was overcome by the Guelfs, and went to Arezzo. On one occasion they asked the man of Christ (knowing he had the spirit of prophecy) how long they would have to be exiles from their homeland, to which he replied, 'When your sins diminish and are fewer than those of your enemies, then you may peacefully return to your homeland.' This was indeed the case; after several years they reconciled themselves better to God and made peace with the opposed party, and thus very peacefully returned home.[23]

22 The bishopric was probably offered to Ambrogio Sansedoni in either 1273 or 1281: Waley, *Siena and the Sienese*, p. 144.

23 There was an attempted pacification and abolition of parties at Siena in 1280–1, which proved short-lived (*ibid.*, pp. 121–2). In 1290, after the defeat of the Tuscan Ghibellines at Campaldino in June 1289 (and after Pier's death), 'the Ghibellines returned to Siena on the terms willed by the Guelfs and made peace'. Both events are recorded by the so-called Montauri chronicler: *Cronache senesi*, ed. A. Lisini and F. Iacometti

Pier was often asked by people to pray for them, and he used always to reply thus: 'Brother, do so also on your side, so that I, praying for you, may deserve to be heard.' And he would also give this illustration, saying, 'If you and I were together at the table, it would certainly not please you if I ate both your portion and my own. It's the same at the table of the divine grace. It's set before us, full of the most delicious and suitable foods for salvation, which are obtained above all by virtue of holy and devout prayer, not just of those who are doing the praying, but also of those for whom the prayer is offered, when they are disposed to receive them.'

A young layman in Siena was instructed to appear before the *podestà* to give testimony which would damage certain people whose friendship he was afraid to lose. On the other hand it seemed to him that that he could not lie without damage to his own conscience, and so he was greatly agitated and did not know what to do. However, he was inspired by God to see Pier's advice; he explained his dilemma to him and Pier replied in this manner: 'Dearest son, it would be better for you to live away from Siena with the friendship of God than to live in it with the friendship of men, or with your conscience corrupted by false witness.' The young man thanked Pier and left him with the intention of following his advice. But Pier the servant of Christ prayed for him, and the dispute was resolved satisfactorily and the young man did not have to give evidence at all.

It was Pier's habit never to exhort his neighbour to the practice of any virtue which he himself had not practised; so he used to say that when anger comes upon us, we must first mortify it prudently within ourselves, before we make any exterior sign and show it outwardly in word or deed; anger thus restrained cannot prevent us, as it sometimes does, from knowing the truth, and if we do this we shall have nothing to confess, at the time for confession, except that first, inward stirring, without having offended our neighbour by evil example.

One summer, when Pier was living in San Francesco, he went around Siena on necessary business, and came back to the convent at the hour of midday, when the brethren rest. Like a godly and tactful person, he did not want to make a noise by knocking, but patiently waited until nones. While he was waiting there were several Sienese also at the door with a pilgrim, talking together. This pilgrim was boasting to them, saying he had traversed many roads and travelled in many regions and

(*Rerum Italicarum Scriptores*, new series, ed. Giosue Carducci et al. (103 vols in 142, Città di Castello, 1908–16), 15:6), pp. 225, 227.

parts of the world, and performed many pilgimages, and in this way he foolishly vaunted himself. Pier listened patiently to all this, but he was sorry, for the sake of the pilgrim's salvation, to hear such vanity. He stopped talking when someone else arrived and knocked at the door, and it was opened. As he went in Pier briefly answered the pilgrim, saying, 'My friend, I don't think it's possible to know the world, nor to make praiseworthy pilgrimages, if a person does not first try to know his own state and interior condition.' And with these words he shut the door and went silently to his cell.

One day Pier was going through Siena and, passing along the road where they dress hides, he saw a friend of his, called Salvi, dressing a hide, and said to him, 'O Salvi, my brother, make sure that you dress that hide well, don't damage your conscience.' The man of God said this to show that one must practise one's trade in such a way as not to offend God or one's neighbour.

Pier had such a reputation for sanctity among the brothers where he stayed that often the novice master brought, or sent, his novices to him so that he could inflame them with his holy words and counsels in the holy resolution to serve God. On one of these occasions Pier was talking and exhorting the novices to serve God fervently and always to talk only of God among themselves, quoting the saying of the holy gospel, that is, 'Where two or three are gathered together in my name, I tell you truly, I will be in the midst of them.' Two of the novices listened to this with especial fervour and, leaving the place (which was a little garden, very pleasant and quiet, reserved solely for the use of the novices) and returning to the cloister, they started to talk together: 'Did you hear what our father Pier said, that if we talk only of God he will be in the midst of us? So I think that tomorrow morning, after mass, let's return to our garden, and there do nothing but talk of God, and like our father Pier has said, he will be in the midst of us.'

One of the two novices said this, and the other replied simply, 'O my brother, it won't be good for our Lord when he comes to sit on the ground like us, so I will bring a stool, for I know where one is, and I'll also bring a little cushion which I have in my cell, on which the Lord will sit on the stool between us, and we will sit on the ground talking about him.' The other novice replied, 'Oh, what a good idea, brother! And I'll bring a towel which our master gave me, and with that we'll cover the cushion which the Lord has to sit on.' And so, the following morning, the devout novices did all this after mass, arranging the stool and sitting on the ground with great fevour, talking of God.

And behold, the Savour came in the form of a most beautiful little boy, and sat on the aforementioned stool; and although the novices did not physically see him, they sensed his presence spiritually, for such was the consolation they felt that they remained for a long period of time as if drunk with him, not knowing what was going on outside; so that the when bell was rung for terce, they heard nothing.

The other brothers said the office, and afterwards the bell rang for the meal and the novice-master realised that two of his flock were missing. Not knowing otherwise, like a good shepherd he was much saddened, fearing that his lambs had been devoured by the jaws of the ravenous wolf or deceived by the cunning of the serpent, although he could scarcely believe it, knowing the unusual uprightness and devotion that was in their hearts and minds. Nonetheless, after the meal he set himself eagerly to see if the two lost sheep were to be found anywhere, and came to the garden, where they still were in this state of devotion. Pier saw him on the point of entering the garden and forestalled him, for he was nearby, and quietly said to him, 'Dearest father, don't reprove your disciples for anything. I will explain how what's happened to them has come about, but see that you keep it to yourself. I was in a place where I could see them, but they couldn't see me, and I saw them sit on the ground, talking about God, as we have been exhorted, and I saw Christ the Saviour sit down between them in human form, and he has been consoling them spiritually up the moment you arrived; they are so intoxicated with his sweetness that they've heard nothing else – so go and call them gently and get them to take some food.' The novice-master believed him and did what he suggested.

Pier had some friends at Florence, who were accustomed to come to Siena to consult him about their most serious affairs. One on occasion they were prevented and could not come. Having need of his advice, for themselves and for others, they sent two of their friends, Bartolomeo and Cerrino of Florence, with a letter in which they begged Pier urgently to write them some words of advice and exhortation to the good, both for themselves and for many others who confided in them. When Pier received this letter he humbled himself and said, 'Who am I to be able to give advice to prudent men? I am an ordinary man, simple, ignorant, unlettered, and so I don't think it is right for me to reply.' And as he thus humbled himself in the sight of God and within himself, the Spirit of God came upon him and he called a friend called Ciano of Siena, and said, 'Dearest brother, I can't write very well and you write well; so I beg you to take down a reply according to what my patron, the glorious

Virgin Mary, will dictate to me, because of myself I shouldn't know how to think or write anything good.' Raising the eyes of his mind and his body to heaven, he began to dictate the reply, and at almost every sentence he said piously, 'O Mary the Virgin, Queen of Heaven, who bore him who is true wisdom, pray him to teach me how I should reply to others, and myself to believe and to do what is pleasing to you and salutary for me'; and he began to write the reply like this:

> To Bartolomeo and Cerrino, citizens of Florence, I, the useless and least servant of Christ Pier Pettinaio, send you greetings in Christ Jesus; and eternal salvation again to our dearest well-wishers and friends of Christ the Saviour in Florence.

> Dearest brothers in the Lord, I have received by your messengers your Christian letter, and read it with pleasure to understand your holy purpose and desire; although you have by writing asked advice from a lowly man who is completely unfit to advise others, being unworthy even to advise himself, nonetheless, putting my trust in the only son of God, our Saviour, who is the true and supreme wisdom, and in his glorious mother the Virgin Mary, I will just tell you what they grant me to write for your salvation.

> First, I think it would be salutary for you to choose for yourselves a spiritual father, from some holy and approved religious order, fitted by goodness and intelligence to give you the advice which is appropriate for your salvation; talking with him every day you would be improved, and in pure and complete confession you would often fully reveal to him your every mishap, with sorrow for past sins and the remorse which is appropriate to true Christians, with the firm intention for the future of totally abstaining from them, so that you may please our supremely good Creator, who is the sum of goodness. You must know that in confession, the sinner seeks out the confessor, that is the vicar of God, before whom he can bring nothing to give to his Creator save abominations and the foulest of deeds; but all the same, when confession has been well made, he derives from the good God, as from the most generous of lords, the most remarkable spiritual contentment, and such sweetness that in that moment he reckons the world as nothing. Just think: if he does us so much good when we lay our wretchedness before him, what would he do if we came before him bearing a sincere and upright conscience? Certainly, we must believe that our spiritual contentment and delight would be much the greater. Anyone who reflected wisely on this as a good Christian would realise how carefully he must guard his soul from offence and be always afire with the divine love.

> You must know, dearest friends in Christ, that a man permits his soul only that expenditure of evil which he himself wishes; and man would have much good through the goodness of God if he himself did not damage himself. I present myself to the Creator, and he, in supreme generosity, always loads me with his gifts; but I, like a bad and avaricious servant, spend his gifts not as I should but as I wrongly wish, working not according to his will but

fruitlessly on the earth. Thus ungrateful, I dare to present myself again to him, and, although he is offended, he still generously restores me with his gifts and renews his friendship with me; I, wicked and ungrateful, at once betray and breach the friendship of so great a lord. Still he in his supreme mercy not only receives me but, as if he had need of me, seeks me out and offers himself to me; and I, stupid and arrogant, still flee from him, and he, like the most generous of lords, still waits for me, giving me time to make my peace with him, as long as this wretched and fragile life lasts.

This time, albeit a great and precious treasure, is ill-appreciated by us and badly spent, although it is freely given to us out of his goodness. But if I, ungrateful and foolish, do not take advantage of it when I have the time to present myself to God, why should he grant me any of his gifts? Rather he can and must justly abandon me as a vile and contumacious creature, since he has visited me with such great gifts and such great friendship and I, supremely ungrateful, have always rejected them. Thus offended by me, when I present myself to him again with humble prayer, he graciously forgives me every offence and rewards me with his ample and gracious gifts.

Therefore we must trust that his goodness will give itself freely to whomsoever faithfully presents himself to him, infusing such devout and sincere minds sometimes with the grace of mental prayer and sometimes only with the grace of vocal prayer; for if his goodness always gave us the virtue and grace of prayer alone, the human mind could (like a fragile creature) easily be already with God in a very lofty state; and therefore he, like a wise and prudent doctor of the human mind, does not always grant that we can mentally taste him in mental prayer, but simply feeds us with himself in vocal prayer; and if we did that with a pure and sincere conscience, we would achieve no less merit than in mental prayer. For there is no doubt that in our vocal prayer the divine mercy deigns to talk with his creature, even if the creature be much more ardently refreshed by his goodness speaking with him in mental prayer. We may say that what happens in vocal prayer is what happens in reading holy theology, in which the good God gives himself freely to the devout spirit; but in mental contemplation, the soul, so exceedingly uplifted, gives itself to God in such abundance of spirit that it cannot of itself bear such fervour.

But what is the stupidity of human weakness, that when the supreme and divine goodness is willing to dwell with us, we always chase it away with our iniquity and malice! Oh! At least we could live with him and do as worldly merchants do, who at the appointed times devote themselves entirely to their business! We must at least on feast-days always work fervently with our sweet God; for we well know that these days were appointed by Holy Church for the faithful for no other reason than to devote them to holy praises, masses, offices, sermons and holy and devout prayers, not forgetting works of mercy towards our needy neighbour; in which holy exercises, there is no doubt, the good God offers himself and his most gracious gifts. We must all the same know that man is composed of two parts, body and soul, and without either of these parts it is possible neither to live nor to live well;

and therefore the prudent Christian must take care of his soul, that it is not at odds with the body, which must be governed and controlled in such a way that it does not dominate the soul, but serves it; for we can see very well that the body is nothing but a rotten thing, which within a few days must return to its beginnings. Throughout its course it drips putrescence and shows us that it is nothing but stinking dregs, in which the soul is placed as in a prison, labouring like a thing spiritual and heavenly until it returns to its most merciful maker, God.

We must always remember that we are creatures and, thinking humbly of ourselves at all times, not be intoxicated by vain and worldly honours nor attribute any goodness or sanctity to ourselves, for 'he who seeks such things obtains not honour but his own disgrace'. O man! Why do you puff yourself up, wanting to be thought good or great, when you are at once saddened by the selfsame desire? Do you not know that God alone is good? and all honour is due to him, by whom alone, through grace, it is granted to us to do any good, if any good we do, as in the gospel he said to his disciples, 'When you have done all these things, call yourselves useless servants.' And the Apostle Paul also warns us, not only that we are not fit to do good, but not even to think it, for all our sufficiency comes from the good God.

Some think there must be something in me, and call me a servant of God; but I tell you truly that when I examine myself justly I find that this opinion is false. And even if there were any little bit of good in me which might be pleasing to God, do we not know that this comes not from me but from God as the giver of all good, from whom comes all beginning and persever-ance in well-doing? No human virtue was ever able to make a millet seed. And so, Christian soul, you must have trust not in yourself or your capaci-ties but in him alone, and try with loving and burning familiarity to unite yourself with him in friendship. In him you will always find every power, every virtue, every goodness and wisdom, with the utmost desire for your salvation. You seek the human friendship of a mutable and unstable creature, subject to many deceptions; why do you not seek rather to unite yourself with your Creator and Saviour, who can never change from his perpetual changelessness and supreme goodness? and with his glorious mother, who never allows those who trust in her to perish? And just as you are unwilling to displease your friend, although a fallible man, so much the more must you with all your might try to avoid displeasing your Creator, who so much loved you that he deigned, for you, to be made, from God, man. From him, just as he cannot be deceived, no deceit can ever proceed; and it is truly a sign that a soul does not love him when he is careless of displeasing him.

We see by experience of human friendships how gladly friends talk together and how willingly, when they are apart, they speak well of one another; how much more, O soul, must you, in presence and in absence, make every effort to think and speak of the Eternal and Supreme God and always to do good? And if on earth you find any false comfort, why do you not raise yourself up to heavenly things, where you can in eternity with Christ and his sweet mother enjoy boundless bliss and jollity? And when it is necessary to associate with creatures, remember always, Christian soul, when you have returned to yourself, that your conversation must be in heaven with Christ, and in your whole way of life always try to choose the conduct which will lead you from earth to the celestial fatherland.

Lift up your sights, gazing always at heaven, and do not let his great distance from you impede you, for the devout and contemplative mind swiftly transcends it. Look and consider again how wonderful is the beauty of heaven, and think how incomparably greater is the interior beauty of that heaven, that is the blessed homeland and paradise of almighty God. Wanting to share in that rejoicing, you must first and foremost reflect on the innumerable benefits granted to you by your Creator, and how he descended to earth from that high heaven for you, to lead you from earth to heaven, and being omnipotent and immortal became for you a mortal man, to lead you to perpetual immortality; so why, vilest of creatures, being nothing with all your pride, do you want to think you are anything? Do you not know that God thwarts the proud and gives his grace to the humble? In the world we see people exerting themselves more or less in various activities, and all the same they get nothing out of all their efforts but food and clothing; and is it not the height of stupidity just to try to feed and clothe yourself by your avarice and obtain these things by improper means, leading your same self to the dark dungeon of perpetual damnation?

Therefore, making judicious use of this world, look always for ways to ensure that you arrive finally at the glory of the eternal king. We know very well that our bodily comforts are causes of damage to the soul, therefore we must seek always to make only just use of them, and [not] to fear that small suffering which goes with living, when it spurs us towards our supreme homeland. Only perpetual suffering is to be feared, and eternal glory sought with every effort; the temporal suffering obtained by patience is to be loved with the utmost longing. Tell me, O man: if you want to have all the good things that are necessary to the body, how much more must you seek what is necessary to the salvation of your soul, for which, as for something precious, the Saviour came to earth and spilt his precious blood? And, just as you avoid bodily illness as much as possible, how much more must you avert from yourself every risk of spiritual illness and damage to your eternal health? As you pursue various bodily sensations and transitory delights, from which in the end nothing comes but illness and death, how much more must you devote yourself to spiritual delights and foodstuffs, through which you can taste your Creator. O soul! Do you not see that in mixing yourself up in worldly pleasures and passing enjoyments, you fill yourself with a mortal poison and befoul in yourself the habitation of the Celestial Bridegroom? We well know that our good God asks nothing other of the soul but that it faithfully serves him with holy simplicity, as even a devout and simple old woman shows, who understands the whole of holy scripture, if she possesses those two necessary texts of salvation, that is, 'Avoid what is evil and do what is good', and this we must believe God permits for no other reason than that he is delighted by holy simplicity alone.

Think often, soul, of your Creator, to what a noble end he has created you, and you will surely find that he has made you for no other reason than to give you eternal nobility. Certainly nothing in this life is greater nobility than to abandon evil, faithfully pursuing the good and serving our sweet God with perseverance; nor does God demand anything of you, but that, departing from evil deeds and working nobly and with virtue, you draw near to him for your eternal good. And you will find no excuse with him, O soul, even if no scripture or divine precept had ever been expounded to you; for do you not have goodness naturally infused in you, that all evil must be shunned and all good pursued? To you, soul, is committed the care of the body, and therefore by you alone can the Creator be offended, for we see very well that the body, without the soul, can do nothing for good or ill, and therefore it is by your indolence that the body gets mixed up in sin, not of itself, and an exact account will be required of you, for you can, with divine grace, do good through the body.

Do not try, O soul, arrogantly to know a great deal, but thinking humbly of yourself, let all your knowledge be in taking pleasure in your good God, and ask of him with humility what is expedient for your salvation. And if you want to be well disposed to him, ensure that in your every action divine grace is uppermost, that is, that in all your works you never want to transgress what is the divine will; when talking, talk gently, avoiding every kind of anger or insult against your neighbour, always trying to achieve perseverance in divine charity; and thus you will have mental peace and steadfastness in well-doing. By these means the soul reposes easily in God. Let its every action be performed by you always in the name of the Saviour, so that he may always be in all things your guide and director. Loved by you above all, and always dwelling in your heart, he will make you a stranger to bitterness, nor will you be able to imagine being disturbed by any adversity, if you serve him humbly and with purity of heart; but guarded always by him in pity and mercy, you will at last be summoned to the true homeland and long-desired knowledge of him, who infuses you in the present life with his light, by which you can discern those things which by displeasing him lead the soul to eternal torment, so that by avoiding them you may always do those things which lead to perpetual glory.

If then, beloved brothers, we desire to rejoice perfectly in the blessed home-land with Christ, let us with longing minds take the narrow path in this life, and persevering in it to the end with the divine grace arrive at the eternal glory, of which the Apostle writes that no human ear can hear, nor the heart of man think, nor the tongue of creature express, how great it is. In this wretched life the rational creature enjoys only the merest spark of it when out of its senses and inebriated by the divine love; not being able in its own nature to endure anything so great, it must become beside itself and, divorced from the body, does not know what is being said or done outside it. And therefore, beloved brothers, so that I may not be cut off from him by my sins, I beg you to pray God for me, and for the scribe of this present ill-composed letter, in which, if you find any spiritual fruit, attribute it to the divine grace and not to me. The peace of the Lord be with you. Amen.

His patience and his passing

Pier was endowed with the wonderful virtue of patience, so that if anything in any way adverse happened to him, either by diabolical suggestion or from the world and those who loved it, he never seemed in the least disturbed but always said, 'Blessed be our Lord and Saviour, and his mother, the glorious Virgin Mary, for love of whom every adversity must be borne, since they have suffered such great things for us.' Everyone who offended him he at once forgave from his heart like a true Christian, remembering our Lord's prayer, the Paternoster, and said silently to himself, 'How can I pray my God to pardon me and forgive the evils and offences, which I commit every day against his goodness, if I do not from my heart pardon my debtors any injury committed by them?'

Once Pier was standing in the piazza with a stall on which he had his combs for sale, and a citizen came by in a great hurry and knocking into the stall upset everything on to the ground. The man of Christ was not in the least upset by this, but in all things blessing God he patiently set about restoring his stall as best he could. The citizen, coming back and seeing the trouble he had given Pier, said to him, 'Dearest father, I beg you to pardon me for the trouble I've given you, upsetting your goods on to the ground amid such a crowd.' Pier answered him kindly, 'Dearest brother, it would be extremely bad for my soul if I had not voluntarily pardoned you, for I know that my Lord wants us to forgive any injury at once, even though in this case I don't think you've done me any harm. So go in peace, my dearest brother, always putting your trust in the Lord God and guarding yourself from all evil and doing with all your might everything that can lead you to salvation.'

The servant of Christ was so much in love with the sweet and benevolent Saviour and with his mother, the ever-immaculate Virgin Mary, that whether he was standing or walking, or was in the house or outside it, he was always thinking sweet contemplative thoughts of them or praying aloud. Once he went, as he often did, to Pistoia and one day, in order to get as far away as possible from other people, the better to contemplate the sweetness of God, he went out of the city and passing through a certain lonely place was seen by a gang of boys as he went along. Stirred up by the devil, either in order to try the patience of the servant of God or to disturb him in his divine meditations, they began to shout at Pier, 'There he is, the bad man who does witchcraft, invoking demons and inviting them to do evil.' Pier took no notice of these devilish and childish jibes, but continued in his devotions as if deaf, showing no sign of hearing. It happened that some men of rank came by and, hearing this abuse of the holy man, of whose sanctity they had the highest opinion, they gravely rebuked the boys, telling them that Pier was a holy man and a friend of God. Hearing this Pier, anxious to preserve his holy humility and desirous of glory that was divine and eternal glory rather than vain and human, immediately secretly left them and returned to his dwelling in Siena.

The time came when it pleased God to summon his enamoured soul to himself, to the perpetual repose of the eternal life, after the many trials he had undergone for his love in this life. Around the year 1289 the man of God was stricken by a very serious illness. It is impossible to relate with what patience the servant of Christ conducted himself, always in word and gesture giving thanks to the supreme God and giver of all good things, seeking and receiving the holy sacraments of the church with the greatest humility. Thus fortified and refreshed by sincere confession and the most holy Communion and extreme unction, he expired to the celestial fatherland. Being thus at his last hour, as a true friend and prophet of God, he uttered many remarkable sayings, the following among others: 'Woe to thee, Pistoia, woe to thee Florence, and woe also to thee Siena.' Having said this, he fell silent, evincing no little wonder in his face and other gestures. A religious brother of San Francesco who was present asked him, 'Father, why do you say such things?' And the man of God repeated the same words; but the friar insisted that he tell him what was going to happen. Pier replied quietly, 'It will be what God wills, and let that suffice.' And in truth we already see his prophecy in large part fulfilled, for the city of Pistoia has been all but destroyed down to the present time, and we see Florence shaken by great factions and party strife, not to speak of the cruel routs which it has suffered, near Montecatini and the place they call Altopascio. May God grant, through his infinite pity and mercy, and that of the Blessed Virgin his mother the ever-immaculate Mary, protector and defender of the city and territory of Siena, that greater evils and disasters do not come upon her than we have seen and heard of; may it be their will, through their own merits and those of the saint and prophet Pier, to preserve it in tranquillity and Christian peace.

While the servant of God was so ill and near the end of this present life, he was often visited by many dear friends, among them a friend called Maffeo, whom we mentioned above as freed by Pier's merits from certain infirmities. Now Maffeo, standing by Pier, said to him, 'O dearest father! I beg you to have faith in the Lord God, and fear nothing; for he wants to call you to himself; therefore prepare your heart and soul to receive him gladly, for soon your salvation will come to you.' Pier answered graciously and with a happy face, 'O dearest Maffeo! How well you speak, and as a true friend! But I tell you, if I had left it to this time to get ready to prepare myself for my dear Creator and Lord God, I would not at this extremity of my life have had much opportunity to prepare myself, for we know very well that with physical illness come many and various difficulties, so that a man can only badly, or not very well, make the preparations befitting faithful and good Christians.' As he spoke, his face became radiant and resplendent, and raising his eyes to heaven, he seemed already to be present where he desired with so much ardour to repose with Jesus Christ; and thus with great fervour he addressed wonderful and ardent words to the almighty and eternal God and to the gracious ever-immaculate Virgin Mary, rendering them infinite thanks that through their goodness they had deigned to bring him to that point without his having become embroiled in the filth and dregs of the world.

When the last hour came at which the servant of Christ Pier passed from this transient and miserable life, if life it can be called, many devout religious stood about him, saying the sacred offices appointed by Holy Church, and that blessed spirit left the earth to the earth and passed to the perpetual rest of eternal life, to which the Lord God Almighty, our Creator, Redeemer and Saviour, with the gracious Virgin Mary his mother and our refuge, guide us in perpetuity with the blessed Pier. Amen.

VII: ENRICO ('RIGO') OF BOLZANO (d. 1315)

Enrico, more often known as Rigo, was a native of Bolzano in what is now the Italian Tyrol; his Christian name was more characteristic of a German-speaking than of an Italian-speaking region. For centuries after his death in 1315 he remained, like many others, a purely 'popular' saint in the sense that his sanctity was recognised by no authority higher than that of the bishop of Treviso, his adopted city and the place of his death. In 1746–7, however, an official enquiry was undertaken at Treviso which in 1750 resulted in papal approval of the cult. In 1759 relics of the saint were bestowed upon his birth-place, and the large baroque reliquary which contains them is still to be seen in the choir of the cathedral of Bolzano.[1] At Treviso his after-fame was marked in 1830 by the building of a neo-classical *tempietto* on the site of the cell where he died; it is now sacred to the soldiers of Italy. In 1909, in anticipation of the sixth centenary of Rigo's death, Carlo Agnoletti published a brief summary of his life and the history of the cult, which was reissued in 1998 in the hope of drawing renewed attention to the saint as the Holy Year of 2000 approached.[2]

The most important published source, apart from the Life which is translated here, is an invaluable collection of documents concerning the beginnings and history of the cult, which was produced in 1760 by a patriotic Trevisan scholar, Raimbaldo degli Azzoni Avogari, as another consequence of the papal approval ten years earlier.[3] These documents convey a great deal of information about the launching of the cult after the saint's death on 10 June 1315. The event created considerable popular excitement, and the commune, in co-operation with the bishop, Castellano Salomoni, made elaborate arrangements for the burial and veneration of the holy man and for the care of the pilgrims who flocked to the scene.[4] One memento of these pious endeavours is still to be seen:

1 The Museo Diocesano at Bolzano preserves other mementoes, including a painting of the solemn procession which accompanied the translation, a nineteenth-century wax figure depicting Rigo with a hat, walking-stick and rosary, and also two axes and a mallet, the tools of his trade as a woodcutter.

2 C. Agnoletti, *La vita del Beato Enrico da Bolzano, autentico testimone di fede* (Treviso, 1909, reprinted 1998). The records of the papal enquiry (cited by Vauchez, *Sainthood*, pp. 236–8) are in the Archivio Segreto of the Vatican, Riti, Proc. 3021, and in Paris, Bibliothèque Nationale, H. 951.

3 R. degli Azzoni Avogari, *Memorie del Beato Enrico, morto in Trivigi MCCCXV corredate di documenti, con una dissertazione sopra San Liberale e sopra gli alti santi dei quali riposano i Sacri Corpori nella chiesa della già detta chiesa* (Venice, 1760). The volume is divided into two parts, separately paginated; the first is devoted to San Liberale and the second includes the documents of Rigo's cult.

4 For accounts of these proceedings, based on Azzoni's documentation, see Vauchez, *Sainthood*, pp. 236–8; Webb, *Patrons and defenders*, pp. 142–5.

the 'beautiful tomb' ordered for Rigo from Venice stood for many years in the *tempietto* mentioned earlier and was then installed in the diocesan museum, but after restoration it has been returned to the cathedral to serve as the high altar. Rigo's body now lies in a chapel on the south side of the nave.

The Life of Rigo published by Daniel Papebroch in *Acta sanctorum* was written by Pietro da Baono, who became bishop of Treviso in 1359. It is dated a little more narrowly by his reference in the preface to Pope Innocent VI (who died in September 1362) as 'of happy memory'. Pietro was made a clerk, he says, by Castellano Salomoni and was a canon of the cathedral before becoming bishop. He was serving the bishop at the time of Rigo's death forty-four years earlier and presents himself both as an eye-witness of much that he describes and as having access to good oral testimony. He remembers vividly the events of the morning of the saint's death, and he was subsequently actively involved in the launching of the cult, in that he sometimes assisted and deputised for his brother Antonio, who was one of the team of three notaries appointed by the bishop to record Rigo's miracles. On the anniversary of the saint's death in 1381, Pietro as bishop performed an exhibition of the relics. The document recording this event notes that Pietro and his brother had registered the miracles and that, on becoming bishop, he 'compiled a legend' of the saint's life 'which he caused to be written in the great books of that church, with the miracles'.[5]

The Life is lopsided. It is overwhelmingly concerned with the old age and exequies of the saint and with the first phases of the cult, on all of which Pietro was in a good position to be informed. There is virtually nothing here about Rigo's early life, no clue to the nature of his occupation when he worked and no indication of his age, except that he was in his last years too feeble to earn his bread, although this only emphasised his wonderful austerities. Agnoletti gives one version of what was known or believed about Rigo's earlier years, supplying his own speculations when all else fails. It is supposed that Rigo's reason for leaving Bolzano was to perform a pilgrimage (perhaps to Rome) and that on his return he passed through Treviso (one version has it that he fell sick there) and decided to stay. He lived with his wife and son, and pursued his trade, not in the city itself but at Biancade, some miles to the east; it was after the death of his wife that he moved into Treviso, accepting the hospitality of a notary who gave him a room in his house. Pietro da Baono mentions Rigo's wife but not his son Lorenzo. On 23 June, barely two weeks after the saint's death, the commune of Treviso resolved that Lorenzo should receive a grant of the necessaries of life, and on 3 July he was also granted certain properties 'so that he can comfortably support his life, and that of his family if it should happen that he has one.'[6] Perhaps Lorenzo, fifty years or so on, was both dead and forgotten, but it is hard to think that Bishop Pietro can have been unaware of his existence. Whether or not his omission was deliberate, it helps to explain the pious contention of a later translator of the Life that the saint had preserved virginity within marriage.[7]

5 *AS*, June, 2, pp. 391–2.

6 Azzoni Avogari, pt 2, pp. 24–7.

7 Quoted by Papebroch, *AS*, June, 2, p. 369.

The Life as we have it is not only lopsided but truncated. Having given some account of the translation of the saint performed by Bishop Castellano's successor, Ubaldino de' Gabrieli (1323–34), and of the present disposition of Rigo's shrine, Pietro embarks on an explanation of the failure to obtain his canonisation. This it seems was intended to include a narrative of the political crisis in which Treviso became embroiled in 1317 in face of the growing ambitions of the della Scala lords of Verona to control a substantial slice of northeastern Italy, but the text breaks off a short way into this narrative, although the author manages to observe that the war lasted 'for three years and more'.[8] It should be noted that Pietro firmly locates Rigo's death in happy times: 'the city of Treviso was flourishing under a communal, popular and peaceful regime', in which Bishop Castellano played an important part.[9] The cults centred on the cathedral also had their political dimension.

On 11 June, the day after Rigo's death, the *podestà* (also praised by Pietro) and ruling councils deliberated about the cult. Impressed by the multiplying miracles, they hoped that God 'through his mercy and the prayers of the blessed Rigo and all the other saints of God will maintain [Treviso] in a good, peaceful and communal state'.[10] Half a century or more later, Bishop Pietro echoed this phraseology. His retrospective account of Rigo's exequies preserves a vivid sense of how very public an event the launching of the cult was. It may be usefully compared with the account of the aftermath of Zita's death that is given in her Life. A similar picture is given of crowd enthusiasm and physical pressure on the relics, but there is much more stress here on official involvement, both communal and ecclesiastical.

For all the popular excitement allegedly aroused by her death, Zita was the possession of one particular community within Lucca. It has already been observed that there is a striking silence about the bishop in the description of the consultations about her cult,[11] and nothing is said in her Life about communal backing for it or any effort to obtain her canonisation. Rigo, by contrast, was to be buried and venerated in the cathedral of Treviso, and a later bishop was now commemorating him; furthermore, his canonisation was to be sought from the pope with the enthusiastic backing of the urban government. Mendicant involvement is also differently handled in the two Lives. Nothing is said to suggest that Zita was in any way involved with the friars in her lifetime, whereas Pietro remarks that Rigo was partial to the Augustinian Hermits, who might have had the burying of him if they had played their cards right. He also tells us, more generally, that Rigo assiduously frequented sermons in both the cathedral and 'the houses of the religious'. However, he has nothing to say about

---

8 The translation here omits this incomplete section. Treviso finally succumbed to Can Grande della Scala in 1329. For a brief outline of these events see Butler, *Lombard communes*, pp. 429–32.

9 See below, p. 252. The city had expelled its da Camino *signori* only three years previously.

10 Azzoni Avogari, pt 2, p. 2.

11 Above, pp. 161–3.

the friars' participation in the deliberations about Rigo's cult, which was in fact instantaneous. The bishop and the superiors of the Franciscan, Dominican and Augustinian orders headed a rapidly appointed commission which reported as early as 13 June on measures to be taken for the saint's entombment and veneration.[12] Zita's hagiographer does inform us that the prior of San Frediano consulted the Lucchese Franciscans and Dominicans before translating her to a stone tomb.

The intervention of the commune in the early stages of Rigo's cult was conspicuous. Vauchez remarks that the officials concerned themselves with things that might not have been thought to be their responsibility. On 13 June it was resolved that two copies of the miracles were to be made, one kept in the sacristy of the cathedral, the other in the communal chancery; this was with a view to the hoped-for canonisation. Here as elsewhere Rigo was associated with an earlier Trevisan holy man, the monk Parisio (d. 1267), whose canonisation the commune had already sought unsuccessfully to obtain; these efforts would now be renewed. On the same day it was declared that the communal officials were to make the same solemn annual offerings to Rigo as they did to Parisio, and on the following day a committee, once again including the bishop and the heads of the Franciscan, Dominican and Augustinian orders, was appointed to write up the lives and miracles of both saints.[13] If they did, their work did not long survive them, for Pietro da Baono evidently knew of no existing Life of Rigo.

Other pious acts on which the government resolved in Rigo's honour in the summer of 1315 included the release of certain prisoners, which was quite commonly done in the Italian cities to mark holy days. There was no wholesale or unconditional amnesty; twenty-four prisoners were named, and each case was separately debated and voted on.[14] The commune's promises of expenditure on the chapel and shrine for Rigo were such as to justify the negotiation, in August 1315, of a loan to help cover the 500 pounds it had pledged. In October, more money had to be found to pay for an image of Rigo, together with the Virgin Mary and St Lucy, painted on the *palazzo pubblico*.[15] The location of the shrine within the cathedral was the subject of lengthy debate in the councils; on 7 April 1316 the bishop even declared that he would take no new action in the matter without the knowledge and consent of the *podestà* and commune.[16]

The times were not propitious for the canonisation. In the summer of 1315 the papacy was in the middle of a two-year vacancy, which lasted from the death of Clement V in June 1314 to the election of John XXII in August 1316. Consideration was given in October and November 1316 to the sending of a

12 Azzoni Avogari, pt 2, p. 5.

13 *Ibid.*, pp. 6–7, 9; B. Betto (ed.), *Gli statuti del comune di Treviso (sec. XIII–XIV)* (2 vols, Rome, 1984–6) (*Fonti per la storia d'Italia*, 109, 111), 2, pp. 204–6. For Parisio see Vauchez, *Sainthood*, pp. 71–2, 193 n. 111.

14 Azzoni Avogari, pt 2, pp. 13–24.

15 *Ibid.*, pp. 31–2, 35.

16 *Ibid.*, p. 49.

new embassy, but in April 1317 it was prorogued for want of funds.[17] Nothing was to come of these hopes, but Rigo remained a local patron. His continuing popularity is obliquely attested in an unlikely source, the *Decameron*. In the first story of the second day, Boccaccio relates how a party of Florentine ne'er-do-wells, observing the crowds around Rigo's tomb, fake the infirmity of one of their number in order to force their way through, and barely escape with their lives when their deception is discovered.

For the purposes of the present translation I have disregarded the division of the printed text of the Life into two chapters. Also omitted is the miracle collection, which, as Pietro explains, he had had copied out as an appendix to his work. Although sizeable, this is not quite complete, for the miracles which occurred on 11 and part of 12 June 1315 are missing. There remain 356, recorded between 12 June and 5 July. The overwhelming majority were cures of what may be termed orthopaedic conditions, involving pain, incapacity or paralysis in one or more limbs or joints. Why Rigo specialised to such a marked degree in cures of this kind is not easy to explain: the blind, deaf, dumb, epileptic and possessed, who normally provide a high proportion of cures, are notably under-represented among his clientele. Taken together with a Life which lays such a strong emphasis on the saint's last years and death, the miracles help to convey the impression that Rigo was remembered above all as a thaumaturge. Vauchez noted that he seems more the contemplative and less the charitable activist than earlier holy men such as Homobonus, Raimondo Palmario or, more recently, Fazio.[18] This may mean that the activist model of lay sanctity no longer enjoyed the favour it had done or it may simply reflect the fact that the Rigo whom Pietro da Baono knew was an old man no longer capable of vigorous physical activity.

The Life of Rigo of Bolzano by Pietro da Baono, bishop of Treviso

Prologue

When the sacred histories and the lives and the deeds of holy men who have passed from this world are read with devout attention, and we study them with due effort, the Catholic faith is strengthened, the mind is edified, and the spirit is inflamed towards heavenly things and receives much increase of consolation. For this reason we see human praises and the heralding of mortals sometimes inscribed in bronze, sometimes conveyed to the memory of posterity in glowing letters. If the authors of such writings had not come forward, posterity would have been totally bereft of these fruitful teachings and examples and

17 *Ibid.*, pp. 65–70, 73–4.

18 Vauchez, *Sainthood*, pp. 205–6.

our faith might have suffered considerable deprivation. Bearing this in mind, we marvel that we are not ashamed to pass over in silence the merits, which are well known to us, of perfect men, and that we do not take care to proclaim, in praise of the Creator of all things, how they lived in this world and struggled with enemies and vices. From the reading of such things proceeds the praise of God; honour is done to the saints, the infidel experiences sorrow, the unbeliever envy, the lax anxiety; the devil laments, and joy is generated for the faithful of Christ.

In view of these considerations, and others besides which could be mentioned, I, Pietro di Domenico of Baono, bishop of Treviso although unworthy (for I had long been a canon of that church, but without my knowledge I was by divine grace promoted to that dignity by the will and provision of the Lord Pope Innocent VI of happy memory), reflected how improper and how ungrateful it was, and had been, that the outstanding merits and marvellous works which divine providence manifested in the blessed Enrico (who originated from Bolzano and lived for a long time in Treviso), both on his death and afterwards, had for so long been passed over in silence, and were still unrecorded. Although inadequate to undertake such a task, I decided to make up for the negligence of our predecessors, especially the worthy men who have officiated and held benefices in that church, and with all due reverence, as best I may, to put in writing what I have seen and heard and witnessed with my own eyes, of that blessed man, and preserve it for the perpetual recollection of those to come, lest knowledge of him sink into total oblivion; for today there is no one left in this church save I myself who can really remember him or better record him.

The Life

This venerable man left his own country and came to Treviso and there lived for a long time as best he could by his own sweat and labour. He earned his living by his labours, and at all times preserved a devout mind and secretly devoted himself to holy works. At length, when he was getting on in years and his bodily strength began to fail, he could no longer supply his physical needs in his accustomed manner and moved to a contemplative life, supporting himself on alms. Whatever he had left when he had eaten, he (himself a poor man) gave to Christ's poor, keeping nothing for himself, by the hour or by the day, unless he left untouched some trifling quantity of what was given to him in charity. And while he was thus living as best he could, a certain Jacopo de' Castagnoli, a notary and a man of good condition and life, who had a wife of similar standing called Catarina, and who knew about the blessed Enrico, took pity on him and took him into their home, which was situated in the Panceria quarter, on the right hand side going towards the gate of Forty Saints, quite near the nunnery of Santa Maria Nuova. They assigned him a little room at the far end of the house, beyond a courtyard, and here for a long time until his death he lived a life of abstinence and penitence, privately and unknown, like St Alexius,[19] as will appear below. If by any chance the blessed Rigo failed to collect adequate alms, Jacopo took care of him in his own household.

And, since a light placed on a mountain-top cannot be hidden, his external and devout works made him known to many people, and charitable gifts and alms were bestowed upon him; the more he received the more he divided among the poor. I remember that my lord and predecessor, Castellano Salamoni, then bishop of Treviso (who made me a clerk and to whose household I belonged for a long time), gave the venerable man money in alms, through me, when he was crossing the piazza in front of the cathedral; and as was his custom he gave it to the other beggars in the cathedral church, which he constantly frequented. And so he always did with other things he was given, as was well known publicly. So his interior and secret life was manifested externally in his humility and conduct.

He had a certain kindly, even gracious, manner of speaking. He always loved to hear about heavenly things; and if he ever suffered any annoyance, in word or deed, perhaps from children or some wrong-headed or stupid person, he bore it humbly, with all patience, betraying nothing by act or sign, even speaking pleasantly to those who insulted him. He was always clad in grey cloth, and wore a surcoat, with leather shoes and a flat cap, as he is depicted; he always carried a stick for the support of his body, which was much worn down with fasts, vigils and other austerities, as will become apparent. He was small in person, but reasonably stout; he had a wife before he adopted this life. He was a most devoted attender at church, at the divine office and above all at mass, and always carried a paternoster on a cord in his hand. Both in the office and elsewhere, he offered little prayers to his Creator according to his understanding, for he was ignorant of letters. He always hastened to sermons,

---

19 On the eve of his marriage St Alexius heard the call to follow Christ and left home to live in pilgrimage, returning only to die unrecognised in his father's house. The similarity to Rigo is remote.

both in the cathedral and in the houses of the religious, never missing one if time permitted; if it had been possible, he would willingly have been present at all of them. An eager listener, he committed to memory as much as he could take in. He so regulated his life and actions, as far as possible in private and in a praiseworthy manner, that no one at the time knew about works of such perfection, or was able to form a true estimate of them, or in any way believe them.

Here is another marvel. A man so old, so worn down by abstinence, supporting himself on a stick, every day visited all the churches of the suburbs of the city of Treviso and there poured out his prayers, lying prone on the ground according to his custom. If by chance he found a church closed, he knelt down outside the door and prayed at length. It was said at the time that, after the cathedral, he visited the church of the Hermit Friars most frequently and talked to the brothers and had such a close relationship with them that, as it was rumoured at the time of his death, he had decided to be buried with them; but either out of the negligence of the brothers, or perhaps because he was poor (and that was being said publicly), they lost him. The dean and canons of the [cathedral] church of Treviso, whose practice it always was and is to go personally and collectively to the funerals of any of their parishioners, of whatever station in life, received that venerable body with all care, according to their custom.

When he had visited all the churches and done everything else, he always returned to the cathedral and stayed mostly in the corner under the portico, towards the bishop's palace, near a certain image of the Blessed Virgin Mary which is painted there. Leaning against the stonework of the portico, with his cap in his hands, he prayed continuously and devoutly, gazing at the image aforementioned, as people looking from the balcony of the bishop's palace could clearly see. Often the above-mentioned bishop, Master Castellano, sent alms to him there. He never missed the divine office in that church and was always early at matins. He had such a conscience that every day he wanted to confess his least sins with the priests of that church, especially with the priest Giovanni Riccio, prebendary in the church of Treviso and afterwards rector of Sant' Agnete, or with the priest Pietro di Zenone, or the sacristan Alessandro, and in between times with the religious, especially the afore-mentioned Hermit Friars. Among other things, I have even heard from the priest Giovanni Riccio, when we were talking about this venerable man's life and conduct, that if he saw a bird flying through the air with any pleasure or curiosity he promptly confessed it; for he had confessed things of this kind, and other trifles, to him.

He was distinguished for many miracles in his lifetime, and other things which I have heard about from people worthy of belief. On one occasion, several people were standing under the portico of San Giovanni Battista, among them the aforementioned priest Pietro di Zenone and a certain layman called Gabo, from the neighbourhood of that church, from whom I heard the story. The venerable man came out of the cathedral and, crossing the cemetery towards the above-mentioned portico of San Giovanni Battista, paused in front of the images which are placed on the wall of the church of San Giovanni, praying devoutly. A sudden torrential shower of rain began; he stood there for a long time in prayer, and the spectators beneath the portico were laughing and making fun of him, for they believed he would be drenched by this rain. When he came up to them, they asked him, laughing, 'Brother Rigo, why did you stand so long in that rain?' And they touched him and his clothes, which were totally free from damp, as if he had been standing in the sun; and they were all dumbfounded and began to marvel at such a miracle and to think that he was a holier man in life and virtues than they had previously reckoned.

And indeed the fame of his life and deeds began to grow. By people of greater seniority, and by almost everybody, he was regarded as a saint, and often, when people saw him they said, 'That man is a saint.' It was no wonder, because his conduct and his continual thought were in heaven, according to the words of the Apostle, 'Our life is in the heavens'. This was clearly shown because he daily meditated with saints and angels. The aforementioned Catarina, wife of Jacopo, who as is usual with women spent more time than Jacopo did in the house (and Jacopo too confirmed this), reported that when she was in the house and the blessed man was shut up in his little room, she often heard him talking with people, as it seemed, and they with him; but she was not able to understand what was being said. When he came out of his room, she asked him, 'Brother Rigo, who were you talking with just now?' But he, pretending not to hear, did not reply, but left the house and went on his way according to his custom.

I have also heard from a trustworthy lady what she was told by the tailor mentioned below. Master ——[20] was a tailor, a poor man of good life, to whom the saintly man entrusted in total secrecy the task of making his hair-shirts. Once he was sewing some shoes of his and putting cords on

20 The name is missing.

them; thanks to the hardness of the cord he transfixed his finger, and about half of the needle went into the finger. The poor man suffered such pain from this that he could not rest; and he thought, crying out and weeping, that he had lost the finger and that he would not be able to use it, or his hand, any more, saying, 'Poor me! Now I shall have to beg, or stay at the hospital, not being able to work any more.' Hearing this and understanding the situation, blessed Rigo began to say to him, 'Don't worry, brother, you will be all right.' He prayed, and touched the finger, and the tailor felt no more hurt or pain and was restored to full health as he had been before.

Who can doubt that he talked with saints and angels? Who would not have to believe, on examining the truth, insofar as human nature can grasp it, that he led a heavenly and perfect life? What the life was that he led in his little room, with what affliction of his body he secretly spent his days, became clear to all after his death; we saw it, and all those then living could clearly see it. For when he died there was an immediate and incredible concourse of men and women; the whole city, in unheard-of wonder, was in tumult. His garments and hair-shirts and the other pious things which were found in his room are still preserved in the sacristy of the cathedral as clear evidence of the truth; but to arouse further the devotion of the faithful we will tell, as briefly as we can, of his way of life in that little room, and of the wonders which occurred on the day of his death and afterwards.

In that poor little room, then, he had three beds, but not stuffed with down, or purple or silks. One was stuffed with vine twigs, and that was hard; the second with cords twisted from thick flax-stems, and that was harder; the third was somewhat softer, that is, it was made with plain straw. On this he would lie for a while when he was worn out with fasting and prayer and afforded his body some repose, so that he could devote himself more vigorously thereafter to fasting and prayer. Always, day and night, he wore next to the flesh a hair-shirt made of the same twisted cord. Similarly he always had the same sort of twisted cords on his boots up to the knee.[21] His sheets were of coarse corded grey stuff. At his head he had a fairly small piece of wood as a pillow, which he always used at night; and he also had a scourge, with which he vigorously beat himself at night, and a certain round stone, with which he beat his breast. All these things are kept as a perpetual memento

21 The word *caliga*, used of Rigo's footwear here, had the classical meaning of the type of 'half-boot' worn by the legionaries; evidently he wore them laced up to the knee with cords which the cobbler was attaching when he suffered the accident.

in the cathedral sacristy, although many people, out of devotion, took pieces out of them. And thus he lived out his penance and his hidden life, entirely unknown, until his death. How worthy of esteem and veneration he was and is, I leave to the judgement of my readers and hearers.

When the day of his death came, as it pleased God, that is, 10 June 1315, the city of Treviso was flourishing under a communal, popular and peaceful regime. The aforesaid Lord Castellano was bishop, a man of great reverence and authority; in the temporal sphere, the worthy knight Magno della Branca of Gubbio was *podestà*. What miracles and wonders almighty God, who gives the good their true reward, clearly exhibited, I could undoubtedly not express if all my members were transformed into tongues, or if I could or would use the speech of the poets.

This is what the Lord performed in him or for him. On the day after his death I was standing under the portico of the cathedral, facing the church of San Giovanni and looking towards the window of the chamber in the episcopal palace where the lord bishop Castellano used to sleep, when the bells of the cathedral began to ring most sweetly and and not in the usual manner. I saw the dean and chapter of the church, with all the officers and chaplains, leave the cathedral and direct their steps towards the Panceria quarter. (All the members of the chapter at that time were present, as will be described below.) And, as it seemed to me and I still believe, before they reached the house where that venerable body lay, and when they did, the word resounded around the Piazza del Commune and the main street, and people without number came running and shouting, 'A saint has died.' This cry was at once taken up and repeated, and they rushed in uproar towards the house of the above-mentioned Master Jacopo. As God is my witness, I had still not moved from my position under the portico. There was such a concourse of people at the funeral procession crying out and praising God that the body could scarcely, and only with great effort, be carried behind the clergy.

So great did the tumult of people grow that before the funeral procession reached the portico of the cathedral the wooden casket in which the body had been placed had been broken on top and at the back, and panels removed from it. The body, wrapped in a coarse cloth, or some sort of shirt, was completely exposed and rocked to and fro with the casket, and I saw this with my own eyes. Someone was following the body, behind the casket, with two crutches in his hands, holding them up in the air; he had been so crippled before that he had not been able to walk by himself, without the aid of these sticks, and I heard that he had come to Treviso to seek a cure. Other sick people besides, similarly following the body, were cured then and afterwards. The bells, while the body was being carried to the church, rang so sweetly, so melodiously, that they seemed to be sounding in the ears of the hearers by themselves.

At last the body was brought into the church, out of the crowd of people, with much pushing and shoving. What can I say? Who would have believed it? In a moment the whole city was aroused and everyone rushed to witness the wonderful event. The *podestà* aforementioned, who had up to then been asleep, arrived accompanied by his whole household and other citizens. Desiring to reach the body, which was placed in the middle of the church, still above ground, he could not manage to do so, with the exercise of all his strength and threats, because of the constant and over-abounding multitude of people. Because of the devotion of everyone who wanted to touch and see that venerable body, it could not be buried; it seemed asleep rather than dead. The aforesaid bishop, startled from sleep and hearing the tumult and uproar from his palace, entered the church as quickly as he could, with an escort. Here he found the *podestà* and, at last, by the exercise of force and intimidation, they reached the body. They marvelled to see the grave-cloths and casket so damaged and, giving thanks to God, had a hole dug in the middle of the church and ordered a sort of wooden grating to be placed over it. The sick flocked to obtain relief, the healthy flocked out of devotion and to witness the exercise of such power. The miracles multiplied and shone forth; the whole church, day and night, remained full of people, with lights and endless uproar. The grating which has been mentioned was scarcely preserved intact.

On the following day they began to build a kind of square enclosure of the strongest timber, with a locked door. The body, entire and flexible, was laid out on a bier on the ground in the middle of this enclosure, covered with a cloth as if it slept, so that it could be seen by all through the aperture in the enclosure. Here it remained, naked and covered by this cloth, for eight days, in such heat, and at a time of year, that corruption should have begun immediately. What more need I say? Another great miracle occurred, and everyone saw it. As it lay there, blood began to flow from the corpse, in such quantity, collected in silver vessels, that it filled several ampullae, which are today preserved in the sacristy. Above the enclosure a platform was constructed of wooden beams, where the crowd of sick people stayed, praying and calling out for the recovery of their health. When the eight days had passed, the venerable body was placed in a stone tomb which was brought from Venice.[22]

In the meantime, and thereafter, news had spread among the cities and nearby places; there was a wondrous concourse of people both from neighbouring peoples such as Venice, Padua, Vicenza, Verona, Brescia and the whole of Lombardy, and from the regions of Trent, Feltre and all of Friuli and Istria and those parts, and also from the Romagna, Ferrara and Chioggia; the word spread through all of Italy, to the extent that even at Rome and in Perugia and thereabouts, the image of the aforesaid most praiseworthy man was depicted in many places; people flocked to these images, and God performed many miracles though the merits and prayers of the said glorious man.

So great did devotion to him grow, and so widely did the story spread, that people came in groups from Verona, Vicenza and Padua to his tomb, beating themselves, and similarly from the whole subject territory of Treviso; such was the concourse of the sick that the church could not hold them. As many of the sick as could stand on the platform were placed on it. And the crowd of poor and infirm so multiplied that they stayed around the cathedral square, and under the fountain, and next to the episcopal palace and on all the cloisters and under the canons' dwelling; there was no place that was not full of them, and they were also scattered in several places around the whole city; devout persons gathered alms for their support. And since the multitude of poor and sick was growing, in the church and outside it and all around, a basket was put in the left-hand part of the church; and good men appointed by the bishop and commune collected bread and wine, sent by the citizens of Treviso for the sustenance of the aforesaid poor; and these officials afterwards every day divided it among the poor and the sick. Thanks to the constant devotion of good men and women, there was no shortage of bread and wine in this basket; indeed (as the officials reported and it became public knowledge) when one day they were distributing wine from a certain vessel, and offering it to the poor and sending it out, as they usually did, to the poor inside and outside the church, the wine lasted and lasted and did not run short for a long period of the day, as they carefully noted. At news of this miracle everyone around the church came running and drank and tasted the wine in large numbers.

Numerous other miracles, by the virtue and prayers of the aforesaid most glorious man, began to shine forth in this church; so that, to obtain a permanent memorial of them, and to obtain information about

22 Still to be seen in the cathedral; see above, p. 243.

the various conditions of the sick, three people were appointed by the
bishop, the *podestà* and the commune, to investigate, verify and put in
writing the said miracles: they were, as president, Master Bartolomeo
di Castagnola, called Becha, expert in canon law, who was afterwards
prior of San Jacopo degli Schinali; Master Antonio da Baono, scribe
and notary to the lord bishop, my brother; and Gerardo di Nerlo,
notary of the commune, who had an arthritic hip. Under the instructions of Master Bartolomeo, they were carefully to examine those who
had been cured and record the cures in writing, how they had been
effected and witnessed, in detail. For when anyone was cured they were
brought before Master Bartolomeo and the aforesaid notaries, with a
large crowd of people present, and full information about their infirmity and subsequent cure was obtained, from their parents or kin or
the [distinguishing] marks of the sufferers themselves, and entered
by agreement by the notaries. I was often present, as a youth, with my
brother, and many times, when he was away, I acted as his deputy, and at
the command of the aforesaid Master Bartolomeo wrote down several
of these miracles with my own hand, according to my knowledge, as
is apparent to the present day in the register which contains them. All
these miracles, recorded thus in writing, I have had appended in order
to this present history, to the perpetual memory and praise of almighty
God and all saints, and in commendation of that most holy man; so that
everyone of sound mind may reflect how greatly the divine clemency
wished to magnify the life which his humble and devoted servant lived
in the flesh by miracles and prodigies at its end, revealing it to the
whole world.

The concourse of people lasted for almost a year, but was at its greatest
for three months and more. Indeed, I believe that during this period,
especially near the beginning, from time to time there were thirty thousand foreigners in this city. Certainly the numbers of people, the noise
and rejoicing in the church, the lighted candles, the offerings of statues
and images, and the sticks which the sick abandoned and had hung up
in the church, which remained hung up for a long time; the repeated
cries of the sick and all the other faithful, praising God for the divine
favours he granted; all were beyond belief. What more can I say? Large
numbers of people, guilty of various offences, rushed to confess their
sins; injuries were forgiven, and peace made between deadly enemies,
both citizens and foreigners; in short, such peace and consolation flourished that year, and even in the year following, that if Homer had been
present, he would scarcely have been able to express it.

So that more adequate thanksgiving and praise could be paid to the Almighty for so great a gift, and out of reverence for the blessed man, an altar was solemnly erected before the shrine in which his body was bestowed, and which was placed (as was said before) in the middle of the church. Here mass was celebrated daily, with the whole people devoutly present. Then, by decree of the bishop and chapter and commune, it was decided that a chapel should be solemnly constructed near the chapel of Santa Maria Piccola in the cathedral church, in which the venerable body, with the shrine in which it rests at present, should remain in perpetuity. The work was begun, as appears today, near the said chapel, but with the coming of war with Can Grande della Scala, and other upheavals in the city, it could not be completed.

At last, however, the shrine was erected, on columns, with angels above, into which the body was translated and lies today, established in the middle church, with a solemn altar before it. Here it remained down to the time of the venerable father Ubaldino de' Gabrieli of Gubbio, bishop of Treviso (of whose household I was a member, and greatly devoted to him), a famous man and worthy of much praise, the immediate successor of Master Castellano. In his time and that of his chapter, the shrine, with its columns and the body remaining inside it, was translated and put in the place where it now is, between the columns of the church on the left side, and today opposite the chapel I have built to the honour of the Holy and Undivided Trinity; and there, at that altar, as is well known, the first mass is always celebrated at dawn, to the praise of God and in memory and veneration of the said blessed Rigo; and at this shrine and in that place, by his merits and prayers, almighty God has performed several miracles and distinguished him with virtues.

However, having regard to the purpose of this work, we have decided, before we bring it to an end, to answer the unspoken question which could be asked: why the clergy and people of Treviso did not see to it that this glorious man, by the divine mercy resplendent in so many miracles, was inscribed by the supreme pontiff and the Holy Roman Church in the catalogue of saints and canonised, in the manner of other saints. The clergy and people and the said bishop Lord Castellano and his chapter were willing and had resolved to put the canonisation into effect; but in the third year after the death of the blessed man, many citizens and inhabitants of the *contado* of Treviso and others entered into a plot with the aforesaid Lord Cane della Scala, the son of the late Lord Alberto della Scala, then lord of Verona and Vicenza, and a horrible war broke out around the city of Treviso; [therefore] the desire of the clergy and people of Treviso could not be put into execution.

SELECT BIBLIOGRAPHY

Bertagna, P. M., *S. Lucchese da Poggibonsi: note storiche e documenti* (Florence, 1969); originally in *Archivum Franciscanum Historicum*, 62 (1969).

Bertoni, G., 'Di una Vita di S. Omobono del secolo XIV', *Bollettino Storico Cremonese*, 8 (1938), pp. 161–76.

Bornstein, D. and Rusconi, R. (eds), *Women and religion in medieval and renaissance Italy* (Chicago, 1996).

Brentano, R., *Two churches: England and Italy in the thirteenth century* (Berkeley, CA, 1988) (reprint of original 1968 edition).

Brocchieri, E., 'Sicardo di Cremona e la sua opera letteraria', *Annali della Biblioteca Governative e Libreria Civica di Cremona* 9 (1956).

Butler, W. F., *The Lombard communes* (London, 1906).

Canetti, L., *Gloriosa civitas: culto dei santi e società cittadina a Piacenza nel medioevo* (Bologna, 1993).

Caretta, A., 'La Vita di S. Gualtiero di Lodi', *Archivio Storico Lodigiano*, 2nd series 17 (1969), pp. 3–27.

Coakley, J., 'Friars, sanctity and gender: mendicant encounters with saints, 1250–1325', in C. Lees (ed.), *Medieval masculinities: regarding men in the middle ages* (Minneapolis, 1994), pp. 91–110.

Cristofani, F., 'Memorie del B. Pietro Pettinagno da Siena', *Miscellanea Francescana*, 5 (1890), pp. 34–52.

Foreville, R. and Keir, G., *The book of St Gilbert* (Oxford, 1987).

Gatta, F. S., 'Un antico codice su S. Ombobono', *Bollettino Storico Cremonese*, 12 (1942), pp. 96–115.

Goodich, M., '*Ancilla Dei*: the servant as saint in the late middle ages', in J. Kirshner and S. F. Wemple (eds), *Women of the medieval world* (Oxford, 1985), pp. 128–30.

Kemp, E., *Canonisation and authority in the western church* (Oxford, 1948).

Lansing, C., *The Florentine magnates: lineage and faction in a medieval commune* (Princeton, 1991).

Miller, M. C., *The bishop's palace: architecture and authority in medieval Italy* (Ithaca, 2000).

Newman, B., '"Cruel Corage": child sacrifice and the maternal martyr in hagiography and romance', in *From virile woman to womanChrist* (Philadelphia, 1995), pp. 76–107.

Noble, T. F. X. and Head, T. (eds), *Soldiers of Christ: saints and saints' Lives from late antiquity and the early middle ages* (London, 1995).

Norman, D., *Siena and the Virgin* (New Haven, 1999).

Orselli, A., *L'immaginario religioso della città medievale* (Ravenna, 1985).

Papi, A., Benvenuti, '*In castro poenitentiae*': *santità e società femminile nell' Italia medievale* (Rome, 1990).

—— *Pastori di popolo: storie e leggende di vescovi e di città nell' Italia medievale* (Florence, 1988).

Petroff, E., *Consolation of the blessed* (New York, 1979).

Piazzi, D., *Omobono di Cremona: biografie dal XIII al XVI secolo* (Cremona, 1991).

Polenton, S., 'Vita beati Antonii Peregrini', *Analecta Bollandiana*, 13 (1894), pp. 417–25.

Thompson, A., *Cities of God: the religion of the Italian communes 1125–1325* (University Park, PA, 2005).

Vauchez, A., 'La commune di Sienne, les ordres mendiants et le culte des saints: histoire et renseignements d'une crise (novembre 1328–avril 1329)', *Mélanges de l'Ecole Française de Rome*, 89 (1977), pp. 758–67.

—— *Les laïcs au moyen âge* (Paris, 1987).

—— *Omobono di Cremona (✝ 1197) laico e santo* (Cremona, 2001).

—— *La sainteté en occident aux derniers siècles du moyen âge* (Rome, 1981); English translation by J. Birrell, *Sainthood in the later middle ages* (Cambridge, 1997).

—— 'Sainteté laïque au XIIIe siècle: La Vie du Bienheureux Facio de Crémone (v. 1196–1272)', *Mélanges de l'Ecole Française de Rome*, 84 (1972), pp. 13–53.

Waley, D. P., *Siena and the Sienese in the thirteenth century* (Cambridge, 1991).

Webb, D., 'Friends of the family: some miracles for children by Italian friars', in D. Wood (ed.), *The church and childhood* (Oxford, 1994) (*Studies in Church History*, 31), pp. 183–95.

—— *Patrons and defenders: the saints in the Italian city states* (London, 1996).

—— 'The pope and the cities: heresy and anticlericalism in Innocent III's Italy', in D. Wood (ed.), *The church and sovereignty c. 590–1918: essays in honour of Michael Wilks* (Oxford, 1991), pp. 135–52.

—— 'Raimondo and the Magdalen: a twelfth-century Italian pilgrim in Provence', *Journal of Medieval History*, 26 (2000), pp. 1–18.

—— 'A saint and his money: perceptions of urban wealth in the Lives of Italian saints', in W. J. Sheils and D. Wood (eds), *The church and wealth* (Oxford, 1987) (*Studies in Church History*, 24), pp. 61–73.

Weinstein, D. and Bell, R., *Saints and society: the two worlds of western Christendom, 1000–1700* (Chicago, 1982).

INDEX

Note: The saints whose Lives are translated in this book are not included in the index.